CONTROVERSY, COURTS, AND COMMUNITY

Recent Titles in
Contributions in Legal Studies

The Sixth Amendment in Modern American Jurisprudence: A Critical Perspective
Alfredo Garcia

Positive Neutrality: Letting Religious Freedom Ring
Stephen V. Monsma

Questioning the Law in Corporate America: Agenda for Reform
Gerald L. Houseman

Reason Over Precedents: Origins of American Legal Thought
Craig Evan Klafter

The Iron Horse and the Constitution: The Railroads and the Transformation of the Fourteenth Amendment
Richard C. Cortner

Between Civil and Religious Law: The Plight of the *Agunah* in American Society
Irving A. Breitowitz

The Death Penalty and Racial Bias: Overturning Supreme Court Assumptions
Gregory D. Russell

The Rehnquist Court: In Pursuit of Judicial Conservatism
Stanley H. Friedelbaum

Parallel Importation in U.S. Trademark Law
Timothy H. Hiebert

John Marshall's Law: Interpretation, Ideology, and Interest
Thomas C. Shevory

Group Defamation and Freedom of Speech: The Relationship Between Language and Violence
Monroe H. Freedman and Eric M. Freedman, editors

Innovation, Reaction, and Atrophy: The Impact of Judicial-Selection Method on Policy in State Supreme Courts
Daniel R. Pinello

CONTROVERSY, COURTS, AND COMMUNITY

The Rhetoric of Judge Miles Welton Lord

Verna C. Corgan

Contributions in Legal Studies, Number 79
Paul L. Murphy, *Series Editor*

Greenwood Press
Westport, Connecticut • London

Library of Congress Cataloging-in-Publication Data

Corgan, Verna C.
Controversy, courts, and community : the rhetoric of Judge Miles Welton Lord / Verna C. Corgan.
p. cm.—(Contributions in legal studies, ISSN 0147–1074 ; no. 79)
Includes bibliographical references and index.
ISBN 0–313–29247–7 (alk. paper)
1. Lord, Miles. 2. Judges—United States—Biography. 3. Law and politics. 4. Rhetoric. I. Title. II. Series.
KF373.L56C67 1995
347.73'14'092—dc20
[347.30714092] 94–39472

British Library Cataloguing in Publication Data is available.

Library of Congress Catalog Card Number: 94–39472
ISBN: 0–313–29247–7
ISSN: 0147–1074

First published in 1995

Greenwood Press, 88 Post Road West, Westport, CT 06881
An imprint of Greenwood Publishing Group, Inc.

Printed in the United States of America

The paper used in this book complies with the Permanent Paper Standard issued by the National Information Standards Organization (Z39.48–1984).

10 9 8 7 6 5 4 3 2 1

To Jeffrey S. Adams, Peter G. Hames, Jr.,
and Virginia Corgan Rengel, my mainstays.

Contents

Acknowledgments

I am grateful to many people who have assisted me in this work. I owe special thanks to the Honorable Miles W. Lord for his willingness to discuss his life, his approach to judging, and his judicial opinions.

I have benefited immeasurably from the criticism and support of Robert L. Scott, my advisor, a fine scholar who demonstrated patience as well as the other virtues in helping me bring this project to fruition; of J. Vernon Jensen, a truly gentle man who first encouraged me in scholarly research; of Karlyn Kohrs Campbell, an insightful critic who gave wise counsel, friendship, and encouragement; and of Joel B. Samaha, who generously shared his legal knowledge. I am especially indebted to Paul L. Murphy, who provided a model of humane scholarship and made publication of this work possible.

Throughout this project I have drawn upon the intellectual, practical, and emotional resources of Virginia Corgan Rengel, Jeffrey S. Adams, Peter G. Hames, Jr., and Tiffany R. M. Corgan, who have sustained me in more ways than I can mention. My thanks, too, to my colleagues Moya Ann Ball, Adrienne Christiansen, Becky Swanson Kroll, Karen Musolf, Patricia Palmerton, Debra Petersen, and Suzanne Walfoort, who were always ready to lend their assistance and encouragement.

1

Introduction

> The truest meaning of the opinion is not its message, but the experience of mind it holds out as a model of legal thought: the language it makes as it places one item next to another, the community it makes with its several audiences.
>
> James Boyd White, *Heracles' Bow*

One hundred fifty years ago Alexis de Tocqueville observed that "[s]carcely any political question arises in the United States that is not resolved, sooner or later, into a judicial question. Hence all parties are obliged to borrow, in their daily controversies, the ideas, and even the language, peculiar to judicial proceedings" (1845, p. 357). In the intervening years the relationship between judicial and public discourse has continued to be a close one. Although opinions differ regarding the appropriateness of the alliance,[1] judicial opinions still affect almost all public discussion of political issues (Hunsaker, 1978; Scheingold, 1974; Wright, 1964). Scholars of rhetoric,[2] law,[3] and political science,[4] are among those who have explored and criticized the nature and scope of the rhetorical connections between courts and communities.[5]

The enduring importance of the relationship between judicial and public discourse has led scholars to pay particular attention to the rhetoric of U.S. Supreme Court justices. They are, after all, the judges who seek to establish the authoritative meaning of the U.S. Constitution; they encourage or discourage arguments about political and social questions, and they provide models of legal reasoning. They also are the judges whose agreements and dissents influence the rhetoric of lower courts. Nevertheless, as J. Frank cautioned, to focus exclusively on the Supreme Court is to succumb to "the false belief about the unimportance of the trial judge's activities" (1969, p. 222).

Although their rhetoric often is overlooked, lower courts do more than affect the fates of individual litigants. What they say and do influences community perceptions of what the courts are, how and how well they function, and whether they are performing legitimate roles in the life of the community. It also may affect relationships among community members. After all, the stuff of people's daily lives furnishes the issues that give rise to legal interpretations, and trial judges are likely to be an important part of citizens' firsthand experience with the courts. Plaintiffs and defendants appear before them, and the public can observe them relatively easily. In addition, local and regional media reporting on legal controversies and the parties involved in them contribute significantly to a community's social knowledge of the courts and the people who appear in them (see, e.g., Hariman, 1990). Lower courts thus have a critical part in developing public perceptions of what life is like under the "rule of law."[6]

Miles Welton Lord is an example of a lower-court judge whose rhetoric was central not only to public debate about specific community controversies, but also to public discourse about the roles of the courts and the community in resolving the community's problems. His approach to judging reflected a conception of a closer reciprocal relationship among the law, the courts, and the community than the relationship envisioned by many of his judicial colleagues. A sometime critic of the appellate courts, Lord advocated modified roles for the courts and the community in the pursuit of justice.

Several of Lord's judicial opinions addressed legal controversies that intersected with public debate about political, economic, and social issues. In these cases Lord directly confronted the need to justify judicial authority over "the people" as well as to explain his decisions. Controversy had divided communities, and he could expect a divided public to be attentive to his arguments in order to criticize them, to employ or refute them in community debates, or to decide whether or not they would comply with the law. In the face of community controversy, the persuasive quality of his rhetoric might help to determine whether the public would accept his judicial resolution of their dispute[7]—that is, whether the public would recognize a fundamental unity underlying their differences and consent to re-form as a community under the "rule of law."

In the context of public controversy Lord also faced appeals of his decisions and complaints about his conduct. In some instances the appeals and complaints resulted in oral and written dialogues with appellate courts. These dialogues afforded opportunities for an interested public to "overhear" the courts' rhetorical responses to internal disagreements about their relationships with each other, with litigants, and with the community. These relationships are, of course, critical to the American judicial system; and Lord's rhetorical attempt to restructure them revealed areas of tension and sources of conflict within the system.[8] This tension and conflict resulted in a complex rhetorical situation. Lord attempted to critique perceived shortcomings of the judiciary and at the same time support the legitimacy of the courts. The courts' legitimacy was necessary to maintain his own judicial authority as he addressed multiple audiences, including appellate courts and the public as well as litigants and lawyers.

Lord's approach to the complex rhetorical obstacles he faced suggests judicial rhetoric as described by James Boyd White. White views judicial opinions as vehicles for educating citizens as the equals of judges (1984, pp. 281-282). Legal rhetoric constitutes a community that "insists to each of the characters [in a dispute] that it will recognize the existence of the other. . . . In doing this, the community claims and performs a meaning for its action or inaction; it defines and maintains a character of its own" (1985, pp. 208-209). Judicial opinions accomplish this task by rhetorically structuring the tension between competing "stories" of litigants. The tension is resolved by using the resources within those stories to invent an "ending" that defines a community's relations with its culture and individuals' relations to one another (1984, p. 273). The judicial ending provides the central terms of praise and blame with which communities "define ourselves, our motives, and our relations with others" (1984, p. 279).

In this way judicial opinions symbolically create a just community that is reconstituted and rededicated as often as judicial rhetoric persuades the actual community that legal principles are just and that judges' decisions are faithful to those principles. Through this process the community affirms the role of judges as spokespersons for their law.

Public discussion of Lord and his activities suggested that his judicial rhetoric stimulated reexamination of the principles underlying the courts by both the legal and larger communities. Although his actions sometimes were viewed as improper by appellate courts and certain of his colleagues, he often enjoyed public support. Furthermore, he was not dismissed as a legal lightweight. He was the recipient of several awards for his judicial performance, and some of his most controversial decisions were confirmed by other judges. His rhetoric suggests the range of choices that judicial discourse may make available to a community as it seeks to define the relationships of its members to one another, to the law, and to the courts.[9]

Lord's participation in controversial cases, his respect for the public audience, his sometimes controversial judicial conduct, his involvement in appeals, and his widely quoted opinions provide opportunities to explore the many dimensions of lower court judges' rhetoric that contribute to the community's understanding of the law, the courts, and themselves.

This work approaches Lord's judicial opinions from a rhetorical perspective that speaks to a general audience. It begins with a brief history of judicial philosophies and conventions that have influenced both judicial rhetoric and criticisms of that rhetoric. Lord's background and the influences on his approach to judging are discussed in an attempt to place his judicial philosophy in the context of historical philosophies and conventions. An overview of Lord's decisions and opinions suggests his general approach to judging and rhetoric; it is followed by detailed examinations of opinions he wrote in cases that involved significant public controversy. The final chapter attempts to summarize the strategies Lord employed to engage and persuade audiences and to shape their perceptions of the courts' and community's proper roles in the pursuit of justice. The point is not to determine whether or not Lord's conclusions were right but to understand more fully how lower-court judges may use rhetoric to influence the relationships between courts and the community. My hope is that this examination may contribute to a deeper appreciation of the possible relationships between rhetoric, law, and society.

NOTES

1. Who are the appropriate audiences for judicial speech, what are appropriate strategies for speaking to those audiences, and who is competent to criticize judicial speech are questions that are debated on a number of grounds. For example, on the one hand J. K. Tulis suggests that judges should not address the larger community, arguing that our constitutional structure was invented in part to remove a measure of demagogic temptation from judges by confining questions of fundamental principles to governmental bodies (1987, p. 31). In his view, the judiciary would do its part to maintain community by maintaining its rhetorical distance from the community. On the other hand, A. F. Westin claims that judges' rhetorical actions and audiences are delimited by individual judgments rather than by constitutional imperatives.(1961, pp. 1-35). In his view, judges' conceptions of appropriate audiences depend on their perceptions of their own and the courts' status and institutional responsibilities. Because these perceptions vary with persons and situations, so does the intended audience for judicial rhetoric. Differing conceptions of judges' proper rhetorical relationship with various audiences increase the complexity of choices to be made by judges who are concerned about both the influence of their rhetoric on the larger community and maintaining their status within the legal community.

2. See, e.g., Bartenan, 1987; Deutsch, 1971; Hagan, 1976; Herbeck, 1984; Hunsaker, 1978; Jones, 1976; LeDuc, 1976; Lindsey, 1985; Makau, 1984; Rabin, 1978; Rodgers, 1982; Strother, 1963; Ulrich, 1985; Wright, 1964; Zarefsky and Gallagher, 1990.

3. See, e.g., M. S. Ball, *Lying down together* (1985); L. H. Carter's *Contemporary constitutional lawmaking* (1985); R. Harbinger's article in the 1971 *Judicature*, Trial by drama; C. Perelman's and L. Olbrechts-Tyteca's *The new rhetoric* (1971); Perelman's *Justice, law, and argument* (1980); and several works by J. B. White, including *When words lose their meaning* (1984); *Heracles' bow* (1985); and *Justice as translation* (1990).

4. See, e.g., Scheingold, 1974.

5. Communication scholars also have manifested an interest in legal communication that is not judicial speech. For example, they have analyzed communication addressed to judges and juries (see, e.g.,Beach, 1985; Bennett, 1978; Dicks, 1981; Hosman and Wright, 1987; Kaufer, 1980; Levison, 1979; Reinard and Reynolds, 1978; Sanbonmatsu, 1971; Washby, D'Amato, and Metrailer, 1976); legal communication as argumentation (Crable, 1976; Dicks, 1976; Hample, 1979;

Strother, 1963; Welch, 1976); the rhetorical dimensions of defendants' communication (Brummett, 1979; Schuetz and Snedaker, 1988); communication between lawyers and their clients (Rieke, 1982); the rhetoric of the U.S. Constitution (Stuart, 1974); mass media approaches to legal discourse (Brummett, 1984; Condit and Selzer, 1985); and popular trials as rhetorical events (Hariman, 1990).

6. This use of the term "rule of law" emphasizes that its symbolic importance transcends legal terms. It implies public acceptance of the written law as being consistent with the demands of justice "beyond" written law.

7. If judicial opinions are to persuade the public, they must be framed in terms the community understands and justified by principles to which the community subscribes, and they must prescribe principles of conduct on which the community will act. As J. B. White has suggested, judicial rhetoric must become "a way of creating a rhetorical community over time" (1984, p. 266). Deutsch (1971) has argued that the Supreme Court's failure to justify its *Miranda* and *Escobedo* decisions in terms of known public values and concerns (e.g., growing governmental power, equal justice for the poor and uneducated, the need to improve law enforcement standards) helps to account for the public's and law enforcement agencies' failure to accept the decisions as consistent with community values and the "rule of law" (see, e.g., pp. 273-286).

8. For a discussion of lower courts' potential for limiting the power of high courts, see, e.g., Murphy (1961), pp. 23-26.

9. I am using Brummett's (1984) distinction to claim that a judge *makes available* to audiences a view of reality they may share, not to claim that they do, in fact, share it.

2

Approaches to Law and Rhetoric

> The "cult of the robe," . . . the judge as a high priest of justice with special talents for elucidation of 'the law,' that sacred and mysterious text . . . inscrutable even to the educated layman, forms a[n] . . . institutional charisma . . . bestowed on judges with their oath of office.
>
> Walter F. Murphy, *Elements of Judicial Strategy*

> Unfrock the judge, have him dress like ordinary men . . . and he may well be more inclined to talk and write more comprehensibly. Plain dress may encourage plain speaking.
>
> Jerome Frank, *Courts on Trial*

Rhetoricians' interest in law and legal practitioners' interest in rhetoric began in ancient times, when decisions about justice were the immediate responsibility of the community. Citizens convened to judge their compatriots' actions and debate the consequences of those actions for the community.[1] Because legal argument was recognized as having political implications, its rhetorical nature was acknowledged. The union between rhetoric and law, however, never was an easy one; acknowledging a relationship is not the same as defining or endorsing it. In fact, disagreements about the community's involvement in matters of justice arose almost from the beginning.

EARLY RHETORIC, POLITICS, AND LAW

About 400 B.C. Plato was an early critic of the relationship among judicial decision, rhetoric, and the ethos of a community.[2] He condemned citizen judges and courtroom rhetoric on philosophical grounds. However, I. F. Stone (1988) has reminded us that Plato's condemnation reflected his political self-interest;

the aristocrat despised the demos. The idea that ordinary citizens should rule themselves was anathema to Plato. He offered Socrates' fate as compelling evidence of the need for an enlightened elite to determine what is just.

In contrast, Cicero, in the first century B.C., was convinced of citizens' judicial competence. His highest praise was reserved for citizen lawyer-orators who demonstrated the interdependence of justice, law, and everyday life (Cicero, 1970). They both protected the community from tyrants and symbolized the community's freedom from tyranny. A champion of the Republic, Cicero followed Plato in tailoring his approach to justice to his politics.

And so from ancient times the relationship between the community and the courts has been a matter of debate. As a result, so has been the role of judicial speech in creating and maintaining community. The debates about judging, judicial speech, and the community continue in the United States.[3]

RHETORIC, POLITICS, AND U.S. COURTS

The Rhetoric of Immutability

Judges as oracles. The roots of the American debate lie in the tension between authority and democracy. Although conceived in and constituted from a citizens' revolt, the American states developed what might be called neo-Platonic jurisprudence. This tradition began with John Marshall, who was appointed the U.S. Supreme Court's Chief Justice at a time when political factionalism had rendered the judiciary vulnerable to attack.[4] To preserve the judiciary's political utility, Marshall resolved to present it as "consciously aloof from direct participation in politics" (G. E. White, 1976, p. 9).

Exploiting the "quasi-religious symbolic quality attached to the doctrine of 'higher law' " (McCloskey, 1960, p. 15), the Marshall court's opinions[5] invested judges with an ethos that represented a univocal judgment of "the people." As the disinterested voice of natural law, judges could decide issues that defied resolution as long as they were discussed by a multitude of voices (J. B. White, 1984, pp. 247-263). Although the federal constitution was an expression of community values and a response to community problems, the law was referred to as an immutable presence independent of community values, to be discovered and pronounced only by judge-oracles (Friedman, 1985, p. 381; Goldman and Jahnige, 1976, p. 156; McCloskey, 1960, p. 19; G. E. White, 1976, pp. 8-10).

That this "ideal" ethos (Bickel, 1962, p. 1) would mask its own political and rhetorical nature is not surprising. Marshall sought profound powers for the judiciary. Federal courts were to determine their own jurisdiction, applying the constitution and laws to each entity they "discovered" within it. Federal legislative and executive acts, and potentially the acts of states, could fall within the judicial purview (Friedman, 1985, p. 122). Political powers such as these could be entrusted only to decision makers who were apolitical, above the multitude of competing interests.[6]

Therefore the Marshall court's opinions employed arguments that, in C. Perelman's and L. Olbrechts-Tyteca's terminology, might be called "convincing." They seemed to proclaim that "the reasons adduced are of a compelling character, that they are self-evident, and possess an absolute and timeless validity, independent of local or historical contingencies" (1971, pp. 31-32).[7] There are several reasons for the appeal of this rhetoric of immutability.

First, Marshallian rhetoric rationalized nondemocratic authority. American independence had been hard won, and arguments for submitting to authority had to be compelling. The need for order alone would not win acquiescence. By rhetorically deriving their power from the natural law that legitimized independence and union, judges with few means for enforcing decisions gained a means of persuasion.[8]

Second, the rhetoric of immutability implicitly eliminated the taint of factional influence. Judges were the medium, not the source, of messages. As individuals, they might be as ambitious, prejudiced, and fallible as other human beings. But so long as they justified their decisions in terms of previous decisions, which in turn had been justified by appeals to natural law, the law's immutability shielded their ethos from accusations of self-interest.[9]

Third, the rhetoric of immutability contributed to the theoretical and political stability of the courts. As long as the natural law expressed in the U.S. Constitution commanded the nation's loyalty and obedience, Marshall's judicial theory could share in that loyalty. This spillover effect enabled the courts to establish a place in the American political tradition that was not destroyed when the nation itself divided. As G. E. White observes, the "oracular theory . . . persisted throughout the great part of the nineteenth century" (1976, p. 2); and biographers still refer admiringly to Marshall's "logic" of law (Stites, 1981, p. 167).

Immutability had a fourth important rhetorical function. It provided a warrant for judges not to address the larger community. By ratifying the federal Constitution, "the people" had assented to be governed under law. Since immutable law did not change, further community discussion was unnecessary. The warrant was consistent with Marshallian assumptions. Marshall, like Plato, distinguished between democratic "chaos" and republican "order" (G. E. White, 1976, p. 15). An enlightened elite was the appropriate audience for judicial speech. The community's ethos, as it related to defining justice and applying law, was placed in the care of the courts.

This neo-Platonic approach to judging was not without its detractors. Thomas Jefferson, with some accuracy, viewed it as a strategy for protecting Federalist interests from Jeffersonian Republicans (Kelly, Harbison, and Belz, 1983, pp. 167-184). Others, perceiving that it made law and justice the monopoly of lawyers and prevented the community from solving its problems with "common sense,"[10] called for simplification of laws and the legal system

(Presser and Zainaldin, 1980, pp. 260-269). In the mid-nineteenth century several states made judicial posts elective. This development, as L. M. Friedman has noted, "undermined the idea that . . . strictly legal principles were the only tools that belonged in the toolshed of judges" (1985, p. 372).[11]

But even as the legal profession retained its authority over the practice of judging and seemed disinclined to demystify the activity, Marshall's oracular style became less viable. Its success had depended in part on the unique opportunity to form rather than follow tradition. So another rhetorical barrier was erected between courts and the community. This was a rhetoric of science.

The rhetoric of science. In the late nineteenth century came the "professionalization" of the legal community. Law schools replaced apprenticeships, and the study of law was separated from the tradition of liberal education. "Scientific method" was adapted to the new discipline, and in 1878 a select membership organized the American Bar Association, in part to support the new scientific jurisprudence (Friedman, 1985, p. 650).[12]

The assumption underlying "legal science" was that a fundamental, coherent "will" of the law existed in each legal area. A properly trained lawyer could identify this doctrine through rigorous analysis of the most important cases.[13] Equipped with an understanding of the doctrine, legal professionals could protect the law's integrity through punctilious application of principles distilled from precedent decisions and their justifications (Johnson, 1981, pp. 20-24).[14]

If not as exalted as the oracular style, legal science, or formalism (Wiecek, 1985, p. 59), was its equal in conveying the law's remoteness from the community. It emphasized abstract "logical" consistency over concrete justice; the political, economic, and social interests reflected in the case law were considered irrelevant to it. The goal of legal reasoning was to establish and maintain the rationality of rules *in terms of* the rules. How the rules operated in the life of the community was not the business of the law.

Justifications for legal decisions were conveyed in judicial opinions that were "bombastic, diffuse, labored, drearily logical, [and] crammed with unnecessary citations" (Friedman, 1985, p. 383). This rhetorical style, "less a way of thinking than a way of disguising thought" (p. 384), underscored the need for a legally trained audience. By speaking of law as a logical process, it maintained rhetorical distance between judges and their decisions, and between courts and the community. It also helped to preserve the "social myth" of law free from outside influences and to support the legitimacy of courts that made unpopular decisions (Kelly, Harbison, and Belz, 1983, pp. 465-466).

Critics noted, however, that judicial decisions made under the scientific paradigm tended to favor the interests of powerful elites against the claims of commoners. The perception of favoritism fostered skepticism about judges' objectivity and the law's logical inevitability. And it was the case that legal scientism coincided with a period of conservative judicial activism during which, for example, judges "discovered" that the Fourteenth Amendment protected the liberty of corporations from regulation (see, e.g., *Santa Clara*

County v. Southern Pacific Railway Co. [1886]) and that workers' liberty of contract required freedom from state maximum hours laws (see, e.g., *Lochner v. New York* [1905]).

Skepticism was intensified by the arguments that justified such discoveries, arguments that sometimes seemed to follow tortuous paths to the least evident conclusion. For example, in *Lochner v. New York* the abstracted principle was that contracts were voluntary agreements between equal parties. Therefore the state of New York's attempt to limit bakers' weekly working hours to sixty interfered unconstitutionally with the bakers' right to earn as much as they wished. Logic demanded that judges ignore the out-of-court reality of contracting parties' differential power.

Reform groups tended to attribute the coincidence of legal formalism and conservative activism to conspiracy. Friedman attributes it to the judiciary's composition. He describes the judges of the period as conservative, white, Protestant men who saw themselves as keepers of legal traditions, values, and social order in a time of fast-paced change, as guardians of true Americanism "holding off the vulgar rich on the one hand, the revolutionary masses on the other" (Friedman, 1985, p. 383). To them post-Civil War societal changes signaled the potential disintegration of the republic. As huge corporations, immigrants, political reformers, farm and labor organizers, Mormons, and assorted others defied long-held religious and cultural tenets, emancipated African Americans and "annexed" persons of color posed the problem of reconciling political and social exclusion with the ideals of freedom and democracy (see, e.g., Wiebe, 1967; Wiecek, 1985, pp. 55-56, 64-74). To men who looked to the past for perfection, chaos loomed.

A. H. Kelly, W. A. Harbison, and H. Belz, however, believe that both conspiracy and class-bias explanations for legal science underestimate the power of ideas. They argue that judicial logic's practical support for laissez-faire economic assumptions, Puritan social assumptions, and elite interests was an accidental outcome of "genuine conviction" that the law and its application were objective (1983, p. 466). Whatever explanation is correct, the rhetoric of science failed to persuade those who perceived that scientific jurisprudence consistently rationalized decisions inimical to their interests. It also failed to persuade scholars and practitioners of law who developed a different approach to judging.

The Rhetoric of Mutable Law

Sociological jurisprudence. In 1881 Justice Oliver Wendell Holmes, Jr.'s, observation that "the life of the law has not been logic: it has been experience" (Holmes, 1963, p. 5) expressed succinctly the view of legal scholars, lawyers, and judges who rejected the ideas that law was scientific and that judges applied it without regard for its political, economic, or social consequences.[15] These legal reformers argued for recognition of judges' susceptibility to bias and for the study of legal decisions' actual effects in the everyday life of the community. From the desire for a meeting of tradition, socially–created law, and extralegal information came an approach to law called sociological jurisprudence (Johnson, 1981, pp. 123-126).

Although sociological jurisprudence was developed as much in law schools as in the courts,[16] Holmes and his fellow Justice Louis D. Brandeis often are singled out as its judicial exemplars. Holmes denied that the law consisted of discoverable, objective rules of timeless validity. He believed that the content and operation of law were dependent upon the values and purposes of the society in which law functioned and that learning how the law worked in society gave insight into its development and meaning. Science was a tool that could be used to ascertain which community values and purposes were strongest at a given time, but it could not determine which values and purposes, if any, were best or should prevail for all time.[17]

Holmes proposed that judges should acknowledge their susceptibility to the influences of their own values, experience, and transitory states of mind; then they should resist those influences by exercising judicial restraint. That is, judges should defer to legislatures as long as legislation reasonably could be expected to achieve its avowed public purposes. According to Holmes, legislatures expressed the majority will of the people who lived under the law, and "in substance the growth of the law is legislative. . . . The very considerations which judges most rarely mention . . . are the secret root from which the law draws all the juices of life. I mean, of course . . . what is expedient for the community concerned" (Holmes, 1963, pp. 31-32; Johnson, 1981, pp. 123-126; Kelly, Harbison, and Belz, 1983, pp. 467-468; G. E. White, 1976, pp. 150-177; Wiecek, 1985, p. 66).

In spite of Holmes's willingness to admit socioeconomic realities into judges' deliberations, he was impatient with social science research. He resisted reading, considering, or using empirical data to support his decisions (Johnson, 1981, pp. 125-126). In this as in other matters, Brandeis, who has been called "Holmes's conscience" (Lerner, 1943, p. xli), provided contrast as well as support.

For Brandeis, there were two kinds of facts, moral and empirical, and he was enthusiastic about both. If Holmes represented sociological jurisprudence's insistence on fair procedures and judicial restraint, Brandeis represented its activist impulses. Unlike Holmes, he did not make sharp distinctions between the proper spheres of law and morality. In his view, some values expressed fundamental moral facts and deserved the law's protection (G. E. White, 1976, pp. 168-169). Convinced of his own righteousness, he did not share Holmes's views that morality could change with time and conditions and that judges should not substitute their own moral judgments for those of political majorities.

Brandeis, however, agreed with Holmes that appropriate rules could not be discovered deductively from traditional legal doctrine. Instead, they must emerge inductively from the examination of empirical data about social conditions and the law's operation under those conditions. Subjected to cost-benefit analysis, empirical data would lead to the correct decision in every case. In contrast to Holmes, Brandeis demonstrated his interest in social reality by using empirical research in his own legal work. As a lawyer arguing before the Supreme Court, Brandeis had presented a brief in *Muller v. Oregon* (1908) filled with research and statistical findings from a variety of scientific and social scientific fields to convince the court to let stand a state law limiting the working hours of female factory and laundry workers (Kelly, Harbison, and Belz, 1983, p. 456).[18] As a Supreme Court justice he continued the pattern set by this famous "Brandeis brief" in opinions such as *Adams v. Tanner* (1917) (Johnson, 1981, p. 128; Kelly, Harbison, and Belz, 1983, pp. 454-479; G. E. White, 1976, pp. 146-177; Wiecek, 1985, p. 60).

The differences in the judicial reasoning of Holmes and Brandeis exemplify the variety of views embraced by sociological jurisprudence. Those viewpoints were subject to criticism. Holmes's juristic philosophy was vulnerable to accusations of moral relativism and denied judges a rationale for mitigating the excesses of political majorities. Brandeis's philosophy made subjectivity's role in legal decisions more overt but did little to temper it. In spite of Brandeis's confidence in empiricism, neither values nor facts spoke objectively or for themselves; they depended on judges to fashion them into coherent justifications. What bound these viewpoints under a common rubric was the idea that realities beyond those found in the casebooks influenced jurisprudence. That idea deprived judges of their grounds for claiming absolute certainty about the proper rules and content of the law. It tied them, individually and inextricably, to their own decisions.

This development had important implications for judicial rhetoric. If sociological jurisprudence was accepted, judges were on their political and rhetorical own. To reject the notion that law resides exclusively in the legal record is to concede that the interpretation of law is a rhetorical rather than a logical activity. If case law does not provide general rules from which to deduce applicable law objectively, the contingency of legal truths would seem to be established. As contingent truth, the law would be the proper subject of rhetoric.

In addition, if case law is not the sole source of information relevant to legal decisions, lawyers and judges may not be the only legitimate participants in debates about the meaning of law. As Brandeis's use of empirical data demonstrated, as the sources for rhetorical invention expand, so do the numbers and classes of people who may compile, interpret, and present data, and so do the ways in which data may be presented. Experts in nonlegal disciplines, and even ordinary people, are admitted to deliberations about law; and the decisions and justifications of judges are opened to community criticism.

At the same time, if jurisprudence is neither oracular nor scientific, judicial restraint takes on new meaning. So long as judges are believed to discover law through "a process independent of one's personal convictions" (G. E. White, 1976, p. 155), there is nothing to restrain. Judicial opinions expound rather than justify. They may speak in the kind of voice that disclaims personal authority in a way that "short circuits the inclination and even the right of auditors to consider claims . . . apart from the particular source of their communication" (Scott, 1984, p. 92).[19] The voice of the judge is the voice of law, and law presumably *is* restraint.

However, once it is conceded that social context and individual attitudes influence judges' decisions, restraint becomes a salient and difficult issue, rhetorically and otherwise. Defining restraint is the first difficulty. According to G. E. White, in the absence of consensual values the term refers to curbing individual subjectivity. It also refers to exhibiting appropriate deference to legislatures that express majority opinions (1976, p. 176). In the first instance, it is hard to envision clearly what can restrain subjectivity when the possibility of objectivity has been rejected. Impartiality may seem a reasonable alternative, but its operational definition may be as problematic as that of objectivity. Judges must make choices, and in the end all choices are partial. In the second instance, as Holmes's critics recognized, deference to legislatures requires judges to condone the errors and evils enacted in the name of the politically powerful.[20] That raises another set of questions about the meaning of constitutional government and the role of judges in it when the constitution appears as eager to restrain legislators as it is to restrain judges.

The difficulties that arise from the abandonment of oracular or scientific authority suggest the need for a different relationship between the courts and the community. Having acknowledged that judges are not decision-making machines and that judicial decisions are grounded in imperfect methods and morality, a community confronts new uncertainties. The uncertainties call for a continuing dialogue between courts and the community to renew and reaffirm the legitimacy of judges who perform unmistakably undemocratic functions. The rhetorical problems presented by such a dialogue are complex. On the one hand, judicial speech that claims objectivity may be seen as deceptive; on the other hand, judicial speech that expresses sympathy or antipathy may be construed as being indifferent to the merits of specific cases. A new approach requires a new kind of rhetorical sensitivity to audience.

To complicate matters further, the development of sociological jurisprudence did not end oracular or scientific theories of law. The contradictory approaches, each with its own standards for legal justification and judicial behavior, existed side by side. To be a good judge according to the lights of one philosophy was to be a bad one in the lights of another. As challenges to the grounds for judicial legitimacy emerged from within the judiciary as well as from without, the range of potential rhetorical responses to legal disputes grew; and so did the potential grounds upon which the responses could be found wanting.

Legal realism. The legal community's disagreements about what is the law and what is good judging were not exhausted by clashes between the oraculists-formalists and sociological jurisprudents. In the 1920s, legal realism upset both camps.[21] Legal science stressed logic; sociological jurisprudence stressed group interests; legal realism stressed the illusion of logic and the ubiquity of idiosyncrasy. If logic is illusion and judging is idiosyncratic, one does well to be skeptical, and legal realism encompassed skepticism of two kinds—"rule skeptics" and "fact skeptics."

"Rule skeptics" asserted that the "truth" about what law is could not be found in "paper rules" of casebooks. The "real" rules inhered in the actual behavior of judges. Analyzing empirical data about that behavior would expose the rules and lead to better prediction of judicial decisions—"real" law. Therefore, legal realism embraced the full-scale reexamination of legal rules rejected by Holmes. To ensure its validity, realists adopted the social scientific imperative to divorce the conduct and conclusions of research from researchers' value preferences. Their approach demanded "suspended judgment . . . the questioning of the plausible, of the respectably accepted and seemingly self-evident; a serene passion for verification . . . 'constructive skepticism' . . . plus an eagerness not to be deceived" (Frank, 1969, p. 219).

"Fact skeptics" focused on fact-making trial courts as well as rule-making higher courts. Jerome Frank stressed the need to debunk the "upper court myths" that law in practice was what the higher courts said it was and that higher courts corrected lower courts' mistakes. He represented realists who condemned the courts' failure to acknowledge that law enforcement and courtroom practices varied; that those practices affected the "facts" presented at trial; and that psychological factors influenced trial judges' interpretations of disputed "facts." According to Frank, rule skepticism meant little without a recognition that the "facts" reviewed by higher courts had been skewed by personalities and practices at lower levels (1969, pp. 146-189, 222-224).

Realists thus made sharp distinctions between the literature of the law and the law itself. They argued that knowledge and honesty about "real" law would strengthen respect for the law and its practitioners. In their view, claims of legal certainty led only to frustration with lawyers and judges who could not agree on the "inevitable" conclusions of "self-evident" doctrines.

The realists' moment in the law schools and journals was brief, spanning a few years between the late 1920s and early 1930s. Enthusiastic proposals for interdisciplinary curricula and ambitious research projects were abandoned as traditionalists outmaneuvered realists in academic politics and the Depression ended funding for long-term research. Then in the political climate of the late 1930s and 1940s, anti-New Deal, Roman Catholic, and other critics linked realism to the totalitarian values of Stalin, Franco, and Mussolini, to Nazism and Marxism. As H. J. Berman argued, "the [second world] war itself required the acceptance of values and symbols sacred enough to die for; and for that, the skepticism of the legal realists was not adequate. . . . for if there is no authority beyond that of the political rulers . . . then we cannot entirely blame those who blindly carried out Hitler's orders. At least they were 'law abiding' " (1971, p. 305). Fear and patriotic fervor threatened to eclipse realism, but two developments extended its longevity.

The first development affected classrooms. Realists published textbooks to compete with formalist casebooks for the legal imaginations of law students. Through the new textbooks, even "nonrealist" law students were exposed to products of realist research and thought.

The second development affected the courtroom. During the Depression several realists became political activists. They supported Franklin D. Roosevelt, and he appointed some of them to the federal bench. Jerome Frank, debunker of the "upper court myth," was appointed to the Second Circuit Court of Appeals. Charles Clark[22] and Thurman Arnold, champions of realist research and interdisciplinary studies at Yale Law School, also were appointed to appeals courts. The U.S. Supreme Court gained three prominent legal realists. Felix Frankfurter was appointed in 1939.[23] He served until 1962. Robert H. Jackson, Attorney General at the time of Roosevelt's court-packing scheme, was appointed in 1941. He stayed until his death in 1954.[24] William O. Douglas, professor at Columbia and Yale law schools, promoter of an interdisciplinary law curriculum, and empirical researcher,[25] was appointed to the Supreme Court in 1939 and remained until 1975. Legal realists lost the battle for the law schools but gained exceptional opportunities to practice what they had preached and so to continue to spread the realist word.[26]

But for legal realists, reality lurked behind, not in, words. "Objective" words veiled judges' values, prejudices, and human nature. When the veil of language was lifted, realists expected to look in the face of subjectivity. To realists this kind of confrontation seemed healthy, even cathartic. In facing the fact of subjectivity, both judges and the community could abandon the futile pursuit of certainty and engage in more "adult" pursuits. They could pursue ways to deal with the absence of absolutes; to mitigate the effects of bias; and to develop economic, social, and legal relationships based on honest, human efforts to do justice rather than on the pretense of perfect justice. Legal realism required an end to the deception of words that constructed an illusion of certainty. Rather than claim mystical or scientific authority, judicial opinions should explain in plain language how judges balanced their perceptions, preferences, and power against the weight of the Constitution, cases, and legislatures. What the community should expect from judges was that they strive to gain self-awareness, to counteract their biases with facts derived from empirical research, and to exercise appropriate restraint (Johnson, 1981, pp. 36, 43-44, 52, 60, 68, 97-110, 123-144, 152-160; Kelly, Harbison, and Belz, 1983, pp. 467, 498; G. E. White, 1976, pp. 154-155, 187-199, 221-254, 262-275, 286-296, 321-339, 345-371).[27]

Legal-realist expectations of judicial opinions gave added dimension to the rhetorical obstacles encountered by judicial rhetors. Warned that judicial opinions would express judges' biases, word-wary audiences would extend their "healthy" skepticism to realists' opinions. And if judges could not be certain of the justice of their decisions, their audiences were in an even more precarious position. Judicial authority would be more difficult to uphold when its objective basis had been denied, especially when judges themselves were called upon to caution their audiences about their fallibility.

According to G. E. White (1976, pp. 232-239), Justice Robert Jackson's judicial speech illustrated the rhetorical tension created by judges' attempts to balance recognition of their fallibility against the ideals of impartiality and restraint. Jackson "[shortened] the distance between judges and mortals" (p. 232) with witty remarks that revealed his personal reactions and individualistic philosophy. "Devastating similes and pejorative metaphors" (p. 235) were among the stylistic devices he used to twit opposing perspectives, express "lofty vision in pungent terms" (p. 238), and demystify precedent. Off-the-bench candor about disagreements among justices further demystified the activity of judging. In White's view, "Jackson the man became a difficulty for Jackson the judge" (p. 239). If White's assessment is correct, it might apply generally to realist judges who sought standards that would justify their undemocratic power, tried to deal with the practical and philosophical consequences of uncertain law, and at the same time refused to conceal their commonality with other fallible human beings.

Reasoned elaboration. First legal science, then sociological jurisprudence, were developed in the context of the unsettling experiences of economic expansion and industrialization. Legal realism was developed against the background of the dislocations of the Great Depression. World War II and the Cold War provided the setting for the development of another philosophy of judging. From reactions against judicial philosophies that seemed to embrace moral relativism (as well as cursory, unsigned Supreme Court decisions of the late 1940s and early 1950s) came the theory of "reasoned elaboration," or "neutral principles." Legal scholars attempted to redirect judicial interest toward legal rules and away from concerns for "real-life" influences. Instead of relying on immutable truths, reasoned elaborationists wanted to create a consistent legal process based on rational thought (G. E. White, 1976, p. 230). Their approach seemed compatible with the heightened interest in rationality and democracy that arose from hot war and Cold War confrontations with totalitarian governments.

Herbert Wechsler, a one-time supporter of realist curriculum reform, supplied the "classic statement" of the approach (Johnson, 1981, p. 159). A "neutral principle" was a rule general enough to be applied to a variety of cases, and one that judges were willing to apply regardless of its result in a specific case. Belief in the principle rather than in the values or policies affected by judicial decision was the crux of the approach (Bork, 1990, p. 78).

Methodology was an automatic check on judicial bias and lack of restraint (G. E. White, 1976, p. 230). Each branch of government was "assigned" defined areas of special competence, and judges avoided usurping power by refusing to consider problems amenable to legislative, executive, or administrative resolution. This weeding process had the advantage of enabling judges to reason about and justify their decisions on the basis of legal rather than political concepts, thereby demonstrating their restraint and supporting the legitimacy of their authority (pp. 315, 322, 370). A problem that survived this first cut was analyzed further to determine whether its resolution could be guided by a society's "mature collective thought." If collective thought had not produced a clear social preference, the judiciary declined to consider the issue until society had pondered it further and made guidance available (Johnson, 1981, p. 159). The overriding issues were judicial restraint and smoothly functioning institutional processes (G. E. White, 1976, pp. 252, 293, 315, 322-323).

A dispute that fell within the judiciary's competence and was the subject of mature collective thought led to more reasoning. The case was analyzed further to unearth the relevant competing issues involved. From this last stage in the analytic process a rational, *legal* solution emerged. The quality of a judicial opinion's articulation of the reasoning process was the test and justification of judicial decisions (G. E. White, 1976, pp. 230-231).

Reasoned elaboration thus attempted to restore argument to the high status it had enjoyed in legal science. Legal realists had disdained words as the helpmeets of deception; reasoned elaborationists considered them the tools of disinterested rationality and principled decisions. In judicial opinions they would clarify the issues, show how issues were weighed, explain the applied principle and the reasons for its application, and elaborate on the general circumstances that would cause the principle to be applied or not. All of this would be done in terms of law rather than politics, economics, sociology, or results; and the terms would be made intelligible and persuasive to a lay as well as a legal audience. In this way reasoned elaboration would enable lawyers to predict legal decisions and the community to understand the rational basis of law. The test of a decision's rightness was its defensibility in a judicial opinion, and it was assumed that the restraint, reason, and principle demonstrated by the processes of reasoned elaboration would strengthen the legitimacy of judicial power in the eyes of a democratic public (Carter, 1985, pp. 75-78; G. E. White, 1976, pp. 315, 367, 370).

In spite of its apparent moral and rational advantages, reasoned elaboration was more popular among academics than among judges.[28] In the late 1950s and 1960s, grave issues divided the public, and government bodies with the "special competence" to resolve them seemed reluctant to address them. The reluctance was understandable. For example, although legislative districts that effectively granted more weight to rural votes than to those of urban populations might seem undemocratic, the legislators who owed their seats to rural voters might pause before sacrificing power to principle. If there was little public interest in addressing abuses of criminal suspects' rights, it was not expedient for legislators to spend political capital on the problem. And although equal access to public facilities might seem right to certain population groups, if they were not the same groups that supported and elected officials they commanded no political allegiance (G. E. White, 1976, p. 324).

Reasoned elaboration's failure to consider the will to act as a factor in its careful calculations may have been an oversight that destroyed its potential for counteracting the force of "might makes right" practices. Its demand for judicial inactivity in the face of apparent legal as well as social wrongs seemed to support the interests of the powerful against those of the rest. Reasoned elaboration came to be associated with political and social conservatism in spite of its developers' desire to avoid bias and partisanship. As had been the case with legal science, the judicial restraint it advocated was perceived to protect the privilege of the powerful and to deny the rights of the powerless. By the decade of the 1960s, the perfect judicial philosophy had yet to be developed.[29]

The rhetorical success of the "ideal" oracular judicial ethos was an important factor in the United States' development of a relatively stable judiciary. In dangerous and trying times, the august authority of immutable law enabled Americans to believe that ultimately they were governed by perfect law rather than imperfect people. However, the very success of this rhetorical persona made it difficult to replace when time and events muted the oracle. The judicial scientist, sociologist, realist, and rationalist all failed to command similar adherence. As unanimity about the "true" nature of judging eluded the legal profession, ambivalence grew in the community. If cumulatively the competing philosophies of jurisprudence weakened belief in an oracle pronouncing immutable law, none matched its appeal. In a sense, subsequent theories of judging have faced a presumption in favor of legal immutability and judicial distance from the community, and none has overcome that presumption.

Uncertainty about the nature of judging is matched by disagreement about the nature of judicial speech and the role of the courts in creating and maintaining community. The oracular tradition continues to influence attitudes toward U.S. courts;[30] although there now seems to be general agreement that judging is not an oracular activity, there seems to be no general agreement as to what it is, what purposes it should attempt to serve, or to whom judicial opinions should be addressed. This profound ambivalence, the result of the unique position, power, and history of the judiciary in American democracy, is a significant part of the rhetorical situation with which every U.S. judge must contend. It is the scene in which the following explorations of judicial character, philosophy, and rhetoric take place.

NOTES

1. Women, slaves, and some others generally had no voice in deciding disputed cases (Cowell, 1967, pp. 9, 18-19, 21-25; Kitto, 1967, pp. 66, 70-73).

2. For a discussion of other critics of justice and the community, see, e.g., J. B. White (1984, 1985).

3. This discussion reviews some major ideas, events, and trends. A comprehensive review of American judicial history is beyond its scope.

4. Marshall was appointed the third chief justice in 1801. His predecessors had divided their attention between the Court and their political endeavors. Their activities and the Court's failure to strike down the Alien and Sedition Acts of 1798 and Federalist court-packing schemes had inspired Republican attacks (Garraty, 1971, pp. 7-13; Stites, 1981, pp. 77-96; G. E. White, 1976, pp. 7-9). Kelly, Harbison, and Belz argue that *Marbury v. Madison* (1803) effected détente; the Court would respect executive and legislative prerogatives in return for independence and noninterference with judicial review (1983, p. 182).

5. Court unanimity ended with William Johnson's 1804 appointment, but a Marshall innovation, the joint majority opinion, endured (Friedman, 1985, p. 134; G. E. White, 1976, p. 8).

6. The background of early federal judges may explain the need for and the adroitness of this rhetorical invention. Before 1829, about 65 percent of the judges had held elective office. By 1861, the proportion increased to 78 percent. It also was relatively common for judges to resign judicial posts to assume other political positions (Friedman, 1985, pp. 137-138).

7. C. Perelman and L. Olbrechts-Tyteca viewed "convincing" arguments as inferior arguments, observing that the "concepts that men [sic] have formed of 'objective facts' and 'obvious truths' have sufficiently varied for us to be wary in this matter" (1971, p. 33).

8. For discussions of enforcement difficulties, see L. C. Berkson, 1978, pp. 69-88; J. Eisenstein, 1973, pp. 216-217; S. Goldman and T. P. Jahnige, 1976, pp. 258-264.

9. For further discussion of distancing, see, e.g., L. M. Friedman, 1985, p. 381; G. E. White, 1976, p. 2.

10. Slavery was just one community controversy that judicial decisions failed to resolve. *Dred Scott* (1857) may be the best known decision to have aggravated volatile political situations, brought notoriety to the Court, and weakened the U.S. Constitution as a symbol of unity (see, e.g., H. L. Trefousse, 1968, pp. 105-106; G. E. White, 1976, pp. 63, 77-83). Interestingly, in spite of *Dred Scott*'s infamy, a 1970 poll of scholars placed its author, Chief Justice Roger B. Taney, among the great Supreme Court justices (Blaustein and Mersky, 1978, p. 37).

11. L. M. Friedman (1985, pp. 373-374) cautions against viewing elections and impeachments as evidence of corruption, noting that some southern states forced African American and "carpetbag" judges from office in spite of distinguished service.

12. W. M. Wiecek identifies a second important ABA purpose: "to better serve its new corporate clientele" by protecting their interests from political majorities (1985, pp. 55, 57-58).

13. Harvard Law School's C. C. Langdell was the leader of legal scientism, publishing selected cases to facilitate instruction in legal science. By the early 1900s, most law schools used the case method as well as Langdell-style casebooks (Friedman, 1985, pp. 616-617).

14. Langdell asserted that law "consists of certain principles or doctrines. To have such a mastery of these as to . . . apply them with constant . . . certainty to the

ever-tangled skein of human affairs, is what constitutes a true lawyer" (In Presser and Zainaldin, 1980, p. 658).

15. J. W. Johnson believes that Holmes may not have been a true adherent of sociological jurisprudence. He points to *American Banana Company v. United Fruit Company* (1909) as an example of Holmes's tendency to treat abstract concepts as facts even when they were contradicted by experience (1981, pp. 125-126).

16. Scholars who contributed to sociological jurisprudence included Harvard Law School Dean Roscoe Pound, who supplied both its name and much of its intellectual grounding (Johnson, 1981, pp. 126-128).

17. According to Holmes, "the logical method and form flatter [everyone's] longing for certainty and for repose. . . . But certainty generally is illusion, and repose is not the destiny of man . . . You can give any conclusion a logical form. . . . But why do you imply it? It is because of some belief . . . of the community or of a class . . . on matters not capable of exact quantitative measurement, and therefore not capable of founding exact logical conclusions. Such matters really are battle grounds where the means do not exist for determinations that shall be good for all time, and where the decision can do no more than embody the preference of a given body in a given time and place" (1943, pp. 79-80).

18. The Brandeis brief's success depended in part on the idea that women were sufficiently different from men to merit special protection (Kelly, Harbison, and Belz, 1983, p. 456). Ironically, his work with able women in compiling data for and writing the brief seems to have persuaded him that women were not necessarily inferior to men (Strum, 1984, pp. 120-131).

19. R. L. Scott, "in passing," suggests that "sounding the authoritative voice" may or may not be rhetorically responsible (1984, pp. 91-92). This issue is of more than passing interest here. I argue that judges' failure to acknowledge their part in declaring the law is a strategy that closes off dialogue and thus abrogates responsibility. My judgment admittedly is influenced by a view of law as socially constructed rather than given and immutable.

20. Holmes suggested that revolution was the alternative for those who failed to gain, or were denied access to, the means for gaining majoritarian power (G. E. White, 1976, p. 159).

21. The appellation "legal realism" probably came from a 1931 law review article, Some realism about realism--Responding to Dean Pound, *Harvard Law Review* 44:1222, in which Frank defended several scholars against Pound's attack. Pound had contributed to sociological jurisprudence, but later seemed to regret his involvement and resent the philosophy (Johnson, 1981, p. 134).

22. Clark's research finding that automobile accident suits accounted for most civil jury trials in Connecticut laid the groundwork for no-fault insurance reformers (Johnson, 1981, p. 103).

23. Frankfurter considered himself a sociological jurisprude, but others identified him with legal realism (Johnson, 1981, p. 149). He coauthored a "Brandeis brief" in *Adkins v. Children's Hospital* (1923), and Brandeis hired clerks on the strength of his recommendation alone (p. 44).

24. Truman was expected to name Jackson chief justice after Harlan Fiske Stone's death, on the advice of former Chief Justice Charles Evan Hughes. However, after an anti-Jackson campaign attributed to friends of Justice Hugo Black, Fred Vinson was appointed (G. E. White, 1976, pp. 236-238).

25. Douglas's major research concerned the reasons for business failures and bankruptcies. Johnson speculates that this research influenced Douglas's appointment to the SEC in 1936 (1981, pp. 102-104).

26. Legal realists did *not* form a Supreme Court voting bloc; they often disagreed. As their philosophy would predict, the realists' respective personalities, experiences, and attitudes led to divergent visions of the law and the role of the judiciary.

27. For example, two Supreme Court realists took judicial restraint very seriously, but developed different ideals of restraint. Frankfurter's ideal entailed self-scrutiny in the pursuit of detachment and rigorous analysis of disputed issues. He insisted that judges respect the limits of their jurisdiction by not "making law" that favored their own preferences over those of legislatures. His was a passive view of law's transcendence. Jackson subordinated the judiciary to the"original intent" of the Constitution's framers. He would permit judges to interpret (and reinterpret) ambiguous constitutional provisions to solve contemporary problems but only if the interpretations were consistent with the founders' purposes, were generally applicable, and followed rather than led public opinion (G. E. White, 1976, pp. 230-250, 317-368).

28. Roger Traynor of the California Supreme Court (1940-1970) was an exception. He was a particularly able adherent of "process jurisprudence" (G. E. White, 1976, pp. 292-316).

29. The decade of the 1960s did not end development of theories of judging. However, the judicial subject of this research was appointed to the federal bench in 1966; later developments were not part of the rhetorical legacy when he donned the judicial robe.

30. For example, K. Dolbeare suggests that "persons subscribing to the 'myths' of nonpartisan, mechanical jurisprudence are more likely to rate the Court highly than are persons who see the Justices as exercising discretionary, policymaking functions" (1968, p. 211). The "professionalization" of the legal community (see, e.g., Friedman, 1985, pp. 689-693) and the large proportion of lawyers in elected or appointed legislative, executive, and administrative offices also have contributed to the distance placed between the law and the people governed by it.

3

Miles Welton Lord

> My mother was a peacemaker and my older brother was very aggressive. And between the two of them I came out with a little of both.
>
> Miles W. Lord, *Portrait: Miles Lord*

In 1966 almost everyone seemed to have a strong opinion about the politics of the federal judiciary. The U.S. Supreme Court was not the model of judicial passivity and precedent envisioned by reasoned elaboration and Cold War conservatism. Instead it seemed to be shifting the grounds of constitutional law. For the first time in U.S. history, civil and individual rights seemed to outweigh property and states' rights on the scales of justice. The federal Constitution reached beyond state lines to mandate one-person-one-vote legislative districts, enforce citizens' constitutional guarantees against state actions, and guarantee equal access to public accommodations. Legal representation was found to be a right of the poor, and courthouse doors opened to persons with previously meager access to the judicial system. Supreme Court decisions were changing the clientele and concerns of the federal courts.

The changes provoked responses. Traditionalists and those whose interests diverged from the courts' views of constitutional justice charged the courts with making law, misreading the Constitution, and meddling in legislative matters. Those whose rights recently had been discovered or implemented rejoiced at the courts' belated recognition of their proper constitutional status. As source and symbol of political, social, and economic change, the judicial system became the focus of controversy.

"What characterizes good judging?" emerged as a central question in the controversy, and competing jurisprudential philosophies offered a variety of answers. Each answer had its influence on the judiciary. Federal judges appointed during this period could interpret the reasons for their appointments from a variety of perspectives. Their interpretations could lead them to model their judicial conduct on that of the Supreme Court or to choose another model from the apparently ever-expanding store of definitions of "good" judging. Their interpretations of their roles contributed to the continuation of debate on standards of judicial behavior.

In 1966 Miles W. Lord was appointed to the federal bench by President Lyndon B. Johnson. He became one of the judges who confronted this interpretive task: why was he appointed, with what mission was he charged, and how ought he fulfill his judicial obligations? Like other judges, Lord was guided by professional training. But also like other judges he looked beyond that training to identify characteristics that might distinguish him as a "good" judge. An understanding of Lord's interpretation of his appointment and mission may be facilitated by a brief review of the background and experiences that figured in it.

THE EARLY YEARS

The Cuyuna Iron Range is a region of northern Minnesota in which people depended on the erratic fortunes of the mining and timber industries for their livelihoods (Klobuchar, 1978, p. 1B). On November 16, 1919, Miles Welton Lord was born into the Range community of Pine Knoll, the eighth of lumberjack Frank Kendall Lord's and Sunday school teacher Rachel Ann Terry Lord's nine children (Chase, 1976, p. 168; Federal judge, 1976, p. 24; Klobuchar, 1974b, p. 1B; McEnroe, 1985, p. 6A). The Lord family endured the financial hardships typical of Range life. Sharing a bed with three brothers, Lord saw nothing abnormal about his family's standard of living: "everybody was poor then; somebody was middle class if he was getting three meals a day" (Grow, 1985, p. 1C; Newlund, 1982, p. 6T). Food, clothing, and shelter were not to be taken for granted.

However, there were important exceptions to the norm of poverty. "Everybody" meant the people *with* whom Lord's family lived and worked, not those *for* whom they worked. Lord has recalled that the mining and lumber "companies were making a profit, but people were suffering" (Lord, 1988a). During his childhood years he perceived that people's suffering was intensified by differences in the rules applied to the poor and the rich; many of his stories about his youth concern those perceived differences.[1]

Differential treatment contradicted the moral standards taught by his mother and the values practiced in his Range community, and those standards and values influenced his judicial responses to inequities. As he commented during a television interview, "When I have problems, when I face decisions, when I consider economic matters, social matters, law-enforcement matters, I take myself back to this little town. 'Wonder what would the people in Crosby/Ironton say about this?' I'm able to get a good deal of help in deciding what I think is right, fair, appropriate and just" (Lord, 1984). It was a judge's duty to see that whatever was "right, fair, appropriate and just" applied to all, regardless of social or economic status.[2]

The vulnerability and values of the working poor were not the only lessons Lord learned during his early years. He also learned how to fight. In the Crosby of the 1930s, school children faced a daily gauntlet of "territories." Each territory was the preserve of an ethnic group—Finnish, Slav, Norwegian, or Swedish—and each group had its champion. Developing an active dislike for bullies (Lord, 1990), Lord participated in many youthful confrontations. Because sprinting was not one of his strengths, he "had to be ready" to fight his way home from school (McEnroe, 1985, p. 6A). At some point Lord's inability to run fast led to an unwillingness to run at all, and he demonstrated what would become a long-lived penchant for applying insights and skills gained in one realm of experience to challenges in another. He applied the skills of the street in an attempt to become a "champion of champions" (Berg and Stone, 1976, p. 1C; Grow, 1985, p. 16C).

In the 1930s, boxing occupied a privileged place in Minnesota's popular culture. People flooded Golden Gloves boxing events, and tournaments were radio broadcast throughout the state. Revealing an enduring preference for being an actor rather than spectator, the sixteen-year-old Lord set his sights on a Golden Gloves championship. Three years later the young featherweight reached the Upper Midwest Regional Championship tournament.

Although he was described as "resplendent in his white robe" (Grow, 1985, p. 1C), Lord failed to become the champion. He did, however, begin to establish a public reputation. Having broken a thumb early in his final bout, Lord was knocked repeatedly to the floor. After each knockdown he laughed to bolster his own courage and to reassure his onlooking family. With the sixth (or eleventh or nineteenth—reports vary) knockdown, Lord lost the fight. The referee recalled that "I think he was down six times. But he got up six times and finished on his feet" (Oslund, 1984, p. 4A). Public reaction to Lord's performance was mixed, seeming to presage responses to his later judicial performances. Some spectators admired his spirit and tenacity; others, including his future mother-in-law, heard his laughter over their radios and concluded that he was a "smart aleck" (Berg and Stone, 1976, p. 9C; McEnroe, 1985, p. 6A; Oslund, 1984, p. 4A).

Regardless of others' reactions, Lord has said that Golden Gloves boxing proved to him that he need not be afraid, and he has been said to appreciate comparisons "between his boxing career and his career behind the bench" (Grow, 1985, p. 1C). More than one commentator has noted that the pugnacity, tenacity, and defiance he displayed as a boxer later seemed to become a part of his judicial character (see, e.g., Federal judge, 1976, p. 24), and Lord himself has said that "if you had to rate the three best things I can do, [I guess] it would be, one, try a lawsuit. Two, fight. And three, politics" (Berg and Stone, 1976, p. 9C).

THE PATH TO LAW

Both censors and admirers of the legal profession might connect Lord's decision to join it with his pugnacity and tenacity. Lord, however, attributes his career choice to his mother. He has recounted how Rachel Lord told her eleven-year-old son that he would make a good lawyer (Lord, 1988a). Notwithstanding this early inspiration, Lord took a meandering road on the way to a legal career. As a teenager he displayed a temperament devoid of the reserve stereotypically associated with judges. By the time he graduated from Crosby-Ironton high school in 1937, he had participated in his share of pranks that ranged from overturning outhouses to drinking moonshine (Klobuchar, 1974b, pp. 1B, 6B; 1978, p. 1B).

When he graduated from high school, Lord was advised that the only way for him to be recognized as an adult was to get out of his hometown (McEnroe, 1985, p. 6A). But he was not ready to leave. Instead he became the only Lord sibling to attend college, enrolling in Crosby-Ironton Junior College with a $20 loan from one of his brothers. He supported himself with a job at the Crosby Armory and service in the National Guard. In 1940 Lord married Maxine Zontelli, the woman with whom he had jitterbugged to a dance championship, and the next year the couple opened the X-L Cafe in Crosby. When the business failed in 1942, Lord finally was convinced that it was time to move on. In 1942 he and Maxine Zontelli Lord moved to Minneapolis.

In Minneapolis, Lord briefly attended the Dunwoody Technical Institute. But in the fall of 1942 he began in earnest the process of becoming a lawyer, enrolling at the University of Minnesota. After a period in the Air Force from 1944 through 1945, Lord received his B.S.L. degree in 1946. By 1948, he had received his law degree from the University of Minnesota Law School, where, he has said, faculty "saw [that] Miles Lord didn't fit" because he saw politics in everything (Lord, 1990). He was admitted to the Minnesota bar and was ready for a career in law.[3]

Lord's journey from undergraduate student to lawyer was eventful in many ways. Two children, Priscilla and Miles, Jr. (Mick), had been born, and Lord worked at a variety of jobs to support the family and to pay off the debts of the failed cafe. As a law student, he also was a welder, janitor, tractor driver, packinghouse worker, appliance salesperson, logger, dishwasher, ditch digger, steam shovel operator, construction worker, insurance adjuster,[4] and bellhop. On the way to a relatively exalted profession, he was maintaining his ties to the working class (Berg and Stone, 1976, p. 9C; Chase et al., 1976, p. 168; Federal judge, 1976, p. 24; Judge ousted, 1976, p. 80; Lord, 1978, p. 241; Klobuchar, 1974b, p. 1B; McEnroe, 1985, p. 6A; Oslund, 1984, p. 4A). He also was forming new friendships and developing interests that were to influence profoundly his future.

Along with religious and community values, a perception that the poor and the rich were subject to different rules, a reluctance to turn away from a fight, the habit of hard work, the experience of failure, and a determination to overcome failure and pay his debts, Lord brought to law school an interest in politics that dated back to his boyhood (Klobuchar, 1974b, p. 1B). It seems fitting that in law school he met Orville Freeman, a classmate who soon became a friend and later became governor of Minnesota. This meeting had far-reaching consequences. Freeman introduced Lord to Eugenie Anderson, who would be the first female U.S. ambassador (Blegen, 1975, p. 578); Eugene McCarthy, a future U.S. representative, senator, and presidential hopeful; and the young Walter F. Mondale, a future U.S. senator, U.S. vice president, and presidential candidate. The most important introduction Freeman performed, however, was to Hubert H. Humphrey, a man whom Lord came to love as a brother,[5] and whose future held the mayoralty of Minneapolis, a successful career in the U.S. Senate, a less successful career as U.S. vice president, and the bitter loss of a presidential election campaign (Klobuchar, 1974b, p. 1B; McEnroe, 1985, p. 6A).

Lord's new friends already were political activists. Under Humphrey's leadership, several had been instrumental in the 1944 fusing of the Minnesota Democratic and Farmer-Labor parties. Lord was struck by the similarities in his own views and their progressive impulses. Although the demands of debts, law school, and family prevented him from taking an early leadership role in the Democratic-Farmer-Labor Party (DFL), he participated in its activities whenever he could.

In fact, Lord contributed to DFL causes even when activism conflicted with financial security. At one time he was working as a hotel night clerk for 35 cents an hour and the use of an apartment. At then-Mayor Humphrey's request, he testified in favor of rent control at the Minnesota legislature.[6] When his employer learned of his testimony, Lord lost his job (Lord, 1988a). As he has remembered it, this kind of risk taking for the good of the community was common among early DFLers: "Times were harder then for working people and hard times make for more unselfishness. We obtained votes on the theory we were going to help each other. We'd appeal to people's goodness" (McEnroe, 1985, p. 6A). Like the poverty of childhood, these hard times had lasting effects on Lord's thought and action; appeals to goodness eventually became a staple of his judicial speech.

LAWYERING AND POLITICKING

The Beginning Lawyer-Politician

In spite of his political ideals and concern for the community, Lord's first task upon admission to the Minnesota bar was to earn a living. With this objective, he started his own private law practice. By 1949, he had accumulated a $900 "safety net" for the Lord family, which numbered five with the birth of James. He was ready to begin a career in politics. His political hopes were dashed when he lost a race for the Minnesota legislature. However, he was able to salvage some good from the wreck of his political ambitions. He had gained sufficient "notoriety" to earn the attention of other party members (Lord, 1988a). When a fellow DFLer resigned his position as an assistant U.S. attorney in 1951, Lord was appointed to the post. He became a winning prosecutor specializing in tax cases (Klobuchar, 1974b, p. 1B).

The tax cases Lord prosecuted were no ordinary cases. He has described being "scared stiff" when, as a neophyte district attorney, he prosecuted "local Al Capones" such as Tommy Banks, Rocky LaPino, and Kid Cann (Lord, 1988a). Lord won convictions in all of these sensational trials while also investigating narcotics traffic in a Minnesota prison (Parsons, 1966a, p. 1A). Nevertheless, he recognized that successful prosecutions were not enough to solidify his government service position. As Dwight D. Eisenhower campaigned for the presidency, Lord predicted for himself a short tenure under a Republican administration. In 1952 he resigned his post rather than waiting to be fired (Lord, 1988a).

Campaigning

But if a federal post under a Republican president was not feasible, there was still a state to serve. In 1954 Lord ran for the office of state attorney general. He campaigned with Orville Freeman, his old law school friend and the DFL candidate for governor who had lost an earlier gubernatorial bid. Lord devoted himself fully to party goals, and the vigorous 1954 DFL campaign became a legend in Minnesota politics. It also marked the emergence of Lord's political persona.[7] According to one report, Lord "was an unquenchable campaigner. A political battle to him was a war, all right, but he liked to fight it with rubber torpedoes and flour bombs" (Klobuchar, 1974b, p. 1B). The joyful pugilist reemerged.

Several campaign "war stories" feature Lord's exploits, and these stories contain three recurring elements: Lord's refusal to be deterred, his use of humor, and his willingness to contribute to others' campaigns. For example, Lord campaigned on behalf of Freeman as well as for himself. At one point he arranged a televised debate with the incumbent Republican governor to discuss alleged irregularities in a state building contract. When the incumbent failed to appear, Lord was undaunted; he debated an empty chair (Federal judge, 1976, p. 24). In a rural district, Lord turned his accidental alienation of a voter to his advantage. When a dairy farmer became annoyed by Lord's amplified "moos" emanating from an unmarked sound truck, Lord quickly entreated the irate man to vote for his opponent, "the man who loves cows" (Klobuchar, 1974b, p. 1B). Stories of Lord's campaigning on behalf of Hubert H. Humphrey, the "fishing buddy" for whom he sometimes acted as a "warm-up" speaker, are numerous; they are filled with examples of practical jokes as well as demonstrations of affection.[8] Although one author has said that "Lord's showmanship . . . strained relations with Freeman, whose approach to politics was disciplined, puritanical, and humorless" (Lewis, 1980, p. 91), Lord sometimes is given major credit for the victory of the entire 1954 DFL ticket—including his own election as Minnesota's attorney general (Oslund, 1984, p. 4A; Parsons, 1966a, p. 6).

Attorney General

Lord's performance as Minnesota's attorney general in some ways typified his career-long approach to political and legal problems. First, his actions often seemed designed to increase the control of farmers, working people, and the less affluent over their own lives. Second, the increase in ordinary people's power often seemed to be gained at the expense of institutional powers. Third, Lord demonstrated a willingness to exercise power strategically, both in public and behind the scenes.

Lord believes that one of his most significant accomplishments as attorney general was to reverse Minnesota's longstanding position that health maintenance organizations (HMOs) violated citizens' right to choose their own doctors. In Lord's view this position, advanced by professional medical organizations, minimized competition among medical professionals and preserved their exclusive control over the delivery and costs of care. Consequently, he prepared a legal opinion that asserted the legality of private citizens banding together to hire physicians. He assigned an assistant attorney general, one with close ties to the state medical association and insurance companies, to support the opinion in the legislature and in court. Privately he gave this assistant incentive to argue persuasively: if Lord's opinion was appealed, the assistant would be fired. Lord's position prevailed.

Although Lord acknowledges that HMOs now may abuse the patient rights they were designed to protect, he also believes that a young attorney general's willingness to exercise power in public and behind the scenes helped to adjust the power relationship between the public and the medical community (Lord, 1988a).

The public apparently generally approved of Lord's approach to politics and law. In spite of some unpopular actions, such as ordering the reinstatement of students expelled from high school because they were pregnant (Lord, 1988b), he was reelected attorney general in 1956 and 1958. Even at the height of his political popularity, however, he was not admired universally. In fact, another pattern typical of Lord's later professional relationships emerged during his terms as attorney general: he faced what he termed a "hostile" Minnesota Supreme Court.

Lord has insisted that the court's hostility stemmed from political differences between the court's majority—"holdover conservative Republicans" who did "nothing but hold the status quo" (Lord, 1988a)—and himself. Again adversity seemed to enliven rather than deter him. His determination to get things done, as well as his willingness to do battle to get things done, exacerbated existing tensions.

After the Minnesota Supreme Court already had reversed several actions taken by Minnesota's governor on Lord's legal advice,[9] the tensions came to a head in the spring of 1959. The state legislature was embroiled in arguments about statewide daylight savings time (DST). This seemingly innocuous issue inspired strong feelings in a state that included metropolitan areas, manufacturing and farming interests, and entertainment and recreation industries along its borders. The DST law would expire on July 1, and the legislature seemed unlikely to resolve the issue during its current term. Attempting to bypass the legislature's division, three metropolitan county boards set April 26 as their DST starting date. On April 25, the Minnesota Supreme Court ordered the counties to "do nothing" about DST. When the county attorneys turned to Lord for his interpretation of the order, he told them that it prohibited counties from passing new policies but not from enforcing previously enacted policies. On April 26, the counties went on DST.

Perhaps not surprisingly, the Minnesota Supreme Court disagreed with Lord's interpretation. However, it reacted even more strongly to peripheral events. One county attorney told the court that its order "accomplished great confusion and the sale of a lot of newspapers," and county board members publicly called the order "silly and asinine" (Hurst, 1959b, p. 11). In addition, Lord's public statements about the affair, delivered at the behest of the governor, characterized the court's involvement in DST as against the public interest. In response, the court summoned the three county attorneys and Lord to appear before them on May 28 to answer charges of unprofessional conduct as officers of the court.

On May 28 the court absolved the three county attorneys of all wrongdoing except bad judgment. All denied knowing that the attorney general's office once had declared that no DST action could be taken until the state law had expired; one apologized for imprudent remarks to the court; and another avowed that he had not advised county board members to criticize the court. Lord's response was different. At the governor's direction Lord evaded notice of the hearing, maintaining that the court long ago had determined that attorneys general were officers of state government rather than of the court. In angry response, the Minnesota Supreme Court censured Lord and effectively placed him on a three-year probation to ensure his good conduct (Hurst, 1959b, p. 1).

In its censuring opinion, the court seemed particularly aggrieved at Lord's public statements. They labeled his public discussion of the DST matter "improper and unethical" and claimed that it was "motivated by an inordinate desire for publicity or by a desire to gain political popularity by undermining confidence in the integrity and impartiality of our judicial system" (Hurst, 1959b, pp. 1, 7). Lord seemed unrepentant, issuing a statement saying that he would continue to use his own judgment in carrying out his official duties. Long afterward he continued to view the controversy as a matter "long in personalities and short on legal arguments" (Parsons, 1966a, p. 6), the consequence of personal and political antipathies between him and the Chief Justice.

So in 1959 Lord collected his first court rebuke. In some respects the DST affair seems to encapsulate his approaches to problem solving, the reactions his approaches provoked, and his own responses to such reactions. When Lord perceived a problem, he would gather information, analyze it, and take direct action to solve the problem, often attempting to enlist public opinion in support of his view. Others would perceive Lord's actions, especially his enlistment of public opinion, as improper, and seek legal remedy for the perceived impropriety. Lord would be unabashed by rebukes and resolve to continue "doing the right thing" in spite of evidence that he sometimes experienced personal as well as professional hurt as a result of these collisions.

In fact, it appears that the DST affair combined with other disappointments to persuade Lord that politics was too bruising a game. During the same period, he had objected to the state conservation commissioner's plan to sell Minnesota's natural peat resources to an oil company. Lord believed that the proposed sale contract would both shortchange Minnesota's taxpayers and lead to environmental damage. He was dismayed when the governor met his objection with a request to keep the peace until after the election. Lord also found fund-raising distasteful. He suspected that seeking and accepting others' money would make it more difficult to act against the contributors' interests. But the biggest disappointment came when the governor, who had been his friend and whom he had helped elect, reneged on what Lord believed to be a promise to appoint him to the Minnesota Supreme Court (Parsons, 1966a, p. 6; Lord, 1988a). As a result, although a 1958 statewide poll revealed Lord to be Minnesota's most popular Democrat (Berg and Stone, 1976, p. 1C), he declined to run for the U.S. Senate (Lord, 1988a). Eugene McCarthy became the DFL's nominee and won the election (Engelmayer and Wagman, 1985, p. 112).

Disillusioned with politics—"If that is all I am, a piece of meat here, I didn't need it" (Lord, 1988a)—Lord made one "last" political move. He advised the governor to appoint one of his part-time assistants, Walter Mondale, to succeed him as attorney general (Berg and Stone, 1976, p. 9C; Lord, 1990). To ensure Mondale's success, Lord told the governor to have the new attorney general "open the Sister Kenny file" (Lewis, 1980, pp. 99-101; Lord, 1988a). Leaving Mondale to prosecute a sensational fraud case that would lead to changes in charity fund-raising laws, the "swashbuckling crusader who hounded mobsters, smote down vested interests, and harangued the state supreme court for being the lackey of big business" (Lewis, 1980, p. 91) resigned his post and returned to private practice, refusing even to consider a position in the U.S. Department of Justice (Berg and Stone, 12/9/76, p. 9C; Lord, 1988a; Parsons, 1966a, p. 6).[10]

FROM U.S. ATTORNEY TO FEDERAL JUDGE

Lord pursued his private law practice for approximately one year. In 1961 he initially said "no" when Hubert Humphrey asked whether he would become a U.S. attorney. But Humphrey had a persuasive argument: he reminded his friend that U.S. attorneys were appointed to the federal bench more often than were other lawyers.[11] Because Lord considered a judicial appointment the "epitome of the legal profession" (Lord, 1988a), Humphrey prevailed. His hopes for a judicial post revived, Lord was appointed a U.S. Attorney by President John F. Kennedy.[12]

Lord performed creditably as a federal prosecutor. He focused on criminals and prison conditions (McEnroe, 1985, p. 6A), successfully prosecuted Teamsters Union associate Benjamin Dranow on a tax fraud charge (Parsons, 1966a, p. 6), participated in amassing the evidence that led to Teamsters Union President James Hoffa's imprisonment (Engelmayer and Wagman, 1985, p. 111), and prosecuted officers of Chicago mailing firms for fraud against the Sister Elizabeth Kenny Institute (Parsons, 1966a, p. 6). But perhaps more important than what Lord did as a federal prosecutor was what he did *not* do: he did not attract the unfavorable attention of the federal courts. He remained a U.S. attorney until 1966, when he was appointed to the federal district court (Klobuchar, 1974b, p. 1B).

Nomination and Appointment to the Federal Bench

When Lord was nominated for a federal judgeship, he became involved in a political process dominated by presidents and senators. According to Article II of the U.S. Constitution, the president nominates and, with the advice and consent of the Senate, appoints federal judges. Regardless of recurring arguments about the meaning of "advice and consent,"[13] students of the appointment process have found that from early times the Senate has played an active role in selecting judges (see, e.g., Abraham, 1980; Chase, 1972; Goldman and Jahnige, 1976; McFeeley, 1987). So it was fortunate for Lord that his long-time friends were successful in politics. Humphrey was vice president of the United States, McCarthy became the senior senator from Minnesota when Humphrey left the Senate, and Mondale was appointed to fill the vacancy created by Humphrey's departure.[14] When a judicial vacancy occurred in Minnesota, all seemed in place to assure that Lord would fill the post.

In fact, Humphrey often has been credited with Lord's judicial nomination and appointment, and his laudatory prediction that Lord would be a "people's judge" has been quoted widely (see, e.g., Engelmayer and Wagman, 1985, p. 112; Peterson, 1979, p. 4B). However, given the Senate's role in appointing federal judges, it was important that Lord also had friends in the Senate.

The Senate has shown itself generally unwilling to consent to a judicial nominee opposed by home-district senators; in the event of their opposition, the Senate Judiciary Committee simply may not act on the nomination.[15] And, although presidents' accommodations to "senatorial courtesy" vary, in Johnson's administration senators usually were consulted even before an upcoming vacancy was made public. Their suggestions were taken seriously (McFeeley, 1987, p. 55; Goldman and Jahnige, 1976, pp. 49-52, 58-59). In fact, according to Goldman and Jahnige, Johnson "was amenable to having his officials defer to the wishes of Democratic Party senators unless the candidates were clearly unacceptable" (p. 50). Thus McCarthy's and Mondale's active support of Lord's appointment was crucial.[16]

However, the senators' support did not operate in a vacuum. It coincided with Johnson's agenda for the judiciary. Succeeding to the "Kennedy presidency," Johnson had respected Kennedy's plans for the judiciary by nominating and supporting Kennedy's judicial selections. As a result of these nominations, Johnson experienced some unwelcome defeats.[17] Then the federal courts became an issue during the 1964 campaign. Barry Goldwater attacked the courts' interest in the rights of criminal defendants (Cortner, 1972, pp. 240-242). Johnson came to the courts' defense, praising their independence and civil rights decisions. After his election, he took an active interest in judicial appointments and was determined to put his own stamp on the judicial selection process (McFeeley, 1987, pp. 35-69). Like presidents before and after him, he established criteria and executive procedures for judicial nominations.

Lord met many of Johnson's criteria, for reasons both beyond and within his control. His age, forty-six, worked in his favor. Johnson had made clear his desire to inject youthful vitality into the federal courts (McFeeley, 1987, pp. 77-80), and in the world of federal judges Lord was young. Humphrey's earlier career counseling also proved its value. It enabled Lord to meet another Johnson criterion, government service. He was one of over 45 percent of Johnson's district court appointees who previously had been prosecutors, most as U.S. attorneys (McFeeley, 1987, p. 74). In addition, Lord's years as a political campaigner and state attorney general were important factors in his appointment. Active political involvement of appointees, Republicans as well as Democrats,[18] was another Johnson criterion (McFeeley, 1987, pp. 82-83).

Lord's political beliefs also served his nomination well, and in this regard timing was crucial. Lord was appointed in 1966, when Johnson's criterion of "loyalty" referred to sharing progressive ideals, believing absolutely in racial justice, supporting civil rights, and perhaps having favored the 1964 Johnson-Humphrey ticket. These requirements Lord easily met. Fortunately, he was not required to meet a criterion that became increasingly important in 1967, that nominees share Johnson's views on Vietnam policy. By 1967, Lord was beginning to believe that a solution to the Vietnam conflict might be found somewhere between the positions held by his friends Humphrey and McCarthy (Berg and Stone, 1976, p. 9C; Klobuchar, 1974b, p. 1B). As it was, Lord was appointed during the period of Johnson's "liberal" appointments (McFeeley, 1987, pp. 85-93).

Although Lord encountered little difficulty in meeting Johnson's criteria, another criterion, merit, caused some consternation. As a University of Minnesota law school graduate, his educational background was acceptable, if not quite imbued with the Ivy League prestige favored by Johnson (McFeeley, 1987, pp. 72-73). However, he found frustrating and demeaning the process of obtaining a third-rung "qualified" rating from the American Bar Association's (ABA's) Standing Committee on Federal Judiciary (SCFJ).[19]

At the time of Lord's appointment, relations between Johnson, the ABA, and the SCFJ were strained. The SCFJ had opposed three of Johnson's "Kennedy legacy" nominees, rousing Johnson's resentment. During the 1964 presidential campaign the ABA gave further offense by seeking both candidates' written agreement that, if elected president, they would attend to the SCFJ in making appointments. Johnson would not give assurances that met ABA expectations. The ABA complained about his manipulation of its ratings. In return, Johnson's Attorney General assigned responsibility for advising on judicial nominees to an assistant deputy with reservations about the ABA. Then the administration and the ABA again clashed over a "Kennedy" nominee (McFeeley, 1987, pp. 60-62). As a result, Lord faced ABA screening during a contest of wills between the president and the lawyers' organization.

Two other factors contributed to a screening process that Lord perceived as hostile and filled with "political machinations . . . that would curl your hair" (Peterson, 1979, p. 1B). First, the SCFJ long has been reputed to favor conservative nominees; its membership has been labeled "Wall Street and Bar Association-establishment types" (Goldman and Jahnige, 1976, p. 52). One of its directors conceded that members "do tend to come from large firms and to rely on personal acquaintances for opinions on candidates" and that "liberal and public-interest group spokesmen [sic]" criticize the SCFJ for representing corporate interests (Peterson, 1979, pp. 1B, 4B; see also, Ball, 1980, pp. 187-188; Grossman, 1965, pp. 106-114, 208-221 on bias in SCFJ ratings). Lord's "liberal" credentials might be expected to receive close scrutiny.

A second factor complicating the screening process was more personal; Lord and SCFJ head Albert Jenner had a previous adversarial relationship. Lord first had encountered Jenner in Chicago, where he prosecuted Jenner's client. A newspaper reported that "during the trial and the following appeals, Jenner bitterly attacked Lord on several occasions" (Parsons, 1966a, p. 6). According to Lord, his one-time courtroom opponent had not left bitterness behind when he examined Lord's credentials: he "had his own ax to grind and he ground it to a fine point" (Peterson, 1979, p. 1B).

Mixed Reactions

Notwithstanding these difficulties, on February 10, 1966, Lord emerged from the screening with a "qualified" rating and a nomination to the federal district court. On May 2 he swore his oath as a federal judge. In a crowded Minneapolis courtroom he remarked that he now had the job he had "wanted . . . for 22 years" (Parsons, 1966b, p. 1). Reactions to the nomination and appointment were as mixed as had been reactions to his previous activities.

On the one hand, an editorial in the reputedly conservative *Minneapolis Star* labeled Lord's nomination "more political than prudent" (Miles Lord appointment, 1966, p. 14), citing Lord's DST censure as evidence that his temperament was not of the judicial sort. Conceding that in seven years "Lord apparently has won respect from both the Justice Department and the federal bench," it nevertheless could only "hope" that he would "earn the esteem—rather than the censure—of his colleagues on the bench" (Miles Lord appointment, 1966, p. 14). On the other hand, Lord's public past also earned him praise; a letter to the *Star*'s editor supported the appointment and cited the DST incident as a credit to Lord's good sense and decisiveness in the face of others' inaction (Nygaard, 1966, p. 4).

Lord himself made no apologies for the politics involved in his judicial appointment.[20] In broad terms, he believed that the political nature of the process helped to protect the public and the judiciary from incompetent judges. In his view, senators staked part of their reputations, and thus their reelection, on the quality of their judicial selections. They had compelling reasons for exercising good judgment. In fact, Lord believed that attempts to depoliticize judicial selection created greater dangers. As he saw it, strong interest groups were likely to use their influence to gain representation on supposedly objective "merit committees." Concerned only with their particular interests and "answerable to no one" (Peterson, 1979, pp. 1B, 4B), these representatives could screen out nominees unsympathetic to their causes. From this perspective, the ordinary person was better off with the selections of broad-constituency politicians having personal knowledge of their candidates' characters.[21]

Lord appreciated the appointment process for yet another reason. He believed that his legal competence, personal character, and conduct all had been examined closely by the Federal Bureau of Investigation (FBI), the ABA, the White House, the Senate, and the public, and had been approved. As Lord has put it, "I had behind me a hell of a track record [and] if they wished to reject me they could have, as they did with Bork. . . . So when I got there I thought they had stamped [my record] and said, 'Miles, you're ok. Do some more of it'" (Lord,

1988b). If not granted a mandate to become "the people's judge," Lord had been given "freedom to do what I had the courage to do" (Lord, 1988b).

THE "REALISTIC" JUDGE

So when Lord began hearing his first case the day after his swearing-in, he already had formed at least a skeletal framework for his answer to the question, what characterizes good judging? This framework seemed to follow the broad outlines of "realist" judicial philosophy. In fact, it seemed to match in several important respects the beliefs and attitudes of Lord's "favorite" judge, realist Supreme Court Justice William O. Douglas (Ackerberg, 1982, p. 11A).

Access and Equality

One of the most important tenets in Lord's philosophy of judging was that everyone, poor or rich, should have a chance to seek justice in a court of law. Before his appointment he had envisioned the judicial life as affording ample time for reflection and leisure (Lord, 1988a).[22] But once he joined the profession, his working hours were as long and hard as any he ever had worked. A new vision of "legions of people lined up for justice [who] waited if I took time off" (Lord, 1990) contributed to a caseload that was the largest in his district even after he became the district's chief judge in 1981 (Zack, 1985b, p. 3B).[23]

Like Douglas (Douglas, 1980,[24] pp. 378-392), Lord rejected the notion that the Warren Court and civil rights movement had lengthened the line by encouraging overlitigiousness and frivolous lawsuits.[25] Instead he supported poor people's access to courtrooms once reserved largely for the rich and organized. He believed that if the number of suits brought by individuals grew, it was because the population grew; and that most people who sued in federal courts did so for serious reasons (Lord, 1988a; 1988b).[26] The courts in their turn should take the people seriously. When asked after his retirement what his proudest accomplishment had been, Lord replied that he was grateful for being able "to do justice without fear or favor . . . and *in the process,* to be able to act out of some of the genuine concerns I have for the people who couldn't ordinarily do it for themselves and who might not be listened to by another judge" (Lord, 1988a).

Some of Lord's harshest criticism was reserved for those, including retired Chief Justice Warren Burger, who sought to limit class-action suits, contingency fee arrangements, and other measures that enabled people of limited means to seek redress for their injuries. He suspected that critics objected as much to the democratization of access and accountability these measures represented as they did to any increase in judicial work load: "they think it's bad because it gives poor people the key to the courthouse" (Lord, 1988a). He argued that if work load were the real issue, corporations that consumed years of court time suing each other would attract the criticism aimed at individuals who contested corporate actions (Klobuchar, 1983a, p. 2B). This suspicion was tied to another of Lord's tenets of good judging, that one of the judiciary's obligations was to "protect the public from the gods we make of success and profit" (Klobuchar, 1974b, p. 6B; Peterson, 1979, p. 4B).

Lord was openly skeptical about the judiciary's success in meeting this obligation. He perceived as relatively rare his own willingness to call powerful corporations to account for their actions. Furthermore, he believed that he had found a specific, if partial, explanation for the phenomenon: the close relationship between the interests of corporations and the ABA lawyers who represented them (Peterson, 1979, p. 1B).

In this belief, too, Lord resembled Douglas, an outspoken critic of corporate influence on the judiciary. Douglas charged that judges "often act as if we are a government of the corporations, by the corporations, and for the corporations" (Douglas, 1980, p. 384). He attributed the phenomenon in large part to a judicial selection process that depended heavily upon the opinions of ABA "mouthpieces . . . of the dominant corporate interests" (p. 42; see also pp. 20, 42, 194-195, 229, 374, 386).[27] To anyone who believed in immutable, scientific, or neutral law, Lord's and Douglas's common concern about corporate influence was unacceptable. Even more controversial were their bluntly stated opinions regarding judicial objectivity.

Judicial Objectivity

Concern about corporate influence on the judiciary stemmed from the realist rejection of judicial claims to objectivity. Lord has stated flatly that "there is absolutely no such thing as . . . an impartial judge" (Lord, 1988a).[28] He believed it impossible for any person to shed his or her interests, values, and distinctive sense of right and wrong simply by assuming the bench. In fact, he speculated that a person for whom such a feat would be possible might be unfit to serve: "If you don't have a heart, you don't have understanding, you don't have compassion, how can you make judgments?" (McGuinness, 1988, p. 261). Douglas had reached similar conclusions, observing that justices' emotional responses, not their intellectual analyses, were the ruling factors in their judicial decision making (Douglas, 1980, p. 8). Disbelief in objectivity aroused in both judges a desire for judges with a variety of interests, values, and moral beliefs. They believed that such inclusion would contribute to recognition of and respect for all parties who entered the courtroom. In this respect both judges found the judicial system wanting.

Lord perceived that the judicial selection process resulted in his own view of justice being underrepresented: "Once in a while you'll run into a fellow like me. But . . . the blow is cushioned by the rest of the judiciary" (Peterson, 1979, p. 4B). He believed that this underrepresentation was exacerbated by ambitious judges' tendency to make conservative decisions and avoid controversy in order to "run for higher office" within the judicial system (Lord, 1990).

Nevertheless, Lord did not believe that underrepresentation entitled him to eschew the responsibilities that accompanied skepticism. If he could not be impartial, he wanted to be fair. The steps he took as an antidote for his own potential prejudice were distinctly realist, involving a thorough examination of the facts to educate himself and others about the immediate and long-term issues they involved. His pursuit of facts earned him praise from some; for example, one judge told reporters that "Miles . . . is . . . a creative thinker, a good judge. All right, an activist. He goes in and probes" (Berg and Stone, 1976, p. 8C). But in other instances this safeguard seemed to increase rather than allay fears about his fairness.[29] His eager pursuit of antidotal information often conflicted with the strategies of attorneys who wished to limit access to evidence; and often the attorneys who most persistently resisted his fact finding represented corporations.

Predictably, this circumstance led to "chicken-and-egg" disputes. On the one hand, Lord sometimes was accused of seeking information *because* of anticorporate bias rather than as a check against bias. On the other hand, Lord sometimes accused corporations of concealing evidence to bias judicial perceptions of the facts in a case. After eighteen years on the bench, he estimated that he had presided over only two civil suits in which the corporations properly had produced documentary evidence to which the court and the opposing parties were entitled (Many firms, 1984, p.14B).[30] Lord's plain speaking on this score did nothing to smooth ruffled feathers, and his plain speaking on other matters ruffled them further.

Lord had little patience with those who equated judicial impartiality with judges' silence or lack of candor about their extrajudicial opinions and activities.[31] For example, he responded to criticism of his support for the political ambitions of Hubert Humphrey's son with the derisive declaration that his critics must be ignorant of history (IRs protest, 1982, p. 4C). He was equally dismissive of protests about his own periodic expressions of interest in running for elective offices or practicing law as an attorney (see, e.g., Berg and Stone, 1976, p. 9C; Dornfeld and Rebuffoni, 1975, pp. 1B, 2B; Klobuchar, 1983a, pp. 1B, 2B; Wilson, 1977, p. 1A). Reporters noted that Lord's candor disturbed the legal community not because its members were unaware of other judges' political leanings but because they felt that the public should not know of them (Berg and Stone, 1976, p. 1C). His comments were controversial because they violated the boundary between professionals and laypersons. Lord's nonconformity in this regard was indicative of another characteristic of his approach to "good judging"—his belief that conventional conceptions of "appropriate" judicial temperament actually interfered with it.

Judicial Temperament

Lord's fundamental attitude toward judicial temperament was that "it can be overdone. To be effective as a judge . . . you don't have to sit there like an undertaker. I think the real core of 'judicial temperament' is fairness. Have you as a judge tried to grant a fair hearing, have you brought all of your resources to bear on a question" (Klobuchar, 1974b, p. 1B). Decorum was a poor substitute for performance. He believed judging to be of great consequence but, at its roots, a practical rather than an exalted activity, performed by human beings rather than demigods (Kimball, 1978, p. 13A). In this he agreed with Douglas, who had admonished that in interpreting law "the overriding consideration was whether the . . . interpretation suited modern needs, modern problems" (Douglas, 1980, p. 121). Lord also believed that facts, not schools of thought, were at the crux of judicial decisions. Again he agreed with Douglas, who had said that once a judge determined the facts in a dispute the law could be applied relatively easily (p. 180).

As a result of this realist view of judging, Lord seemed to extend to judicial power his general observation that power tended to bestow on its possessors an undeserved aura of right and venerability. He expressed his view on the "cult of the robe" and judges' august ethos with characteristic debunking candor. For example, in discussing the possibility of his own retirement, he commented, "When you're gone as a judge, lawyers will look at you on the street and say there goes that scrawny s.o.b. If you're still on cases, they'll tip their hats and act like you just saw a vision" (Klobuchar, 1983a, p. 2B). Although as a judge Lord wanted to be right, and often believed wholeheartedly that he was, he did not believe that wisdom came from compliance with conventional definitions of judicial temperament. In his view, those who associated aloofness with authoritativeness and showed more interest in manners than in the substance of adjudicated disputes served badly both the law and society. As he put it, "I enjoy being respected, sure, but being right is far more important" (Klobuchar, 1974b, p. 6B). This emphasis on facts and function is "realistic," and in Lord's case as in others it has implications for the judge's approach to judicial speech.

Judicial Speech

Lord believed that all judges had a duty to justify their decisions as fully as possible. This was so for two reasons. The first reason was that any judge might be the only judge to hear a specific plea for justice: "Very often you *are* the Supreme Court. You're the last person they get to. That is, they don't ever appeal, they accept it. So . . . you might as well write [your opinion] like it is [a Supreme Court opinion]" (Lord, 1988b). This view was consistent with his insistence that judges should try to take the cases before them as seriously as the disputants did.

An equally important reason for full justification was that Lord considered judicial opinions part of a vital educational process for which all public officials shared responsibility. He has recalled that he and Humphrey often discussed the role of judges as well as elected officials in providing citizens with the information they need to run the country (Lord, 1988a). Lord viewed judicial opinions as addresses to several audiences—the disputants, appellate courts, the public, and, potentially, posterity (Lord, 1988b). Given these diverse audiences, opinions should attempt to clarify judges' perceptions of facts, values, and justice for laypersons as well as to share interpretations of the law with other professionals.

This perspective on the educational purposes of judicial speech helps to explain some of the speech characteristics that provoked the ire of Lord's more decorous detractors. One of these characteristics was Lord's plain language. Related to it was his willingness to speak that language to the press and other mass media. A telling example of both characteristics can be found in a 1984 "60 Minutes" interview. Interviewer Mike Wallace asked Lord whether Lord could accomplish his aims in a less provocative manner. In response, Lord posed his own questions, questions that revealed his impatience with Wallace's conception of appropriate judicial style: "The point is, are the statements true? Are they justified? Is it more important that you look impartial and let [wrongdoers] get away with something, or that maybe you'll get out of . . . character a little bit and just say, 'Hey, that's enough of this; stop it'" (Lord, 1984). Lord's response demonstrates his insistence on saying what he meant in language that was not only accessible but arresting. In addition, the fact that he was being interviewed for a popular television program with a national audience demonstrates his success in attracting the mass media attention that could help him reach the widest possible audience.

As Lord's response also indicates, he rejected the notion that circumspect language necessarily furthered the cause of justice. In his view, the emphasis placed on scholarly judges who could "rub words together like a cricket" (Lord, 1988a) was misplaced. Scholarly words gave little evidence of a person's character, philosophy, disposition, or empathy, the qualities that Lord believed determined one's fitness for making judgments (Lord, 1988a). He criticized the judiciary's sometimes deliberate "couch[ing of] its message in terms that hide the true meaning from the people" (Lord, 1988b). Although he conceded that even those who agreed with his opinions sometimes wished that he had expressed them differently (Lord, 1988a), he seemed to consider his mode of expression both a counterweight to judicial obscurity and a sign of his willingness to make himself accountable for his opinions. According to Lord, what judges ought to provide in their opinions were good reasons for their judgments and clear explanations of what their remedies would accomplish. Without these reasons and explanations, the technical aspects of judicial opinions could be a subterfuge, and citations might function as "an excuse, a justification for doing something that [judges] may not have the courage to do themselves" (Lord, 1988b). Plain speaking seemed to be equated with standing up to be counted in debates about justice.

Plain speaking also served to attract media attention, and Lord courted that attention. The mass media were the channels through which Lord reached the public he wished to educate and stimulate; on his retirement he commented that he owed his status as a judge to the media, which should "appreciate how powerful [they] are" (McAuliffe, 1986, p. 12B). As he has admitted, he would "have to plead guilty to [playing to the gallery]. . . . A public official must put on a performance. He's like an actor, an educator. If the public is in the dark, then democracy can't function" (Berg and Stone, 1976, p. 1C). Embedded in this admission are the notions that legal issues are political and social issues, and that their long-term, just resolution depends on the public's ability and willingness to take responsibility for them. In Lord's view, "public acceptability is really what's behind the law" (Klobuchar, 1974b, p. 1B). And it is up to judges to ensure that the public knows what it is accepting.

In attracting the media attention that would help educate the public, Lord employed language strategically. Although he admitted to pontificating from time to time, he did not admit to being boring. One of the differences he perceived between himself and "conservative" judges was that "they just cite more cases and act more pompous and never use any exciting language" (Lord, 1988b). Because of its predictability, pompous judicial language was not likely to encourage wide reading of judicial opinions, and Lord wanted his opinions to be read. Not only did he try to write opinions in terms that would be used by newspapers and understood by the general reading public, he "even put in some little catchy phrases that would catch their attention" (Lord, 1988b). In fact, he has described having a "fight" with a law clerk who objected when Lord injected "a little juiciness" in an opinion (Lord, 1988b). In that specific instance the clerk won,[32] but Lord continued to try to write judicial opinions that newspapers would quote, that the public would want to read, and that almost everyone could understand—opinions "with a minimum of legal mumbo jumbo" (Newlund, 1982, p. 6T).

In other ways as well, Lord tried to understand and accommodate media needs. Believing that what makes it into the media is what is called specifically to their attention, he made active efforts to position himself to highlight cases he viewed as important. He maintained generally amicable relations with reporters, and his language combined with accessibility almost ensured that an interviewing reporter would get a usable quote. As local reporters once commented, "He loves to talk to [us], handing out what he calls 'tidbits' " (Berg and Stone, 1976, p. 1C). On a slow news day Lord's down-to-earth style made for a good human interest story, whether it involved his handing out change for soda pop to children in his courtroom (Judge pops, 1973, p. 6B), swearing in three of his children to federal law practice (Swearing in, 1981, p. 11A), or declaring a mistrial after a drug-sniffing dog's courtroom demonstration attracted more publicity than he had anticipated (Klobuchar, 1979, p. 1C).

Lord's accessibility and quotability, and his quality of being not-boring, helped him to establish the reputation and relationships that enabled him or his clerks to suggest to reporters what cases might be newsworthy (Lord, 1988b) and to be believed. If his critics saw this as grandstanding, Lord saw it as fulfilling his role as an educator.

This chapter presents the background and philosophy of a judge who believed that he tried to help create a just community through nonconformity. Lord's "realistic" approach to judging in an era of uncertainty about the nature of judging might have ensured a measure of controversy about his judicial opinions within the legal community. However, it was Lord's individual approach, involving candor, plain speaking, and publicity, that ensured controversy in the larger community. The following chapters will examine how Lord attempted to create relationships between the courts and the community in applying his philosophy of good judging.

NOTES

1. For example, Lord was scandalized by the contrasting treatment of "Indian Joe," a boy born in jail after his mother's incarceration for whiskey selling, and that of "a Minnesota multi-millionaire" whose highly praised philanthropy rested on the profits of a whiskey-sale monopoly (Lord, 1988b). According to Lord, such disparities left a mark on him (Lord, 1988b) and as a result, "it's not hard for me to empathize with the poor and downtrodden" (Newlund, 1982, p. 6T).

2. Lord has made distinctions off the bench that he would not make as a judge. For example, when asked about his attitude toward extending insurance coverage to domestic partners, Lord replied, "I'm a little too old for that. I let [gays and lesbians] have a dance on Hennepin Avenue, but I don't believe in it. It's not in my bag" (Lord, 1990).

3. A University of Minnesota Bachelor of Science in Law degree signified completion of two years' liberal arts study and two years' study of law. A Bachelor of Law degree signified the completion of two years of liberal arts study and four years of law school.

4. Lord lost his job as an insurance adjuster after he obtained a $500 settlement for an injury-disabled elderly woman who had demanded only $50 (Oberdorfer, 1987, p. 11A).

5. The quality of Lord's love for Humphrey is reflected in such statements as "Being around him was to be touched like the guy in the Bible who climbed the tree to see Jesus: their eyes met and his life was changed" (Solberg, 1984, p. 228).

6. Soldiers' return from World War II led to housing shortages. The legislative hearings concerned proposals to prevent landlords from evicting current tenants to charge higher rents to new ones.

7. According to one writer, in Minnesota's legendary political "golden era" Humphrey, McCarthy, and Lord "strode forcefully onto the national political landscape, taking over the Democratic party and almost the country" (Carr, 1990, p.

26). In urging students to become politically active, Lord joked that the 1940s DFLers "sat around here on campus and decided to take over the state government! We did!" (Tubert, 1986, p. 8B).

8. See, e.g., Berg and Stone, 1976, p. 9C; Engelmayer and Wagman, 1985, pp. 112-113; Klobuchar, 1974b, p. 1B; Oslund, 1984, p. 4A; and Solberg, 1984, pp. 229-231.

9. For example, on Lord's advice Governor Freeman had declared martial law during a 1959 labor strike. His order was reversed by an appeals court (Miles Lord appointment, 1966, p. 14).

10. Humphrey earlier had given Lord a similar "gift"; some of Lord's successful prosecutions resulted from racketeering investigations during Humphrey's anticrime mayoralty. See, e.g., A. Eisele, 1972, pp. 57-58.

11. J. Eisenstein reported that "nearly one out of four [U.S. attorneys] has gone on to another governmental post. Nearly half . . . became federal judges" (1973, p. 48).

12. For a discussion of the U.S. attorney appointment process, see Eisenstein, 1973, pp. 36-42.

13. Article II, Section 2, states in part that the president "shall nominate, and by and with the Advice and Consent of the Senate, shall appoint . . . Judges of the supreme Court" (in Kelly, Harbison, and Belz, 1983, p. 754). For criticism of the Senate's advice giving, see, e.g., Bork, 1990, pp. 278-293.

14. Lord urged Mondale's appointment as Minnesota attorney general in 1954 and his later appointment to complete Humphrey's Senate term (Engelmayer and Wagman, 1985, p. 113).

15. Until Senator Edward Kennedy became its chair, the Senate Committee on the Judiciary automatically eliminated a nominee if a home-district senator failed to return a comment request printed on blue paper. The "blue slip" stated that failure to return comments would be construed as approval, but in practice it was interpreted as disapproval. See H. J. Abraham, 1980, pp. 161-162; Goldman and Jahnige, 1976, pp. 51-52; McFeeley, 1987, pp. 19-20, 58-59.

16. Support for Lord was enthusiastic. McCarthy claimed that Lord's appointment was his doing and was "one of the better nominations I made for any position" (Furst, 1985, p. 3B). Mondale called Lord his "choice for chief justice" (Engelmayer and Wagman, 1985, p. 113).

17. See, e.g., Goldman and Jahnige, 1976, pp. 54-55; McFeeley, 1987, pp. 28-33.

18. Sensitive to his relations with the Senate, Johnson made more nonpresidential-party nominations (twenty-three) than had the six preceding presidents (McFeeley, 1987, p. 83).

19. The rankings are Exceptionally Well Qualified, Well Qualified, Qualified, and Not Qualified. According to H. J. Abraham, "the lowest ranking is not necessarily a reflection on the nominee's character and ability" because it also reflects age, trial experience, and years in legal practice (1980, p. 163).

20. By 1988, Lord had formed the opinion that judges should be elected rather than appointed (Lo d, 1988a).

21. Lord's opinion of merit committees did not prevent his postretirement participation on the fifteen-member Minnesota Judicial Advisory Board that recommended state judicial nominees to the governor (Miles Lord named, 1989, p. 3Bw). Lord expressed surprise that "we're hearing the same things [about potential nominees] from Democrats and Republicans" (Lord, 1990).

22. Lord described how, as a young lawyer, he observed federal judges with no cases to hear for months at a time. It was a surprise to him that judging is "grinding, grinding dedication to listening to [and trying to solve] other people's problems" (Lord, 1988b).

23. Lord could have decreased his caseload in recognition of his administrative work load, but he chose not to do so.

24. Douglas died January 19, 1980, approximately four years after retiring from the Supreme Court and three months before this volume's publication (see, Publisher's Note in Douglas, 1980, pp. ix-xi).

25. Douglas noted that justices on the Burger Court heard fewer cases and did less case-related work than ever before, relegating such tasks as research and reading *in pauperis* appeals to an increasing number of clerks. He viewed this development as a derogation of judicial duty, feeling that justices, not their clerks, were appointed to judge (Douglas, 1980, pp. 384-386).

26. Research has confirmed Lord's belief in part. Except for business versus business and asbestos-related personal injury suits, all categories of lawsuits have increased only at the rate of population growth (Galanter, 1988).

27. Douglas suggested that undue corporate influence could be prevented by squarely confronting the bias in judicial appointment processes and deliberately appointing "sharecropper judges and labor judges" (Douglas, 1980, p. 194).

28. Neither Lord nor Douglas used skepticism to excuse himself from the obligation to avoid conflicts of interest (Douglas, 1980, pp. 253, 344; Lord, 1988a). Although Lord felt that conflict-of-interest concerns sometimes were overblown (Lord, 1988a), he acted on his obligation. For example, he sold his wife's public utility stock when the company appeared before him (Judge takes stock, 1973, p. 1A); removed himself from a suit challenging an abortion-restriction law for which his legislator son Jim had voted (Abortion hearing, 1974, p. 15B; Judge Lord's sense of propriety, 1974, p. 10A; Rebuffoni, 1974b, p. 4B); interrupted a trial to allow a criminal defendant he had criticized to appeal his decision not to disqualify himself (McCabe, 1976, p. 16A); and reassigned a sentencing after a criminal defendant claimed that he had broken Mick Lord's leg during a high school football game (Peterson, 1980a, pp. 1A, 9A; 1980b, pp. 1A, 8A).

29. Lord proposed the routine use of special masters to perform document searches and issue requests for document production. He believed that this procedure would facilitate fair and efficient discovery and help judges avoid the appearance of partiality (Anderson, 1984c, p. 10A). He vigorously opposed Chief Justice Burger's and others' proposals to "streamline" the discovery process by limiting access to documents, refusing repeat requests for document production, and penalizing requests for documents that an opposing party claimed did not exist. The reasons for Lord's opposition will be explored in later chapters.

30. Some of the cases discussed in later chapters will explore this issue in greater depth.

31. An example of Lord's controversial activities was his 1977 call for prominent DFLers to organize opposition to the DFL governor in a primary election (Maybe Judge Lord, 1977, p. 6A).

32. It is not surprising that Lord's clerks could win arguments concerning judicial opinions. Lord has immense respect for law clerks and has speculated that they are responsible for "90 to 95%" of judges' writing tasks, although most judges

are reluctant to admit that fact. Lord has described his approach to judicial opinions as a process of reviewing evidence, reading briefs, and listening to arguments in order to reach a decision. He then would marshal his reasons and compose a justification, often while driving. Lord's clerks were charged with drafting an opinion based on his arguments, which Lord would edit. Lord particularly credits his clerks for their attention to technical aspects of his judicial opinions and for help with organization. However, he takes responsibility for the final form of his opinions, especially with regard to the reasoning and language that became his rhetorical hallmark (Lord, 1988b).

4

The Honorable, Rhetorical Miles Welton Lord

> Men of most renowned virtue have sometimes by transgressing most truly kept the law.
>
> John Milton, *Tetrachordon*

The day after swearing his judicial oath, Miles Welton Lord began his first case. Over the next nineteen years his work load sometimes swelled to almost 1,000 cases of varying gravity and scope (Lord transfers, 1982, p. 7B). He considered the constitutionality of the U.S. bankruptcy courts (Judge overturns, 1982, p. 9C; *Marathon Pipeline Company* [1981]; News Services, 1982, pp. 5C, 10C), and of closing prostitution-plagued health clubs (Foley, 1985, p. 6B; Tubert, 1985, p. 5B). His decisions earned him honors for "deep devotion to . . . justice and . . . the inalienable rights of the people" (Worth Noting, 1975, p. 2C), for "being in the forefront of judicial innovation" (Stone, 1981, p. 1A), and for "judicial independence, courage and integrity of purpose, and commitment to our legal system" (Associated Press, 1984b, p. 10B; McEnroe, 1985, p. 6A). They also earned him judicial rebukes (see, e.g., *Reserve Mining Company v. Lord* [1976]); and scathing editorials (The best, 1980, p. 21).

Not every decision Lord made was controversial, not all of his opinions were distinctive, and only some of his cases attracted public attention. This chapter will examine a sample of the disputes he heard in order to explore the application of his judicial and rhetorical philosophy, identify patterns that contributed to contradictory judgments of his judicial character, and begin the consideration of his rhetoric of law and the community.

THE "MOST IMPORTANT" OPINION

Interviewers variously have suggested that Lord's most important opinion was written in a bankruptcy case, an environmental suit, an antitrust action, a product-liability litigation, or a criminal sentencing. Lord invariably has rejected their suggestions, saying that his most important opinion concerned a dispute between two high school students and their schools and that his greatest source of pride was ruling in favor of equal opportunity for girls and women in *Brenden v. Independent School District 742* (*Brenden*) (1972) (see, e.g., Klobuchar 1974b, p. 1B; Lord, 1988b; Lord, 1992; Lord, 1988a; Lord, 1984; McAuliffe, 1986, p. 12B).

Brenden's significance was personal as well as professional, producing a fundamental shift in Lord's perspective. It enabled him to understand more fully the reasons for "tremendous social change" (Klobuchar, 1974b, p. 1B) and to comprehend more deeply how legal norms affected the people closest to him. *Brenden* expanded the limits of Lord's "old-fashioned humanis[m]" (Lord, 1984).

Brenden involved tennis player Peggy Brenden and cross-country runner and skier Tony St. Pierre,[1] high school students who wanted to compete in interscholastic sports.[2] Their schools did not have girls' teams in their sports, but they did have boys' teams. When Brenden and St. Pierre asked to try out for the boys' teams, the schools said no. They belonged to the Minnesota State High School League (League), a voluntary organization that regulated state high school sports. League rules provided that "equitable competition" precluded girls playing on boys' teams or girls' teams competing with boys' teams (*Brenden*, at 1227). If schools allowed girls on boys' teams, the League could force them to forfeit games or even suspend them (*Brenden*, at 1228). Brenden and St. Pierre, claiming that they were being denied equal educational opportunities,[3] asked the federal court to permit them to try out for boys' teams and prevent the League from sanctioning their schools.

When Lord first heard about the dispute he found it amusing. A self-described "typical male chauvinist. . . . just the same unthinking male supremacist as most people" (Klobuchar, 1974b, p. 1B), he joked to his son-in-law that the girls probably just wanted to wrestle with boys (Lord, 1988b). But some family members were not amused. His daughter angrily reminded him that her high school athletic opportunity was cheering for boys (Klobuchar, 1974b, p. 1B). His sister reminded him that she and her friends were forced to play in long bloomers with inferior equipment, and even then could play only until "the coach would chase us off as soon as the boys came. . . . You think about that," she ordered (Lord, 1988b).

The Rhetoric of *Brenden*

Consequently, when *Brenden* was assigned to Lord he took it seriously, and he has described his ultimate decision as "so easy, so natural, and so right" (McAuliffe, 1986, p. 12B). He decided that the schools must provide equal athletic opportunities for female and male students; Peggy Brenden and Tony St. Pierre could compete with boys.

Although Lord later recognized his decision's far-reaching implications, his opinion seemed to disavow them. He carefully limited its scope, making it "emphatically clear" (*Brenden*, at 1231) that it did not address issues of fundamental rights, suspect classes, general application, and constitutionality. His negating strategy had a practical advantage; it limited the decision's vulnerability to appeal. The issues Lord enumerated as *not* being decided were those that exceeded his jurisdiction (see *Brenden*, at 1228, note 4). Lord insisted that he would decide only whether the application of League rules to Brenden and St. Pierre was valid; given the facts of the case, did banning the girls from boys' teams "rest upon some . . . difference having a fair and substantial relation to the object of the rule" (*Brenden*, at 1232).

Lord's limits did not banish broader issues; scrupulous negation was counterbalanced by strategic footnotes. For example, one of his footnotes observed that "[i]n another context, education has been held to be a fundamental interest" (*Brenden*, at 1231, note 12), and in another he quoted extensively from a California decision holding that sex was a suspect classification (*Brenden*, at 1231, note 13).[4] Lord used others' words to say what he could not say himself.[5]

Having limited his own decision, Lord likewise limited the arguments of the schools and the League. According to Lord, the arguments rested on three assertions: first, physiological differences made participation on boys' teams dangerous for Brenden and St. Pierre; second, allowing the girls to play on boys' teams would impede the development of girls' athletic programs; and third, if the girls were allowed to play on boys' teams, the League would be inundated with challenges to its "no girls on boys' teams" rule.

Lord's refutation clarifies his characterization of the opinion as "easy." He sounded a derisive note regarding safety concerns. Pointing out that the girls' athletic prowess eliminated concerns about fair competition, he declared that presumed female "physiological disabilities . . . have little relevance to Tony St. Pierre and Peggy Brenden" (*Brenden*, at 1233). Further, concern about male coaches treating "a young lady's charley-horse does not require further discussion. The rules provide that men may coach girls' teams . . . and separate but equal facilities hold no promise of resolving that alleged dilemma" (*Brenden*, at 1233, note 15). Therefore, Lord concluded, neither girls nor boys would be damaged by Brenden's and St. Pierre's participation on boys' teams.

Even more dismissive of the claim that Brenden's and St. Pierre's participation on boys' teams would retard girls' athletic programs, he scolded the schools: "The law presumes that public officials will do their duty and thus they should not rely on this Court for inspiration" (*Brenden*, at 1233-1234, note 16). In any case, the girls "should not be sacrificed upon [the] altar" of "vague and undocumented fears" (*Brenden*, at 1233-1234). Officials were to accept their responsibility for providing equal opportunities, not assign it to the girls.

Finally, Lord found elements of hysteria and hypocrisy in the fear of administrative "chaos." First he noted that fewer than ninety girls wished to participate in mixed-sex competition, which the League already permitted in some cities (*Brenden*, at 1234, note 17). More important, however, was the principle that administrative convenience could not justify invalid discrimination. To Lord it was "obvious that allowing such a justification . . . would . . . prevent contesting the validity of any . . . rule on the grounds that such challenge might upset [a] regulative scheme" (*Brenden*, at 1234).

Given what he found to be transparent flaws in their arguments, Lord declared that the schools had denied Brenden's and St. Pierre's requests to try out for interscholastic competition on the basis of their sex alone. As a result, he ruled that applying the League's prohibitions to the girls was "arbitrary and unreasonable, in violation of the equal protection clause of the fourteenth amendment" (*Brenden*, at 1234). He ordered the schools to declare Brenden and St. Pierre eligible for the boys' teams and ordered the League not to apply sanctions. If girls wished to compete, Lord would cheer them on.

Brenden and "Realistic" Rhetoric

The *Brenden* opinion in some ways illustrates Lord's general judicial and rhetorical approaches. First, Lord's "realistic" admission that it was influenced by his experience seems typical of his approach to law. The admission was not a confession of prejudice. Instead Lord's family anecdote was an example of how personal experience opened his mind to more careful consideration of a case; it gave tangible form to abstract notions of justice. It reminded him to consider how law works in the community as well as in the courtroom. Many of Lord's opinions reflect a respect for experience and incorporate similar attempts to reconcile legal principles with everyday life.

Second, Lord's language in *Brenden* is typical of his "plain speaking." Readers seldom need sophisticated knowledge of the law or its technical language to understand Lord's justifications. When such knowledge is required, explanatory footnotes often increase the likelihood that readers will acquire it.

A third element in *Brenden* is typical of Lord's rhetoric and related to his habit of plain speaking. In *Brenden* he uses language to establish a unique tone. The tone amplifies his assessment of issues, his appraisal of motives, and his evaluation of arguments. Sardonicism reflects his impatience with the defendants' arguments and his linking of unworthy argument to unworthy motives. Tone often is a strong element of Lord's rhetoric; his language tends to convey not only what he thinks but that he feels and how he feels. Because feeling often is regarded as separate from rather than integral to thought, tone may help to account for the attention Lord's opinions have attracted and the responses they have evoked.

Another important feature of Lord's *Brenden* opinion is its positioning of Brenden and St. Pierre as vulnerable victims of institutional power. Institutions transformed the girls' modest athletic ambitions into the oft-cited federal case. Were Lord willing to play Abraham, the girls would be "sacrificed" to amoral institutional interests. *Brenden* is representative of Lord's rhetorical response to such uneven contests; Lord would pick David over Goliath almost every time (Lord, 1988a).

Finally, Lord's off-the-bench comment also is typical of his attempts to "educate" the public as to the significance of legal disputes. Although Lord had limited his opinion legally, publicly he did not. More people read newspapers and watch television news than read judicial opinions. Determined that people should know what their courts were doing and the implications of what they had done, Lord created and exploited opportunities to present his version of judicial developments through mass media. Because judicial attempts to speak directly to the public may be perceived as inappropriate to the judicial ethos, Lord's eagerness to speak publicly also helps to account for the responses he and his opinions evoked.

Lord's "most important" opinion thus illustrates some of the ways in which his judicial philosophy influenced his rhetoric in concrete cases. Other cases also aid the understanding of Lord's rhetorical patterns.

THE ENVIRONMENT: RHETORICAL RULES AND EXCEPTIONS

Lord's tenure coincided with a period of significant environmental legislation, and as environmentalists clashed with economic enterprises, disputants turned to the courts to interpret untested laws. Lord's consistent response to such cases[6] earned him the sobriquet "judicial godfather to [a] troubled environment" (Klobuchar, 1974b, p. 1B). One environmental lawsuit, *United States of America v. Reserve Mining Company* (*Reserve-a*) (1974), became one of Lord's most controversial cases; in it the rhetorical patterns already suggested by *Brenden* emerged in higher relief. However, *Reserve-a* was not the only significant environmental dispute over which Lord presided, and the *Reserve-a* and *Brenden* opinions were not the only kind that Lord wrote.

Among other important environmental disputes over which Lord presided was a series of cases involving the Boundary Waters Canoe Area Wilderness (BWCAW). Lord's opinions in those cases illustrate consistency in his analysis and variability in his rhetoric. The cases also suggest an irony in Lord's association with environmental disputes: they often focused on Minnesota's northern region, where forests, lakes, and rivers provided both natural beauty and economic opportunity, and where the youthful Lord had experienced economic anxiety. Nevertheless, Lord consistently tried to protect the environment.

In the early 1900s, President Theodore Roosevelt created the 1-million-acre Superior National Forest. In the 1920s and 1930s the federal government restricted roads, logging, and dams to preserve the area's primitive character, and over the years thousands of acres were added to it. Eventually lakeland areas along 110 miles of the Minnesota-Canada border were named the Boundary Waters Canoe Area (BWCA)[7] and were closed to motorized vehicles. The Wilderness Act of 1964, however, prohibited motor vehicles in almost all U.S. wilderness areas *except* the BWCA.

The Act also made the Secretary of Agriculture responsible for protecting *and* harvesting over 500,000 acres of virgin forests. When the U.S. Forest Service sold BWCA land to logging firms in 1972 (Picone, 1975, p. 1A), the Minnesota Public Interest Research Group (MPIRG) sued. Charging that the Forest Service had not submitted an environmental impact statement or a forest management plan,[8] it asked Lord to enjoin logging in the BWCA (*Minnesota Public Interest Research Group v. Butz* [*MPIRG*] [1975]; Rebuffoni, 1974k, p. 10B). In February of 1973 Lord issued a temporary injunction and warned that logging would be banned permanently if it threatened the area's primitive character (Rebuffoni, 1974k, p. 10B).

After an appeals court upheld Lord's injunction, the Forest Service filed the required documents. It also announced that logging would be permitted in virgin forest (Picone, 1975, p. 1A). MPIRG filed a new complaint charging violations of the 1964 National Wilderness Act and the 1969 National Environmental Policy Act, and asking Lord to continue his injunction (Rebuffoni, 1974k, p. 10B). After Lord observed that "the U.S. Government is acting like a timber baron" (Judge to rule, 1974, p. 14B; Rebuffoni, 1974k, p. 10B), his September injunction came as no surprise (Picone, 1975, p. 4A).

In August of 1975, Lord ruled that the Forest Service's logging decisions were arbitrary, illogical, and environmentally unsound. He made his injunction permanent; almost all virgin-forest logging was prohibited. Lord also advised the Secretary of Agriculture that the law allowed the Secretary to ban all logging in the BWCA (Picone, 1975, pp. 1A, 4A). The Eighth Circuit Court of Appeals reversed Lord's ruling (Rebuffoni, 1980a, p. 1B), but within three years new legislation seemed to support his position. Shortly thereafter, BWCA issues were back in his courtroom.

In 1978 Congress transformed the BWCA into the Boundary Waters Canoe Area Wilderness (BWCAW), adding more than 45,000 acres, halving the lake area accessible to motorboats, limiting snowmobile routes, limiting logging, and providing protection against mining. Because of the legislation's effects on area resorts, it also enabled resort owners to force federal purchases of their land (*National Association of Property Owners v. United States of America* [*Property Owners*] [1980], at 1229).

Three sets of plaintiffs—in all, twenty-nine organizations, communities, and individuals—challenged the legislation. They requested that Lord rule on summary judgment motions in all three cases (*Property Owners*, at 1230-1231; Rebuffoni, 1980a, p. 1B). At an April 1980 hearing, Lord wondered aloud whether the plaintiffs were subsidized by "a wolf in sheep's clothing" in the form of logging or mining interests and made light of their complaint that the environmental impact of creating a wilderness had not been studied: "I don't even have to look in a lawbook to tell you that you don't need an environmental-impact statement to leave something natural alone" (Rebuffoni, 1980a, pp. 1B, 4B).

Three months later Lord dismissed the suits (Rebuffoni, 1980c, pp. 1A, 4A).[9] He invited the people gathered in his courtroom to witness the "historic moment" of his signing the decision. As photographs were taken in his chambers, Lord explained that his ruling would prohibit mining from "tearing up the BWCA" (Rebuffoni, 1980b, p. 4A). One of the photographs made it to the front page.

The drama of Lord's signing was not repeated in his opinion. *Property Owners'* technical subject matter included the preparation of boundary maps, federal regulation of nonfederal land and water uses, and international treaty issues. Lord found answers to the technical questions in the BWCAW Act itself, in the legislative history, and in legal precedent; extensive quotations overshadowed his voice. Only occasionally do echoes of his more engaged rhetorical style emerge in isolated words or phrases. For example, a hint of the more familiar Lord resides in his note that if "the physically disabled are not accorded special treatment, it follows that the less physically fit—the out-of-shape—are accorded even less protection" (*Property Owners*, at 1243, note 12).

Lord's *Property Owners* opinion is interesting for reasons other than its eloquence or rhetorical typicality. The absence of a distinctive voice suggests a detachment that contrasts to Lord's active engagement in other opinions and encourages speculation regarding the reasons for the contrast.

Two important contextual features of the *Property Owners* case may distinguish it from those in which Lord demonstrated rhetorically greater engagement. The first concerns Lord's judicial status. When he made his decision in *Property Owners,* his prior ethos (Campbell, 1982, pp. 123-125) presented obstacles arising from two audiences, the Eighth Circuit Court of Appeals and the public. The appeals court had overturned one of Lord's earlier BWCA decisions, and he could anticipate that his decision would be more acceptable if it were steeped in statute and precedent rather than in his more distinctive rhetorical brew.

In addition, a lawyers' magazine recently had characterized Lord as the worst federal judge in the Eighth Circuit,[10] and newspapers had reported on the article. Although laudatory letters to editors from well-known members of the legal community may have counteracted some of the criticisms, Lord was "not the guy to stand there and bleed with my robes on" (Klobuchar, 1980b, p. 5C). His chances for regaining the public's confidence in his judging might be greater if he relied on newspapers to make his decision known rather than on the public to read a highly technical opinion. That is, Lord's signing ceremony might have been rhetorically more important than his opinion.

The second major contextual factor at work was the relative power of the litigants. The plaintiffs included organizations that Lord apparently considered allies of two powerful economic forces, the mining and timber industries. The defendants included the U.S. government, also a powerful entity. In an important sense, each party was capable of fending for itself; neither was needful of strong rhetorical intervention to prevent an otherwise inevitable crushing of the weak by the strong. In *Property Owners* Lord rhetorically matched the kind and level of judicial support he gave to the "right" side's kind and level of need.[11]

RHETORICAL RESPONSES TO THE PEOPLE AGAINST PUBLIC INSTITUTIONS

The People Against the Government

Lord chided government agencies as well as supported them. Targets of his chiding included the U.S. Office of Economic Opportunity (OEO), which had frozen funds appropriated for Native American schools. Asking it not to "punish the children" for the American Indian Movement's occupations of a Washington, D.C., government building and Wounded Knee, South Dakota, he observed that "I know OEO has cut out some of its programs, but I'm not sure it has cut out its heart" (Parsons, 1973, p. 6B; *Red School House, Inc. v. Office of Economic Opportunity* [1973]). His reference to "heart" was typical of comments aimed at discussing institutions in human terms.

Human vulnerability and government fairness were central to Lord's various decisions to reinstate benefits terminated by the U.S. government. For example, in ordering the continuation of disaster loans to farmers in *Berends v. Butz* (1973), he declared that the "people have a right to expect better treatment from their government" and that government highhandedness "offends all traditional notions of fair play" (Associated Press, 1973a, p. 23). Similar judgments were evident in his order that frozen food stamp funds be released. In *Bennett v. Butz* (1974), he accused the Department of Agriculture of "total failure . . . to do what Congress clearly intended" (Food stamp fund, 1974, p. 19). In such cases, Lord insisted that the nation's poor be treated as worthy citizens.

Cases involving children also found Lord on the side of "the people." For example, in ordering Aid to Families with Dependent Children (AFDC) restored, he accused Minnesota of "leading the charge against the poor" (Newlund, 1981a, p. 1A) and trying to "out-Reagan Reagan" (Newlund, 1981b,

p. 8A) with stringent eligibility requirements. These requirements, he charged, reflected a "deliberate decision to let people go hungry" (Newlund, 1981a, p. 1A). The Eighth Circuit Court of Appeals disagreed and overruled Lord's order.

Nevertheless, Lord continued to decide for the vulnerable. Several courts ruled Health and Human Services (HHS) Secretary Margaret Heckler's wholesale termination of workers' disability benefits illegal (Associated Press, 1985a, p. 13B), but Lord issued the most far-reaching order. In addition to enjoining terminations, he required the Secretary to continue benefits until individual hearings were held, to notify those who had been denied benefits that HHS may have erred, and to consider pain in determining disability (Associated Press, 1985a, p. 13B; *Kiphuth v. Heckler* [1984]; Parsons, 1984, pp. 1A, 8A; *Polaski v. Heckler* [1984]).[12]

Lord voiced outrage at the tactics of those who ordered the terminations. In *Kiphuth v. Heckler* (*Kiphuth*) (1984), he charged that an administrative law judge was able to deny benefits "only by distorting both the law and the evidence . . . and displaying a shockingly contemptuous attitude toward the plaintiff" (*Kiphuth*, at 1569); the offending judge "only thinly veiled his . . . attitude that only the dead can be disabled" (*Kiphuth*, at 1571). He answered the government's hardship plea with harsh words, commenting that "[Heckler] will have to live in her own mess" (Parsons, 1984, p. 8A). As in *Brenden*, Lord linked faulty reasoning with faulty motives, and in the tone of his comments revealed his feelings as well as his judgment.

Vickerman v. Hennepin County Probate Court (1982) brought high praise for Lord's "earnest, creative side" and "legal technique" (Wehrwein, 1981a, p. 7A). Lord had mediated the settlement of class action suits brought by psychiatric patients who charged that their due process rights had been violated. As the admiring editorialist commented, this was a case that "does something for a lot of people rather than making a lot of money for a few [and has] a democratic flavor . . . that stirs Lord's populist reformer's soul" (Wehrwein, 1981a, p. 7A). Once stirred, Lord not only helped to settle the case but retained jurisdiction by means of a consent decree. He counted the case as one that taught him to value public service lawyers (Lord, 1988a).

The People Against the University

Rajender. A consent decree also was the outcome of a class action against another institutional power. *Rajender v. University of Minnesota* (1982) (1983) originally was filed by a female chemistry professor who charged the University with discriminating on the basis of sex and national origin. After seven years, the University's rejection of three negotiated settlement proposals, and eleven weeks of trial, an agreement was reached.

Lord approved a consent decree that provided, among other things, that a special master for the court would resolve future issues relating to the decree, that the University would institute internal grievance procedures, and that the fees of attorneys representing women for whom the internal procedures failed would be limited to $6,000 (*Rajender* [1982] [*Rajender-a*]; [1983] [*Rajender-b*]).

Although the decree became a model for settlements in other discrimination suits and Lord was applauded for "requir[ing] nondiscriminatory pay for University of Minnesota women" (An institution, 1985, p. 14A), the *Rajender* opinions suggest Lord's distrust of the institution. The first opinion (*Rajendera*) makes clear Lord's concern that the University would use its greater resources to tax actual and potential plaintiffs out of court.

For example, the University objected to the amount of the fees for plaintiffs' attorneys. Its protest against paying for two class attorneys' presence at a settlement conference with three University attorneys earned Lord's rebuke: "If the University is so solidly represented . . . is it not proper for the class to be equally represented by its co-counsel of record? Zealously representing one's client does not include drawing straws to see who goes to crucial settlement talks in the event clients don't prevail and counsel won't be adequately recompensed" (*Rajender-a*, at 166). The "duplication" was a sign of virtue rather than of greed. Lord was especially dismissive of the University's contention that plaintiffs' attorneys had won few benefits for the class. Lord declared himself "compelled to point out the fact that prior to this lawsuit whatever rights properly belonged to the class were largely illusory because . . . the defendants were ignoring them. As a result of the *Rajender* action, procedures have been established to ensure that the University of Minnesota is purged of discriminatory employment practices. From this Court's perspective . . . that accomplishment is far from insignificant" (*Rajender-a*, at 171).

One year later Lord saw evidence that his misgivings were justified. The University's internal procedure did not address all grievances adequately, and *Rajender* claimants sued for relief. However, attorneys would not accept their complex cases for only $6,000 in compensation. Lord cried foul, contrasting the University's willingness to pay $118,000 to defend a case to its insistence that claimants' attorneys receive only $6,000 (*Rajender-b*, at 407). According to Lord, the University was using its financial power to defeat the consent decree's purpose: the "disparity in resources underlines the inequity in the very system designed to promote equality" (*Rajender-b*, at 407). To equalize resources, Lord granted the special master's request to remove the fee ceiling.

After the appeals court overruled Lord's decision, he considered *Rajender* a failure. Years later he commented that the "Rajender case helped 200 to 500 women. . . . but as far as changing the university permanently, I don't think it changed it a bit" (Smith, 1989, p. 8A). In Lord's view the University had prevailed over the people in *Rajender*. But in another controversial case the individual outweighed the institution.

Hall. Mark Hall was a University of Minnesota basketball player. Denied admission to a degree-granting program, he was declared ineligible to play intercollegiate varsity basketball. If he did not play, he could not become a

National Basketball Association draft pick in the spring of 1982. With a "no-cut" contract in jeopardy, Hall sued, asking Lord to force the University to accept him (Associated Press, 1982a, p. C11).

Lord depicted Hall as a victim of the controversial relationship between university athletics and scholarship. Conceding that Hall "will probably never attain a degree," Lord pointed out that he had been "recruited to . . . be a basketball player and not a scholar. His academic record reflects that he has lived up to those expectations" (*Hall v. University of Minnesota* [1982], at 106). Having lived up to the University's expectations, Hall was entitled to expect something from the University—the opportunity to play ball.

Lord found evidence that Hall was a pawn in internal University power games. Academicians broke the rules to prevent him from playing. He was denied admission because a dean accused him of misconduct and program directors interfered with committee decisions to admit him. Because the interference was unprecedented (*Hall*, at 106) and Hall had no opportunity to answer misconduct accusations (*Hall*, at 110), Lord viewed the admissions process as "a disciplinary proceeding" (*Hall*, at 108). Further, he criticized the University's arbitrary refusal to consider twenty-six summer session credits evidence of academic progress, pointing out that, although the "courses were not the most esoteric in their nature, they were offered for credit" (*Hall*, at 110).[13] Their rejection suggested that either the University's courses or its rejection of Hall did not meet academic criteria.

Lord believed that he "must view with some skepticism the defendant University's claim, regarding [harm to its] academic integrity" (*Hall*, at 109). In fact, the only harm it faced was National Collegiate Athletic Association sanctions if an order to admit Hall later were overturned. And, Lord noted, "in this regard, the defendant University's destiny is in its own hands. [It] does not have to appeal" (*Hall*, at 109-110). Clearly Lord believed that Hall had been mistreated. He laid the blame largely on the institution's doorstep, declaring that "[i]f this situation causes harm to the University, it is because they have fostered it" (*Hall*, at 109). Lord determined that Hall's rights had been violated; once more an athlete was to be rescued from the "altar" of institutional interests.[14]

The University may have considered Lord's opinion strong stuff, but a law clerk had intervened to spare it even more caustic comment. In Lord's private opinion, "Hall was hired as an athlete and [the University] should treat him like one"; if the University truly wanted to educate athletes it would "take them in on . . . the basis of ability to read and study and understand, and motivation, and make students out of them" (Lord, 1988b). He had no patience for what he perceived to be the institution's willingness to "sell" Hall a future and to renege on its deal after he had paid for it in the coin it demanded.

Public comment suggested that Lord's audience had gotten part of his censored message. The University's student newspaper editorialized that "The U's neglect of due process . . . enabled Lord to tell all of higher education something it should already know: *You* got yourselves into this; you get yourselves out" (Mark Hall, 1982, p. 4). One columnist noted that "Lord's position . . . can be boiled down to: 'Aw, come on, guys. What do you mean, academic integrity?'" (Wehrwein, 1982, p. 8A). Another observed that Lord "forces us all to look at the recruiting of athletes for what it is: sheer hypocrisy" (Hodowanic, 1982, p. 8A).

However, the commentators' focus on institutional betrayal of the public trust also suggests that another part of Lord's message was less persuasive. Lord had characterized the public's attitude toward college athletics as "equally ambivalent" to that of the University (*Hall*, at 110); through its acquiescence, the public shared responsibility for Hall's predicament. But the public seemed to reject his depiction of Hall as a victim.

Thus, with only partial persuasiveness, Lord had identified an individual who needed protection from institutional power. He had responded to the individual's need and warned both the institution and the public of the corruption they courted by act or omission. Lord found equal danger in the power of another kind of institution. The public had less influence over these entities, and Lord sometimes stepped into a void that was created by the absence of public influence.

THE RHETORIC OF CORPORATIONS AND CONSCIENCE

From time to time, newspaper articles pondered whether Lord was antibusiness. His speeches to gatherings of the American Lutheran Church (Thorkelson, 1976, p. 10A), the Minnesota Council of Churches (Judge Lord will address, 1981, p. 10A; Thorkelson, 1981, p. 10A), an Environmental Health Conference (Associated Press, 1981, p. 16B), the Hennepin County Bar Association (Many firms fail, 1984, p. 14B), and the Unitarian Society (Carideo, 1985, p. 3B) alerted audiences to the danger of corporate misdeeds. And in interviews as well as in court Lord excoriated corporations such as Reserve Mining Company and A. H. Robins Company (see, e.g., Klobuchar, 1974b, pp. 1B, 6B; Lord, 1984).

Yet Lord protested the antibusiness label, saying, "Christ, I'd like to own one" (Oslund, 1984, p. 4A). He insisted that those who applied the label failed to distinguish between corporations and corporate abuse of power. Corporate power was immense—"short of government, corporations have control" (Lord, 1990)—and when corporations used it wrongly often only the power of the courts could check their abuse.

In becoming a judge, Lord believed that he had accepted a special responsibility to detect and correct corporate abuse. In 1973 he performed that function in a suit brought against a public utility company. After quickly selling his stock in the utility company, Northern States Power Company (NSP) (Judge takes stock, 1973, p. 1A), he heard a reform group's complaint that the company had "fraudulently and intentionally" misled the group about procedural changes for electing directors. After NSP admitted that the changes were intended to frustrate representation of small shareholder groups opposed to management (Fuller, 1973, p. 5A), Lord delayed the changes for one year. He would not insulate the corporation from the community.

Lord considered financial penalties one of the most effective means for controlling corporate abuses. In 1980 he imposed a record $3.5 million penalty against the United States Steel Corporation for collecting illegal rebates (Associated Press, 1980, p. 4). He also upheld a $170.4 million jury verdict in *McDonald v. Johnson & Johnson* (1982). A jury had made the award to the inventors of an electronic pain-killing device after being convinced that the makers of Tylenol had purchased the rights to their device to subvert competition. Although in the pretrial phase Johnson & Johnson's attorneys almost had persuaded Lord that the lawsuit was a "dumb case" (Lord, 1990), by the trial's end he had "no doubt as to the wisdom and propriety of the jury's verdict" (Associated Press, 1982b, p. D11). As in the *Brenden* case, Lord had been willing to open and change his mind.

However, one of Lord's most controversial corporate cases, the Consolidated Antibiotic Antitrust Actions, ended in settlement rather than a verdict.[15] It won him praise for legal innovation and condemnation for presiding over a legal circus. The class-action suit against companies that produced and sold broad-spectrum antibiotics[16] also provided a model for other class-action settlement distributions and became the subject of a book.

The antibiotics cases arose from the complicated history of tetracycline's patenting and marketing. In 1952 Chas. Pfizer and Company (Pfizer) obtained a patent for tetracycline. It licensed American Cyanamid Company (Cyanamid) and Bristol-Myers Company (Bristol) to produce the drug and sell it in bulk only to Squibb-Beechnut Company (Squibb) and Upjohn Company (Upjohn). After Senate investigations and an eleven-year Federal Trade Commission (FTC) action, an appeals court affirmed that Pfizer's patent was obtained through fraud by Pfizer and Cyanamid. In 1967 a jury convicted Pfizer, Cyanamid, and Bristol of criminal monopoly and restraint of trade[17] (Bartsh, Boddy, King, and Thompson, 1978, pp. 1-4; *Coordinated Pretrial Proceedings in Antibiotic Antitrust Actions [Antibiotics-b*] [1974], at 670-671).

More than 140 plaintiffs filed civil suits, and the cases were consolidated for discovery in New York. In 1970 sixty cases were assigned to Lord.[18] In 1971 he transferred them to Minnesota[19] and certified as plaintiff classes farm, insurance, union and health and welfare, and state cases. Five attorneys from each class formed a Plaintiffs' National Steering Committee to coordinate pretrial discovery, with states acting on behalf of institutions and consumers (*Antibiotics-b*; Bartsh et al., 1978, pp. 1-10).

In 1972 the Eighth Circuit Court of Appeals denied the drug companies' motion to remove Lord (City bank wins, 1972, p. 72).[20] Lord had suggested an investigation of the Patent Office, which he called "the sickest institution that our government has ever invented" (Lundegaard, 1972, p. 5B), and had warned a Cyanamid witness that "[t]hat's not an answer to the question, and you are going to have to straighten out and fly right or the court is going to impose a little fine on you" (Lundegaard, 1972, p. 5B). Lord's determination to garner facts and resolve "mountainous litigations" (Lundegaard, 1972, p. 5B) had led to activism and impatience.

Lord's determination also led him to appoint special masters to facilitate pretrial discovery. Among other duties, the special masters reviewed thousands of objections to producing documents[21]—the number of discovered documents reached over 1 million—and helped to manage activities such as monthly hearings attended by up to a hundred lawyers. At the same time, court-appointed economic and statistical experts performed studies and mediated negotiations (*Antibiotics-b*; Bartsh et al., 1978, pp. 5-11; *Coordinated Pretrial Proceedings in Antibiotic Antitrust Actions* [*Antibiotics-a*] [1974]). Most of the plaintiffs settled their claims before the October 1973 trial date (Agreement backed, 1973, p. 58; Associated Press, 1973b, p. 50).

Over the drug companies' objections, Lord had established an "opt-out" consumer class[22] and appointed special masters to notify class members, process claims, and distribute funds. Media announcements and claims forms were test marketed to increase potential responses, and two computerized claim centers were established. At relatively modest cost, the largest class-action settlement program ever attempted processed almost 1 million qualified claims (Agreement backed, 1973, p. 58; *Antibiotics-b*, at 679; Bartsh et al., 1978, pp. 19-76).[23]

Lord's attention to administration in matters of justice had a purpose: demonstrating the manageability of class actions supported access to the courts. Lord believed that class actions and contingency fees were a "key to the Courthouse" (Lord, 1988a); without them lawyers could not afford to represent the poor. Lord incorporated a defense of those "keys" in *Antibiotics* opinions that approved settlements and attorney fees.

In his opinions Lord maintained that computers and other technologies removed size as a legitimate factor in limiting classes (*Antibiotics-a*, at 668; *Antibiotics-b*, at 680). In fact, he said, in the huge *Antibiotics* classes "[a]ll . . . were treated with courtesy [and] dignity and given every opportunity to appeal" (*Coordinated Pretrial Proceedings in Antibiotic Antitrust Actions* [*Antibioticsc*] [1975]). Therefore, he declared, "Class size alone should never be used to permit wrongdoers to retain the fruits of their unlawful actions. . . . A judicial system which places a higher premium on convenient administration than on redress of grievances soon ceases to be just" (*Antibiotics-a*, at 668-669; *Antibiotics-b*, at 680).

Lord also supported contingency fees. He pointed out that the antibiotics cases represented "at least eight years of labor for some of the Plaintiffs' lawyers" (*Antibiotics-c*, at 693), who would not be compensated unless they won or settled the cases (*Coordinated Pretrial Proceedings in Antibiotic Antitrust Actions* [*Antibiotics-d*] [1975], at 732). In complex litigation, attorneys who represented plaintiffs "risk[ed] financial ruin" (*Antibiotics-c*, at 693), and those who were willing to persist under those circumstances deserved compensation (*Antibiotics-c*, at 693).

Lord underscored the attorneys' risk by referring to the resources arrayed against them, including money and time. The drug companies were "multinational corporations . . . involved in antibiotic litigation in one form or another for the past twenty years. They have spent millions of dollars defending these actions. The Court . . . has personally met and seen in the courtroom, at least 150 [of their attorneys]. . . . For every attorney in the courtroom, at least five more must be involved behind the scenes. . . . The Plaintiffs' attorneys have been up against the best" (*Antibiotics-c*, at 692). Overall the companies had "used over 520 foreign law firms and 180 U. S. law firms" (*Antibiotics-c*, at 692, note 2); they had all the help that money could buy. Implicit in this enumeration was the need for a check on enormous power. Class-action suits and contingency fees were a part of that check.

Lord considered the *Antibiotics* cases proof that class actions could be effective and that "manageability" did not have to translate into an unwritten rule that "if you hurt more than five hundred people you'd get away with it" (Lord, 1990). As he observed, "Hard work and imagination will be required, but these two requirements . . . should [not] be new to any parties before any Court in any litigation" (*Antibiotics-b*, at 680). Hard work and imagination made the *Antibiotics* settlements "a triumph" (Weinstein, 1975, p. 51) in which Lord had a part.

However, these settlements did not end all of the cases. There were more settlements (Associated Press, 1976b, p. 55; Pfizer and others, 1975, p. 49), further judicial innovation, and an anticlimactic end to Lord's involvement. The trial was delayed until November. To avoid duplicate trials for government and private claims[24] Lord impaneled two juries. Observers considered this measure an effective innovation; drug company lawyers branded it a "two-ring circus," complaining that it made it "extremely confusing to know which way to face" (The best, 1980, p. 27). Over the trial's eighteen months "people had operations, babies, and divorces" (Lord, 1988a), but they persevered (The best, 1980, p. 27; Engelmayer and Wagman, 1985, p. 123; Lord, 1992; United Press International, 1976b, p. 45).

In 1976, after more than fifty newspaper stories about the cases, Lord dismissed nine jurors on the grounds of prejudice resulting from publicity. Finally he declared a mistrial (Associated Press, 1976g, pp. 55, 64; Stone, 1976c, pp. 1A, 8A), saying that the publicity was "certainly sufficient to cause doubts about the objectivity in the mind of any juror" (Stone, 1976c, p. 1A). In November he dismissed a major part of the federal government's claim, finding that in purchasing drugs after the companies' fraud was revealed it had waived its right to damages (United Press International, 1976c, p. 83). Ultimately the cases were settled out of court (Engelmayer and Wagman, 1985, p. 123).

The largest civil case over which Lord presided brought him both satisfaction and frustration. At the cost of criticism, it presented an opportunity to introduce new tools into judges' trial kits. In contrast, criminal cases seemed to bring him criticism but few opportunities.

LORD AGAINST CRIMINALS

Lord's support for individuals against institutional power seemed to reach its limit in criminal cases. There were exceptions. Lord was willing to order tolerable living conditions for prisoners, deriding Minnesota's objection to spending $70,000 to provide showers and opportunities for exercise with the observation that the state "spill[ed] that [in gasoline] every day on the way to the legislature" (Associated Press, 1976f, p. 4B). He supported an imprisoned draft resister's right to his chosen counsel (Associated Press, 1974c, p. 34), and in the interests of fair trials and sentencing he sometimes facilitated motions for his removal (Associated Press, 1976c, p. 7A; McCabe, 1976, p. 16A; Peterson, 1980b, pp. 1A, 8A; Peterson, 1980a, pp. 1A, 9A; Stone, 1979b, pp. 1B, 5B; Stone, 1979a, p. 2B). He threatened U.S. attorneys with contempt when they shipped an American Indian Movement activist from jail to jail, and finally to Leavenworth, Kansas, to avoid a hearing for his release in Lord's courtroom (Cassano, 1973b, p. 9C; Cassano, 1973a, pp. 1A, 4A). And he lectured a prominent attorney in open court for failing adequately to defend one of his clients (Peterson, 1980c, p. 12A).

More often, however, Lord seemed to prefer the prosecution in criminal cases; the meticulous concern for individual rights evidenced in civil cases often was absent. For example, in 1980 five defendants were convicted of marijuana trafficking in Lord's court. The Eighth Circuit Court of Appeals overturned the convictions after learning that Lord had coached the prosecutor, whom he considered too inexperienced to try the case (Klobuchar, 1983b, p. 1B; Zack, 1983b, p. 1A; see also, McEnroe, 1983, pp. 1A, 10A; Zack, 1983b, p. 1A; Zack and Phelps, 1983, pp. 1A, 8A).

Even Lord's supporters criticized his conduct regarding another alleged criminal. In 1972 Lord ordered the incarceration of a man whose status as mentally ill and dangerous had prevented his prosecution for murders. In 1979 the man escaped from a security hospital and called Lord's home. Although the judge had received previous threats on his life calmly, this time he requested protection and filed a complaint about an earlier call from the man (Armed guards, 1979, p. 3A). He also publicly called for the man's apprehension, accusing the "mass murderer" of nine killings (Wehrwein, 1979, p. 8A). After the man was found in Missouri, Lord's complaint enabled police to arrest him and return him to Minnesota (Armed guards, 1979, p. 3A; Berg and Stone, 1976, p. 1C; Escaped patient, 1979, p. 3A; Judge under, 1979, pp. 1B, 8B; Klobuchar, 1980b, p. 5C; Wehrwein, 1979, p. 8A).

Lord's actions in this case, which he called "fully justified" (Klobuchar, 1980b, p. 5C), inspired protests. His response to one reporter's objections—"Give him his rights when you've got him in irons" (The best, 1980, p. 27)—was cited by the *American Lawyer* as one of its reasons for naming him the Eighth Circuit's worst federal judge. A writer whose previous columns had supported Lord's controversial stands declared that his "inflammatory and prejudicial comments are atrocious. . . . No matter what [the man] has done . . . he's innocent until proved guilty. . . . the judicial council should call Lord to account" (Wehrwein, 1979, p. 8A).

The defense attorney in the drug cases found Lord "hard not to like" (Klobuchar, 1983b, p. 6B), but he preferred not to try criminal cases in front of him: "I think he's usually decided before we walk into the courtroom that the guy is guilty" (R. Meshbesher in Lord, 1984). Although another lawyer who tried civil cases before Lord disagreed, saying "I don't think he makes up his mind beforehand any more than any other judge" (Berg and Stone, 1976, p. 8C), the defense attorney may have been right about criminal cases. Years later Lord explained why he would not practice criminal law: "After . . . telling juries to ignore lawyers when they [bring] phantom, shadowy figures into the scene of the crime, I'd look silly trying to pin it on shadows myself" (Klobuchar, 1983a, p. 1B).

Lord's cases and opinions suggest several patterns in his judicial and rhetorical conduct. First, they suggest his consistent concern for those whom he perceived to be victims of powerful institutions, his apparent emotional engagement and distinctive tone in opinions affirming their rights, and his rhetorical creation of "big-bad vs. small-vulnerable" scenarios in those opinions, as in *Brenden* and *Hall*. Second, they suggest Lord's willingness to address issues broader than those presented by concrete disputes, as in his reference to public ambivalence in *Hall* and his defense of class actions and contingency fees in *Antibiotics*. Third, Lord's willingness to comment publicly on his attitudes and opinions has emerged clearly in his remarks about several of the cases. And, finally, this review strongly suggests Lord's preference for plain speaking and acting: "I do exactly what I think is the right thing. [If] I get censured, that's a price I have to pay" (Oslund, 1984, p. 4A). These characteristics of Lord's conduct and rhetoric focused public attention on controversial cases and invited reconsideration of the roles of the courts and communities in doing justice. The following chapters examine three of Lord's most controversial opinions to learn more about the characteristics and consequences of his rhetoric.

NOTES

1. Brenden was the Northwestern Lawn Tennis Association's top ranking area eighteen-year-old female tennis player. St. Pierre participated in Amateur Athletic Union and United States Ski Association events (*Brenden* [1972], at 1226).

2. "Interscholastic" was the term for scheduled competition between coached teams representing different schools. Athletics' "educational" mission was an essential element in *Brenden.*

3. See *Brenden* [1972], at 1228, for a fuller discussion of the claims.

4. The quotation's length suggests its importance to Lord. In reduced-size print, it occupies more than one-half page of the reported opinion.

5. Compare Lord's use of precedent here with his observation that judges use precedent to do what they do not have the courage to do themselves.

6. It is not unusual for courts to develop reputations for consistent responses. For example, newspapers reported that environmentalists filed suit against the Bush administration in Minnesota "because the Eighth Circuit Court of Appeals was considered sympathetic to [environmental] claims" (Hamburger, 1992, p. 1A); and that the U.S. Supreme Court "shows [a] decided tilt in favor of the White House over Congress" (Savage, 1992, p. 7A).

7. The story of the Boundary Water Canoe Area Wilderness is long and complex. The background given here has been simplified considerably.

8. The Sierra Club joined the suit as a plaintiff in August 1974. The defendant logging firms were Consolidated Papers, Inc., the Northwest Paper Company, Northern Forest Products, Ltd., Kainz Logging Company, Emil Abramson, and Boise Cascade Corporation.

9. Two additional aspects of Lord's opinion are of interest. First, Lord did not dismiss all of the plaintiffs' concerns. His order did not preclude damage claims by landowners if federal action clouded title to land or diminished property values (*Property Owners*, at 1250). He later disallowed a commission established to set purchase prices because landowners would be denied jury trials on the fairness of the prices (Associated Press, 1979, pp. 2B, 4B). Second, at least one *Property Owners* plaintiff should not have been surprised by Lord's ruling that the government could regulate activities on nonfederal land and water adjacent to federal property. It was similar to his ruling on the plaintiff's earlier complaint that the National Park Service cited him for hunting in a national park when he was actually in a boat on state-owned waters (*United States v. Brown*, [1977]).

10. The 23,000-circulation *American Lawyer* magazine based its selection of Lord as "worst" on interviews with approximately thirty lawyers, including "several" involved in an antitrust trial over which Lord presided (Judge called, 1980, p. 15A; Stone, 1980, pp. 1B, 5B). Lord called the magazine a "no-class legal trade paper" and attributed his selection to the animus of its editor, whom Lord had found offensive, "called . . . a jerk and hung up on" a year earlier (Klobuchar, 1980b, p. 5C).

11. Lord also presided over environmental cases not discussed or cited here. Examples are disputes over the U.S. Army Corps of Engineer's dredging in Lake Superior and the Mississippi River (Lord delays decision, 1976, p. 8B; Nelson and Furst, 1982, pp. 1C, 4C) and over the killing of wolves (Rebuffoni, 1984, pp. 1A, 4A; 1985, pp. 1A, 6A).

12. Disability benefits were terminated when doctors made conflicting diagnoses or health problems were back-related or psychological (Associated Press, 1985a, p. 13B).

13. These courses would have brought Hall's completion rate up from 48 percent to 72 percent. Hall did not complete four additional credits for which he had enrolled in the summer session.

14. Lord also "rescued" a first-year hockey player with a temporary restraining order. The student's agreement to be represented by an agent after he turned professional led to his ineligibility to play for the University of Minnesota (New York Times, 1974, p. 25).

15. The controversy over A. H. Robins Company will be discussed in a later chapter.

16. "Broad-spectrum" antibiotics are effective against a wide range of organisms.

17. An appeals court later overturned the conviction, and the judge who retried the companies found them not guilty.

18. Forty-three states had settled with the drug companies. North Carolina had tried its case and lost. California, Hawaii, Kansas, Oregon, Utah, and Washington remained as plaintiffs.

19. Lord had been on special assignment to the Southern District of New York.

20. This was one of five pretrial appeals filed by the drug companies.

21. An important special masters' ruling was a finding of prima facie fraud in obtaining the tetracycline patent. This eliminated many objections to document production based upon work-product or attorney-client privilege (*Antibiotics-c*, at 685).

22. Qualified consumers in plaintiff states were members of the class unless they notified the court of their intention to "opt out" of the class.

23. For the consumer class alone, 9 million households were notified, almost 11 million claim forms were mailed, pharmacists were supplied with information to assist customers in completing the forms, and consumer education programs were implemented. Over $20 million were refunded to consumers in six states (Bartsh et al., 1978, pp. 19-55; Weinstein, 1975, pp. 51, 57).

24. Foreign governments' claims presented some unique issues, such as how to handle South Vietnam's claim after the government ceased to exist (Associated Press, 1976b, p. 55).

5

Lord Against the Reserve Mining Company

I knew that in the end the mining company would win, but they'd have to climb over me first.

Miles W. Lord, *Portrait: Miles Lord*

In January, 1976, it seemed that for Lord, as for Justice Robert Jackson, "the man became a difficulty for . . . the judge" (G. E. White, 1976, p. 239). The Minnesota Trial Lawyers Association planned to honor him as "trial judge of the year" (Stone, 1976a, p. 4B), but he felt impelled to refuse their testimonial. The award could be construed as defiance of the Eighth Circuit Court of Appeals, which earlier that month had punished Lord, seemingly for the same conduct the lawyers admired (Lord rejects, 1976, p. 7B; Stone, 1976a, p. 4B; Trial lawyers, 1976, p. 9A). As the case of *United States of America v. Reserve Mining Company* (*Reserve-a*) (1974) neared its end, the court denied Reserve Mining Company's (Reserve's) request for Lord's removal. It then ejected him on its own initiative. The court had not subjected a trial judge to such humiliation in twenty years (Judge is removed, 1976, p. 1; Wehrwein, 1976, p. 14A).

Clearly the legal community's opinion about Lord's conduct was as strong as it was divided. Public opinion reflected similar strength and division. In 1976 two-thirds of Minnesota's public knew about Lord's judicial troubles. Approximately 83 percent approved of his conduct; 70 percent disapproved of his ejection from *Reserve* (Poll shows, 1976, p. 11A). Letters to the editor praised Lord's "guts" (Johnson, 1976, p. 14A) and willingness to act (Lofstrand, 1976, p. 14A), criticizing the "appalling" acts (Wargin, 1976, p. 14A) of the "uncaring" judges who removed him (Doliner, 1976, p. 14A). Less united, newspaper columnists called Lord's actions necessary and even courageous, but many also considered his ejection warranted (see, e.g., Klobuchar, 1976a, p. 1B; 1976b, p. 9A; Judge Lord was right, 1976, p. 38; Lord removed, 1976, p. 8A;

Now let's get moving, 1976, p. 6A; Reserve scandal, 1976, p. 24; Wehrwein, 1976, p. 14A).

The case that generated such controversy has been called "a classic . . . in the politics of values in transition" (Bartlett, 1980, p. 6). It tested the limits of private rights to public resources, pitted scientific against humanistic standards of proof, and threatened the viability of long-standing political alliances. Underlying all other issues was the question of how to value human life in weighing the costs and benefits of risk.

In all of Lord's career, *Reserve-a* was the case he was most reluctant to try. He predicted that it would land any presiding judge "on the slag heap" (Ackerberg, 1982, p. 11A) and tried to persuade other judges to take it (Lord, 1988a). His prediction required no particular gift of foresight. After years of frustrated negotiations between ambivalent public leaders and uncooperative corporate executives, the court was to referee the contest between industry and environment. Its decision surely would disappoint bitterly some important player. That disappointment would be only one consequence of a long and complex relationship between Reserve and the state of Minnesota.[1]

BACKGROUND

Reserve Mining Company had come to Minnesota in the 1950s at the state's invitation. In the 1940s, wartime demand nearly had exhausted the rich iron ore that provided jobs for Minnesota's Mesabi Range and more than half the iron for America's vital steel industry. Only low-grade iron ore, taconite, remained. Confronted with the loss of a major industry, the state devised tax incentives,[2] University of Minnesota engineers developed a "beneficiating" process for taconite ore,[3] and Minnesota campaigned to return mining to the Mesabi Range (Bartlett, 1980, pp. 16, 51-53; Greene, 1974, pp. 17, 95).

Reserve was the first mining company to respond. Its proposed operation faced only one serious obstacle. Approximately two of every three taconite tons it mined would constitute waste, taconite tailings. Disposal could be costly. However, a low-cost dumping ground lay about forty-seven miles from the proposed mine. The company agreed to build its beneficiating plant there *if* the state agreed to the disposal site—Lake Superior's Silver Bay (Bartlett, 1980, pp. 20-21).

Accepting Reserve's claim that density currents would localize tailings,[4] Minnesota dismissed conservationists' protests and issued permits[5] allowing Reserve to discharge tailings directly into the largest and cleanest Great Lake.[6] In exchange, Reserve assumed exclusive liability for any unanticipated consequences of its discharge (Bartlett, 1980, p. 23; Hill, 1974a, p. 28). Once the permits were granted, Armco Steel Corporation (Armco) and Republic Steel Corporation (Republic) bought out other shareholders to become equal co-owners of the company. Reserve reactivated an open-pit mine, constructed processing facilities on Silver Bay, and erected company towns near its facilities (Bartlett, 1980, pp. 23-24; Farrell, 1974c, p. 26). In 1956 Reserve formally opened its plant.

Production doubled by 1961 (Bartlett, 1980, p. 25).[7] Reserve operated twenty-four hours each day except Christmas and Labor Day, employed more than 3,000 workers, earned a daily profit of $60,000, and produced 15 percent of the nation's iron ore (Brody, 1974, p. 39; Farrell, 1974b, p. 37; 1974c, p. 26). Its plant also discharged 67,000 tons of taconite tailings into Lake Superior every operating day, and its smokestacks emitted 20,000 pounds of particulate every hour (Bartlett, 1980, p. 111; Brody, 1974, p. 39). The company denied responsibility for deteriorating lake conditions, and for fourteen years Minnesota was satisfied with its denials (Bartlett, 1980, p. 26).

BECOMING A POLITICAL AND LEGAL ISSUE

But eventually Minnesota was forced to reexamine Reserve's tailings disposal. In the 1960s the environment became a "hot" issue. Congress enacted new laws, including the Water Pollution Control Act of 1965 (WPCA),[8] and authorized environmental studies, including a study of tailings in Lake Superior.[9] In late 1968 the study's findings, published as the Stoddard Report,[10] raised concerns about increased turbidity, eutrophication, and chemical concentrations. The report recommended a three-year deadline for Reserve to dispose of its waste on land (Bartlett, 1980, pp. 64-65).

Citizens, including newly influential environmentalists, demanded protection for vulnerable Lake Superior[11] and revocation of Reserve's discharge permit. These demands galvanized U.S. Representative John A. Blatnik. Called Mr. Pollution Control for his strong support of environmental laws, Blatnik had helped bring Reserve to Minnesota.[12] Now, faced with a choice between constituents' jobs and clean water, Blatnik opted for jobs. He prevailed on Secretary of Interior Stewart Udall to suppress the Stoddard Report. When it was leaked to the press, he convinced Udall to "fudge it by saying it wasn't an official report" (Greene, 1974, p. 96). But Blatnik could not protect Reserve from scrutiny. In 1969 Reserve's smooth sailing was disrupted by roughly concurrent state and federal actions.

In June 1969 Minnesota ended four years of negotiating for exemptions and passed WPCA-required water quality standards. In July the Minnesota Pollution Control Agency (MPCA) asked Reserve to comply with the standards or to appeal within thirty days. The company did neither. So in September, two environmental groups filed suit in Hennepin County, far from the Reserve site, to compel enforcement of Reserve's permit conditions. In November a state court ordered that permit hearings be held before May 30, 1970.[13]

The hearings never were held. On December 24 Reserve finally appealed the MPCA request,[14] filing its appeal in Two Harbors, approximately thirty miles from the company's plant. Judge C. Luther Eckman refused to return the appeal to Hennepin County. He also prohibited permit hearings. The Reserve controversy would be considered *only* in Two Harbors.

However, interest in Reserve had spread beyond state borders. Udall included Reserve in a call for a federal enforcement conference on interstate pollution of Lake Superior.[15] In May 1969 alleged polluters and representatives of the federal government, Michigan, Minnesota, and Wisconsin met in Duluth, Minnesota, approximately fifty miles from Silver Bay.

The conference was charged with negotiating voluntary pollution abatement plans.[16] Reserve, however, repeatedly failed to comply with orders to produce such a plan. Challenging every study that suggested that tailings harmed Lake Superior, the company answered charges of bad faith[17] and demands for revocation of its discharge permit by repeating its claims that taconite tailings were harmless and that on-land disposal was impossible (Bartlett, 1980, pp. 63-64, 68-77, 81-83, 87-92).

On December 15 Eckman decided that applying water-quality standards to Reserve would be unreasonable: the standards would halt tailings discharges, and Reserve might halt its operations. He ordered Minnesota to grant a variance. Eckman also found, however, that tailings escaped the density currents. He gave Reserve until May 15, 1971, to design a conduit to carry tailings directly to the bottom of Silver Bay's Great Trough. The MPCA was to negotiate plan modifications and allow Reserve two years for implementation.

Eckman's order did not end the Reserve controversy. First the MPCA appealed to the Minnesota Supreme Court.[18] Then, on January 14, 1971, the conference moved to enforce its order for an on-land disposal plan. Reserve refused. Instead it proposed to thicken the tailings slurry with chemicals and pipe it to the bottom of the lake (Rebuffoni, 1975c, p. 4A; Schaumberg, 1976, p. 114). In the face of Reserve's continued insistence that it could not dispose of tailings on land, the conference appointed a committee to evaluate the deep-pipe plan.

When the conference reconvened in April, the public was noting its failure to abate Reserve's discharge,[19] and critics were attributing its patience to Reserve's political connections.[20] In this context the evaluation committee reported that deep-pipe waste disposal would add to the problems associated with tailings by introducing chemicals into the lake. Reserve stood firm: its plan satisfied Eckman's order, and on-land disposal was not feasible.[21] Attempts to compromise were at an end.

The conference closed, recommending that the Environmental Protection Agency (EPA) require Reserve to abate its discharge. On April 28 the EPA called on Reserve to comply with WPCA provisions. The company failed to respond. On February 2, 1972, after months of negotiating and lobbying by Reserve (see, e.g., Bartlett, 1980, pp. 107-110), the U.S. Department of Justice filed suit in U.S. District Court (Bartlett, 1980, p. 110). Judge Miles W. Lord was assigned to the case.

JUDGING PUBLIC HEALTH ISSUES

Over the years the complexity of the Reserve controversy had increased. At the beginning of litigation that eventually involved over 139 trial days, 100 witnesses, 18,000 transcript pages, and 1,600 exhibits (Bartlett, 1980, p. 130; *Reserve Mining Company v. United States of America* [*Reserve-b*] [1974], at 1074), the trend continued. Seventeen parties intervened,[22] and even after years of studies and reports, all were hard pressed to complete their scientific reports by Lord's January 1973 deadline (Bartlett, 1980, p. 112). At first the complex case attracted only local media attention. But on June 15 the nature of the case changed, and so did media coverage.

On June 15 the EPA and MPCA announced that cummingtonite-grunerite fibers from taconite tailings, highly concentrated in the drinking water of Lake Superior's north shore communities, were identical to asbestos.[23] Unsure of the findings' significance and determined to avoid premature public alarm, Lord earlier had prohibited public discussion of this new issue. But his initial anxiety proved largely groundless. Although some north shore residents began to drink bottled water, others dismissed the announcements as "politics" (Bartlett, 1980, pp. 126-127); Reserve had assured them of their safety, and the Minnesota Department of Health (MDOH), feuding with the MPCA and pressured by Duluth Mayor Ben Boo, disputed the health warnings.

Others showed more concern. The National Water Quality Laboratory searched for effective home-filtration devices, the COE flew a mobile water filtration system to Duluth, and the Office of Economic Opportunity (OEO) granted $100,000 to provide bottled water for low-income families. Lord ordered the EPA to expedite studies on the health effects of tailings and announced that health implications would have first priority when the trial began on August 1. High stakes and division in the community promised to rivet attention on the Reserve trial.

The public health case focused on several issues. Key questions were as follows: (1) Were the taconite fibers sufficiently similar to asbestos to justify concerns about their health effects? (2) Was Reserve the source of the fibers in Silver Bay's air and north shore communities' water? (3) Was there any evidence that ingesting asbestos fibers would have negative health consequences? (4) Was there any "hard" evidence associating the tailings fibers with actual human diseases (Bartlett, 1980, p. 131)?

Whether or not the answers to these questions could be proved depended partly on scientific evidence and partly on the standards of proof applied to that evidence. Not surprisingly in view of the Reserve controversy's history, the litigants contradicted each other on each point.[24]

In this situation, Lord the fact seeker took a characteristic action. He appointed Dr. Arnold Brown, of Mayo Clinic's Department of Pathology and Anatomy, to review the scientific evidence. Brown's testimony reflected the conflict between scientific and social truth (Campbell, 1982, pp. 3-6) embedded in *Reserve*. He testified that the available evidence did not allow him to say as a scientist that taconite fibers caused disease. However, asbestos fibers were carcinogens with no known safe exposure level, and cummingtonite-grunerite fibers appeared to be identical to asbestos. As a medical doctor, Brown wanted the fibers eliminated from the air and the water.

Brown's testimony encapsulated the choice Lord would have to make. If he allied the law with scientific truth, Reserve might continue its discharge indefinitely in the absence of *absolute* proof that tailings caused disease. If his choice was social truth, Reserve's discharge would be stopped unless the company proved that tailings posed no substantial health risk to the public.

Lord came down on the side of social truth. On February 5 he ruled that the government had established a prima facie case that Reserve's discharge constituted a public health menace.[25] Earlier he had requested a Reserve proposal for on-land tailings disposal in the event of such a ruling. The company had responded that only the deep-pipe plan was feasible. Now Lord ordered Reserve to produce a proposal and warned that noncompliance might result in a plant closing. Reserve replied that it could not produce a plan without court-specified design criteria (Bartlett, 1980, p. 142; Brody, 1974, p. 39; Company is ordered, 1974, p. 34; Associated Press, 1974b, p. 32). The New York *Times* labeled Reserve's position "arrogant" and declared that "the poisoning of [Lake Superior's] waters [is] too great a price to warrant the continued indulgence of an enterprise that rates its private budget so far above a decent concern for the public good" (Pollution with Reserve, 1974, p. 26).

March 1974 began a showdown. On March 1 Armco and Republic responded to a subpoena with documents relating to Reserve's deep-pipe plan. They demonstrated that the plan continually advanced as the only feasible disposal alternative had been judged unworkable by company engineers. They also showed that the company had developed on-land disposal schemes and had considered them technologically and economically feasible (Bartlett, 1980, p. 143). Lord accused Reserve of abusing the public and the court by concealing information and prolonging the trial (Farrell, 1974a, p. 18).

On March 4, Reserve informed Lord that on-land disposal problems could be solved and submitted an on-land disposal "concept." However, it warned that "it does not mean it's a plan Reserve is offering" (Farrell, 1974a, p. 18). Lord recessed the trial to try to facilitate settlement negotiations (Bartlett, 1980, pp. 142-143; Farrell, 1974a, p. 18).

Lord hoped for a settlement in *Reserve*. However, he also was concerned that north shore communities still had no filtration systems[26] and that public exposure to tailings would continue during protracted negotiations and construction of on-land disposal facilities. Troubled that "everyone is more concerned about not disturbing the population than about attacking the problem," he decided to "alert people to danger and let them make decisions for themselves" (Lord, 1988a). Lord turned educator.

With Reserve's consent, Lord transformed his courtroom into a public hearing room. There he lectured on the dangers of unfiltered water, warning that Reserve's discharge could not continue if drinking water remained unfiltered. Failure to filter would mean that "people will be out of work" (Minnesota communities, 1974, p. 46). Certain of his own judgments, Lord offered information he believed the public needed. By doing so he risked making himself as well as Reserve a subject of controversy. As one columnist noted, *Reserve* was becoming "not only a legal battle but a public relations battle, and the judge is no foreigner to either arena" (Klobuchar, 1974a, p. 1B).

The trial situation continued to deteriorate. On March 29 Reserve defied a subpoena by failing to produce documents. Then its president testified that he had known that Reserve's denials of on-land disposal plans were false. He also had known that disposal plans were being withheld from the court. The EPA moved for an immediate injunction against Reserve's tailings discharge. Lord delayed a decision in order to send Reserve's president to fetch his personal files on the plans. The next day the president testified that, with Lord's "tremendous help," engineering problems relating to on-land disposal had been solved. Unimpressed, Lord joined Armco and Republic as defendants to ensure the availability of funds to implement any court orders mandating on-land disposal (Hill, 1974a, p. 28; Strick, 1974, pp. 1A, 2A).

In the following weeks Reserve offered to implement on-land tailings disposal if the federal and state governments would exempt it from air emission standards, help finance the changeover, and issue irrevocable operating permits for the life of the mine. In addition, the court must rule that its operations had posed no public health risk. In Lord's estimation, these demands demonstrated Reserve's bad faith. On April 20, he ordered Reserve to close down by 12:01 A.M. the following morning (Farrell, 1974b, pp. 1, 37).

RHETORIC IN *RESERVE*

Lord had witnessed what he perceived to be a clear and immediate danger to the public. He believed that he was in a unique position to end it by "striving to right [the] wrong and to tell the public how wrong it was" (Lord, 1988b). Lord's rhetorical approach to righting the wrong was in many ways typical.

Plain speaking was one strategy Lord used to simplify a complex situation to his rhetorical advantage. Plain speaking occurred on two levels. On an educational level Lord attempted to make scientific, engineering, and economic evidence accessible to his audience. He explained it in detail and in commonplace words, defining technical terms and providing footnotes to amplify his explanations. On a judgmental level he polarized the issues, discussing Reserve's motives and acts in ordinary language that separated good from bad. He rhetorically erased the middle ground, offering an either-or choice.

Also typical was Lord's rhetorical escalation of the stakes involved in his judicial decision making. He portrayed *Reserve* as a test of the judiciary's integrity as well as a deliberation on the life-or-death issue of cancer risk. Introducing the longer-than-life integrity issue did more than provide a dramatic focus for audiences awaiting the courts' decisions. It also positioned Lord as the champion of judicial integrity and challenged reviewing courts to maintain the high ground he had claimed for them.

This strategic escalation was important in a number of ways. It rhetorically painted Lord into a corner from which honorable escape was impossible; there was only one right decision. This strategy involved risk; Lord could anticipate that appellate courts might resent receiving challenges. But he could increase his credibility by taking the risk. By transforming his decision into a species of reluctant testimony, he might enhance the prospect of "winning" in the long if not the short term, and of persuading the public if not the courts. The strategy also involved risk for others: it "cornered" appellate courts as well as Lord. It signaled Lord's unwillingness to recant in the interests of judicial harmony. If a higher court overturned his decision, it would assume the rhetorical burden of proving a negative—that it had not sacrificed its integrity. In cases he perceived to be profoundly important, Lord judged the risks to be worth taking.

Finally, Lord did not depend on his formal opinion alone to accomplish his goals. On and off the bench his statements and activities drew media attention to himself and thus to the issues he judged. Lord became the symbol of a larger conflict. As a symbol he made the conflict more understandable to a lay audience. The battle between the environment and industry became a choice between Lord and Reserve.

Memorandum of April 20, 1974

Lord's *Reserve* memoranda were written in three installments: April 20, May 11, and August 3. The first was a brief outline of his reasons for ordering Reserve's shutdown. At the least, the dramatic order would focus attention on the Reserve controversy and encourage settlement. The memorandum presented an opportunity to help shape the controversy's ultimate resolution. If Lord was persuasive in characterizing the motives and strategies of actors in the controversy, he could offer his desired outcome as the only acceptable and just one.

Lord attempted to do just that. He fixed responsibility for the controversy firmly on Reserve. According to Lord, the company had forced its own shutdown: "the court was only used as an instrumentality to close that mine" (Farrell, 1974c, p. 26). Thus Reserve was responsible for the Range residents' suffering. As Lord explained, he issued his order only after "exhaust[ing] every possibility . . . that would alleviate the health threat without a disruption of operations" (*United States of America v. Reserve Mining Company* [*Reserve-a*] [1974], at 20-21).

To support this contention, Lord enumerated the steps he took to find a less disruptive solution and recounted how Reserve had frustrated them. First he studied the evidence, hearing "from substantially all of the world's experts in the area" (*Reserve-a*, at 18). Learning that tailings exposed the public to cancer-causing substances, he sought Reserve's cooperation. He asked the company to plan for the contingency of an on-land disposal order. But Reserve insisted that Lord reconsider the deep-pipe plan, claiming that it "had no alternative method for disposing of the tailings" (*Reserve-a*, at 18). Later Lord learned that his reconsideration had been "superfluous"; "Armco had long since disregarded [the plan] on the basis of engineering infeasibility alone" (*Reserve-a*, at 18).

Lord again asked Reserve to develop on-land disposal plans to avoid a shutdown. Reserve protested "that little had been done in the way of devising an alternative and . . . [it] knew of no feasible way to accomplish such a system" (*Reserve-a*, at 18). Again it dissembled. Weeks later Lord learned "that several plans had been developed dealing with the possibility of on land disposal" (*Reserve-a*, at 18).

To demonstrate that Reserve could have cooperated, Lord emphasized its profitability: "the daily profit in the operation . . . is in the neighborhood of $60,000.00 per day" and "there is a 90 percent return on owners' equity" (*Reserve-a*, at 19). Company documents showed that it "could afford *at the very least* a $180,000,000 to $200,000,000 capital outlay . . . without substantially changing their economic situation" (*Reserve-a*, at 19). In Lord's view, Reserve consciously made a decision to imperil public health and victimize workers rather than invest in an affordable waste-disposal scheme. The peril was stressed through repetition, with twenty-three references to the dangers of taconite tailings. And Reserve's deliberate disregard of workers was stated as fact: "It was their choice whether they would make the investment or abandon their employees" (*Reserve-a*, at 20).

However, as Lord observed, "The Court has been constantly reminded that a curtailment in the discharge may result in a severe economic blow to the people of Silver Bay" (*Reserve-a*, at 17). Audiences might consider a plant closing almost as devastating as a cancer risk and believe that Lord was punishing innocents rather than Reserve. Demonstrating Reserve's past wrongs might not be sufficient to convince them that his order was just. Lord faced the necessity of persuading his audiences that Reserve had not exhausted its will or capacity to do harm. An essential ingredient of his message was deterrence: because neither exposure of its wrongs nor a reasonable opportunity to correct them had convinced Reserve to change its ways, stronger measures had to be taken to prevent further harm.

Lord found proof of Reserve's dishonorable intentions in the actions that precipitated his shutdown order. Reserve had submitted an on-land disposal plan that would violate air emission standards and continue tailings discharges for at least five years; the plan was "rejected by the plaintiffs because it is not environmentally sound" (*Reserve-a*, at 20). The company had underscored its contempt for the public in its demands that the government compensate it for abating its discharge, that Lord order the company's exemption from future environmental standards, and that he make a judicial finding that its operations never had endangered the public health.

Lord depicted Reserve as a company determined to subject the public to carcinogens and to corrupt those whose duty it was to protect the public. He labeled Reserve's settlement conditions "totally unacceptable," "preposterous," and "absurd," stating that even "if [the court] had the power it would not grant such an order" (*Reserve-a*, at 20). In particular, Reserve's proposal that he find its discharge harmless was "shocking and unbecoming in a court of law. To suggest that this or any other court would make a finding of fact without regard to . . . the evidence is to ask that judge to violate the oath of his office and to disregard the responsibility that he has not only to the people but also to himself" (*Reserve-a*, at 20).

In identifying Reserve's acts and uncovering its motives, Lord increased the stakes in *Reserve*. The litigation now concerned values associated with judicial integrity as well as competition between industry and the environment. Nevertheless, his order was stayed by the Eighth Circuit Court of Appeals in fewer than forty-eight hours. In a late-night meeting in a Missouri motel room, the three-judge appeals panel complained that not "one shred of evidence of anyone getting sick" (United Press International, 1974a, p. 55) was offered to justify putting 95 percent of Silver Bay's adult population out of work (Associated Press, 1974c, p. 70; Farrell, 1974c, p. 26).

Although Lord anticipated this outcome, he declared that he could not postpone his decision because "the Court is faced with a situation where a commercial industry is daily exposing thousands of people to substantial quantities of a known human carcinogen" (*Reserve-a* at 17). He had "no other alternative but to order an immediate halt to the discharge which threatens the lives of thousands" (*Reserve-a*, at 20). Lord "figured I would be reversed, but I knew I was right" (Lord, 1988b).

Supplemental Memorandum of May 11, 1974

Lord's brief April 20 memorandum did not end the trial, which continued to consider whether Reserve polluted Lake Superior. Lord and the appeals court disagreed as to the relative importance of the public health and pollution issues, and the appellate court's stay began a dialogue that may be characterized as a contest of wills. The contest demonstrated how differing views of "good judging" can test the judiciary's ability to resolve legal issues.

Predicting that Reserve would prevail on the public health issue, the appeals court asked for Lord's findings on pollution. Lord, however, did not limit his second memorandum to that issue. He had made his stand on April 20, and on May 11 he defended it. He resolved to "put in the record . . . . a complete justification for everything I did" (Lord, 1988b). To Lord it was clear that, in spite of what the New York *Times* called "overwhelming evidence of grave environmental abuse" and the "profoundly irresponsible and anti-social behavior of corporations" (Showdown at Superior, 1974, p. 20), his hopes for a just resolution of *Reserve* could not rest with the appeals court. So he wrote an opinion with the Supreme Court in mind (Lord, 1988b). Rather than admit defeat, he attempted to expand his audience.

Before explaining his reasons for closing Reserve, Lord reviewed the parties' claims against one another. This review was important in two ways. First, it justified Lord's joining of Armco and Republic as defendants in the context of conflicting case law. Second, and more salient to this analysis, it contributed to the rhetorical construction of Reserve's character in the *Reserve* drama.

Declaring that "this Court cannot allow the interposition of corporate entity to frustrate the implementation of a judgment that is required by justice" (*Reserve-a*, at 27), Lord depicted Reserve as an empty shell. Reserve's decisions, even decisions about whether to close and how much to invest in waste disposal, were made by its parent companies. In spite of round-the-clock operations, Reserve never made a profit for itself. Instead it passed its product to its parents in return for reimbursement of costs. Reserve was a conduit, not an independent entity; it could not cover costs that might be assessed as a result of its dumping and survive as an entity. Only by selling itself, thereby destroying itself, could Reserve meet such obligations: "in effect . . . the Court . . . may not levy fines and penalties without shutting down the plant" (*Reserve-a*, at 29). Because it lacked independent substance and will, Lord maintained, "Reserve is the personification of Armco and Republic" (*Reserve-a*, at 29).[27]

With this depiction Lord did more than suggest that no remedy would exist without joining Armco and Republic as defendants. He also offered a view of Reserve as the barren creation of absentee owners, incapable of developing allegiance to the people it affected and from whom it demanded loyalty and support. As this rhetorically invented creature loomed in the background, Lord began his "educational" effort.

Educating the audience. The remainder of Lord's memorandum followed in form well-known principles of public speaking.[28] It began with an introduction that previewed its three main points: (1) the properties and transportation of ore and tailings, (2) the health implications of taconite tailings, and (3) applicable law. Each main point was separated into labeled subpoints, facilitating readers' understanding of Lord's argument and signaling changes in his tone.

The memorandum's first two sections accomplished several rhetorical purposes. Perhaps most important, they contributed to Lord's credibility. In a case that tested the law's capacity to judge scientific matters, it was essential for Lord to demonstrate that he understood those matters. His ability to explain them was a practical test of his competence.

Lord seemed to recognize this rhetorical opportunity. He established the foundation for his expertise, noting, for example, that "[t]his Court after many months of expert testimony and after personally studying a great number of transmission electron microscope (T.E.M.) photographs feels itself knowledgeable" (*Reserve-a*, at 32-33). He observed that "[t]he scope and depth of the review of the literature and scientific knowledge in this area . . . presented to this Court has not been approached either in the field of science or in law" (*Reserve-a*, at 45) and that his findings "rest upon weeks and months of careful investigation" (*Reserve-a*, at 48). He also referred to expert witnesses more than 120 times, using the testimony of Reserve witnesses to provide "reluctant" force to his findings (see, e.g., *Reserve-a*, at 31, 32, 33, 37). But as "the Court," Lord was the authoritative speaker; scientific experts merely supported his findings. This rhetorical reversal of expert roles conferred heightened credibility on his instruction.

In addition to enhancing his credibility, Lord's explanations empowered his audience. Even nonscientists among them were likely to understand his plainly worded, step-by-step explication of the issues. Each finding was preceded by accessible description and, particularly in the first section, largely dispassionate elucidation. Supported by references to scientific experts and definitions of technical terms, they seemed to lead inexorably to Lord's conclusions. Through Lord's explanations the audience could develop a perception of their own competence, which they might attribute to Lord's expertise and instructional ability. As a result, they might be receptive to Lord's findings—an essential outcome for him because these findings were the foundation on which the remainder of his conclusions rested.[29]

The rhetorical use of numbers. In Lord's first memorandum numbers had emphasized Reserve's financial resources. In the second they underscored Reserve's size and the magnitude of its harmful acts.[30] Lord described Reserve's operations in terms that stressed size, e.g, "Jet piercers sink 40-foot deep holes," "trucks . . . haul . . . about 90,000 tons per day," and "150-car trains carry the materials on Reserve's 47 mile long intra-plant railroad" (*Reserve-a*, at 30).

The size of Reserve's waste discharge corresponded with the size of its operations. For example, using "2,062,500 tons of water" each day, Reserve processed "1227.60 L.T.P.H. (long tons per hour) of amphiboles" (*Reserve-a*, at 31) and discharged "60,000 long tons or about 67,000 short tons on the average day" (*Reserve-a*, at 33). A particularly arresting figure dramatized the enormous number of fibers in the discharged tons. Lord observed that if the fiber particles were spheres of five-micron diameter, "Reserve would be dumping 1.5×10^{19} particles in Lake Superior each day (15,000,000,000,000,000,000)" (*Reserve-a*, at 36).[31] The solid discharge capacity of all natural sources paled in comparison; together they could contribute a mere 12,000 tons per day.

Lord also used spatial measurements to stress the magnitude of Reserve's discharge. For example, he reported that the discharge created a density current that was "a force to a depth of 300 to 500 feet" and spread out to form a layer "37 miles wide, 3 miles long and 100 to 300 feet in height" (*Reserve-a*, at 37). But the current did not hold all of the tailings. After taking "lost" tailings into account, Lord found, "it is reasonable to assume that the actual area of Lake Superior despoiled by the waste from Reserve is . . . approximately the size of the State of Delaware" (*Reserve-a*, at 38).

Lord's rhetorical use of numbers extended to his discussion of asbestos. There the numbers emphasized alarming measurements by contrasting enormous health effects to the miniscule fibers that caused them. Many studies Lord cited discussed fibers measuring five or fewer microns.[32] Smaller fibers caused greater harm. For example, "most fibers found at the center of the workers' lungs, and nearly all . . . at the periphery, where pleural mesotheliomas occur, are shorter than five microns"; and "manufacturing workers, who are generally exposed to shorter fibers . . . have a worse record as to health in general and mesothelioma in particular" (*Reserve-a*, at 43).

Lord emphasized that exposure to the fibers often was minimal. Asbestos victims included people who worked with the substance for "six weeks" (*Reserve-a*, at 41) or "less than three months" (*Reserve-a*, at 40). In fact, some did not even work with asbestos. They included family members who merely "handled asbestos products brought home" (*Reserve-a*, at 40) or "lived with someone who worked with asbestos" (*Reserve-a*, at 41), and community members "liv[ing] within one-half mile of an asbestos plant" (*Reserve-a*, at 41). There were "500 cases of pleural calcification in a county where anthophyllite asbestos was mined . . . and no such cases . . . in another county" (*Reserve-a*, at 40); and after twenty to thirty years "[t]hirty-nine per cent of the people [in households of amosite workers] had x-ray abnormalities characteristic of exposure to asbestos" (*Reserve-a*, at 45).

Regardless of the nature of their exposure, victims who did not die of asbestosis were at extremely high risk for other diseases. For example, Lord cited studies indicating that lung cancer killed over three and one-half times as many asbestos workers with less than three months' exposure as it did people in unexposed populations, and that "[f]orty-five to fifty per cent of asbestos workers die of cancer, whereas in the general population 15 to 20 per cent die of cancer" (*Reserve-a*, at 40). Decreasing asbestos levels did not eliminate its effects. Although concentrations sometimes were no greater than five fibers per cubic centimeter, "workers in low and moderate classifications did show a significant excess in deaths by cancer" and research had "found excess deaths from cancer at every level of [asbestos] dust exposure" (*Reserve-a*, at 47).

The impact of these numbers was heightened by another kind of enumeration. Lord listed the diseases caused by asbestos, including asbestosis; mesothelioma; cancers in "the larynx, lung, pleura, peritoneum, and gastrointestinal tract"; and "interstitial scarring (fibrosis) of the lung, pleural plaques, and pleural calcification" (*Reserve-a*, at 41).

Lord argued that the high incidence and variety of asbestos-related disease were particularly salient for communities such as Duluth, where, unlike workers, 200,000 residents "are subjected to contamination 24 hours a day, every day of the year, and their exposure begins at birth, not some twenty years later" (*Reserve-a*, at 43); and "even a very small increase in mortality rates would result in many deaths to people who have never benefited from Reserve's profits or payrolls" (*Reserve-a*, at 47).

All of these numbers, statistics, and enumerations emphasized the perniciousness of three other characteristics of asbestos exposure: its effects are irreversible, they "are not apparent until 20 to 30 or 45 years after the initial exposure" (*Reserve-a*, at 41), and "*there is no known safe level of exposure*" (*Reserve-a*, at 47). Convinced that taconite fibers were identical to asbestos fibers, Lord sought to illustrate the catastrophic consequences he believed Reserve's conduct would bring.

The shifting tone. In the first section of his memorandum, Lord's "objective" tone enhanced his credibility and empowered his audience. He criticized some of Reserve's testimony, but in relatively restrained language. If the objective tone persuaded Lord's audience that he was a conscientious, accurate, and knowledgeable observer, analyst, and instructor, he had established his credentials for judging. It was then appropriate that his tone became more judgmental in the second section, largely with regard to Reserve's testimony. Lord's evaluation of testimony was based on several factors, including accuracy, sufficiency, and consistency. According to Lord, some of Reserve's testimony was erroneous, some was insufficient, and some was simply incredible.

Error led to the rejection of witnesses' findings but not to highly negative characterization; after all, some of the court's studies also were flawed.[33] For example, Lord dealt relatively gently with four Reserve witnesses who had testified that their studies confirmed the safety of the occupational standard for asbestos exposure. Dr. Knox had erred in viewing a mere decrease in excess disease risk as sufficient grounds to apply the occupational standard to the community (*Reserve-a*, at 46). Dr. Enterline's and Dr. McDonald's errors were similar; for example, McDonald had found only "that those with greater exposure had a higher death rate," not that "those of lesser exposure suffered no ill consequences" (*Reserve-a*, at 47). The fourth Reserve witness, Dr. Newhouse, had reached conclusions prematurely; "when she was able . . . to cover 25 years of exposure [she found] . . . a significant excess in deaths by cancer as well as total excess deaths" (*Reserve-a*, at 47).

Other grounds for rejecting testimony led to harsher criticism. For example, Lord discounted the testimony of Dr. Wright, who "as late as 1972 was of the opinion that the amphibole fibers were more carcinogenic than chrysolite" (*Reserve-a*, at 42) but in the *Reserve* trial changed his mind. By observing that Wright's initial opinion had coincided with his testimony on behalf of Johns Manville, Lord implied that Wright's opinions changed with his employer. His testimony was impeachable as well as erroneous.

Lord also dismissed Dr. Bristol's testimony. Bristol had monitored Reserve workers' x-rays for more than twenty years. Although one worker was receiving compensation for hardening of his lungs, Bristol "testified that since 1952 he had not seen any sign of asbestosis or a single case of parenchymal[34] change" (*Reserve-a*, at 53). Bristol's testimony was contradicted by company records and by another Reserve witness, Dr. Morgan. Morgan found that "approximately 5% [of workers employed 15 years or more] have x-ray signs of minimal non-specific fibrosis" (*Reserve-a*, at 53). He could not testify regarding a hundred recent x-rays because Reserve had withheld them from him. Given these contradictions, Lord found Bristol's testimony "somewhat incredible" (*Reserve-a*, at 53).

These judgments are representative of Lord's shifting tone. When errors and omissions appeared accidental, he corrected them. When they seemed to be intentional, he met them with stern language, using strategies of implication and sarcasm to emphasize his umbrage. By matching his tone and treatment of witnesses to their perceived probity, he worked rhetorically to preserve his objective persona. Preservation of this persona was essential in laying the groundwork for the memorandum's final section. If Lord's audience accepted his statements of facts, probabilities, and criticisms as objective, they would find his more judgmental conclusions reasonable and proper.

The final paragraph of the second section suggested the judgments to come: "Defendants are exposing thousands to significant quantities of a known human carcinogen. . . . Nonetheless the Court is asked to permit the present discharge until such a time as it can be established that it has actually resulted in death to a statistically significant number of people. The sanctity of human life is of too great value to this court to permit such a thing (*Reserve-a*, at 54). Lord, protector of the sacred, was moving to a higher plane. Reserve would be left behind.

Conclusions of law. Lord's conclusions of law amplified the judgments he had made on April 20. They also comprised many of the same rhetorical strategies. Lord emphasized Reserve's responsibility for the failure to resolve the controversy and for the shutdown of its plant. He enumerated Reserve's obstructive tactics and attributed them to economic motives. He warned that Reserve would continue on its present course unless forced to change direction. Required by law to "consider the practicability [and the] physical and economic feasibility of securing abatement of the pollution [and] also . . . the public interest and the equities involved in the case" (*Reserve-a*, at 55), at each point Lord sought to demonstrate that Reserve had done wrong and was determined to continue its own wrongdoing and to involve others.

Lord's conclusions of law also followed the rhetorical model of earlier sections, using numbers and comparisons to dramatize contradictions between Reserve's hardship claims and its actual condition, to explain the steps that had led to his conclusions, and to justify his decision. What was different about Lord's conclusions was the language he used to present them.

Lord described Reserve's obstruction as almost obsessive. By enumerating Reserve's obstructions he attempted to convey a sense of the difficulties that the court must overcome in order to do justice.

One obstruction was Reserve's false claims. For example, although the company complained of the ruinous costs of on-land disposal, records unearthed in spite of its "refusal . . . to cooperate with the Court" (*Reserve-a*, at 60) contradicted its complaint. They showed that implementing on-land disposal would mean that a "net profit per year assuming 100% debt financing would be $14,814,000. The rate of return on funds furnished by participants, therefore, is . . . 41.3%" (*Reserve-a*, at 64). After financing on-land disposal, Reserve's return on assets would exceed the rates of return from the parent companies' other assets, and "[u]nder no set of costs . . . would it have been more profitable for the parent companies to leave Reserve and buy [taconite] on the open market" (*Reserve-a*, at 61).

Lord used the amount of money Reserve generated and the rate of return it earned to demonstrate its comfortable economic situation and its duplicity in claiming hardship. He concluded that Reserve could afford on-land disposal. It did not need $100 million from the government to make the conversion (Court to permit, 1974, p. 26).

Reserve's character and culpability were further indicted as Lord described how it had exposed its own people to humiliation. For example, the company had withheld company documents from a University of Iowa professor it hired to analyze the economic impact of on-land disposal. As a result, the professor's analysis erred by $20 million, "an error of extraordinary proportions" (*Reserve-a*, at 62), and it was contradicted by the testimony of Armco and Republic executives. In rejecting the professor's evidence, Lord absolved him of blame, saying, "[I]t is as unfair to Dr. Soldofsky as it is unhelpful to the Court to deprive him of the very evidence he needs as foundation for his opinions" (*Reserve-a*, at 62). Along with taconite workers and the public, experts had fallen victim to Reserve's obstructive and destructive pursuit of profit.[35]

According to Lord, this obstruction was representative of Reserve's overall litigation approach.[36] It covered a long period of time and involved ever larger numbers of people. As the only Minnesota taconite company discharging waste into Lake Superior, Reserve had "steadfastly" maintained a stance that "was taken . . . in bad faith . . . was contrary to the facts as they knew them, and was pursued for the sole purpose of delaying the final resolution of the controversy" (*Reserve-a*, at 64). Particularly damning was evidence of Reserve's consistent obstruction regarding on-land disposal plans.

According to Lord, Reserve's deep-pipe plan was a chimera. After Reserve had maintained in state court, in the federal conference, and in federal court that the deep-pipe plan was the only feasible alternative to density currents, Armco's president finally admitted that Reserve could not build such a conduit. The company had used false promises to deflect all attempts to change its disposal system: "if the Court had gone along with Reserve's proposal . . . the end result would have been months and years of further delay without any assurance that there would ever be a satisfactory resolution of the problem" (*Reserve-a*, at 65).

It appeared that the months and years of delay could be brought to an end only because Lord had persevered in his pursuit of the truth. Reserve already had turned aside less exacting pursuers. It had duped Eckman into ordering a plan that could not work. It had defied the federal conference, refusing to present an abatement proposal. Then it had both defied and deceived Lord.

On January 11 Reserve had refused to tell Lord whether it would close its plant if he ordered on-land waste disposal. The company's attorney, Edward Fride, evaded the same question; he "did not use the opportunity . . . to purge his client of its failure to respond in full to earlier discovery requests" (*Reserve-a*, at 66). In February, Fride claimed that engineering changes had enabled Reserve to offer the deep-pipe plan. Reserve vice president Kenneth Haley followed his example, testifying that the conduit was "the best viable alternative"; he said that "he had received no written memorandum from Armco . . . or Republic . . . concerning complete on land disposal" and knew of no serious discussion of such a plan (*Reserve-a*, at 66). Reserve's attorney and its officers were implicated in defiance and deceit. Only when Lord ordered Armco's and Republic's officers to testify was the web of deceit broken: "These high officers . . . produced a flood of documents, 255 of which are now exhibits in the case, many of which bore the Reserve stamp, and were admitted at a later time by Reserve President Mr. Furness to be in Reserve's files" (*Reserve-a*, at 67).

According to Lord, Reserve's attorney, officers, and expert witnesses had participated in this deception. Some also were implicated in deception regarding alternative disposal plans. When Reserve's vice president denied knowing of any such plans, Reserve and its parent companies already had possessed at least one plan for over a year. Armco and Republic officers had known about it, and they also had known that it was being withheld from the court. Reserve's attorney had "attended . . . meetings when the on land disposal plan was discussed and was lead counsel . . . when the Court unsuccessfully called for those very plans" (*Reserve-a*, at 68). Further, three days after the documents finally were submitted to the court, Reserve's vice president had made the "incredible" claim that "it was only after the Court's suggestion [that cooling water be returned to the lake] that the engineers were able to overcome the problem that had been plaguing them for years" (*Reserve-a*, at 68). Lord caustically commented that "[i]f in fact [Reserve] had not previously considered the alternative . . . it could only be because they did not wish to solve the problem" (*Reserve-a*, at 68).

Lord had uncovered the deception, but the problem of ending the discharge remained. The judge portrayed Reserve as unwilling to change its conduct even after the revelation of its "intolerable" and "obvious misrepresentations" (*Reserve-a*, at 68). The company would not comply with air emission standards. It would implement on-land disposal only if the government and the court rewarded its wrongdoing by ensuring its "receipt of public assistance and the Court's issuing of an opinion contrary to its true findings" (*Reserve-a*, at 69). Because "Defendants' answer to the Court's inquiry shows that there is no middle ground," Lord's alternative was clear. Because Reserve would "continue exposing thousands to the carcinogenic effects of its discharge until such time as ordered to stay by this Court, or some other Court" (*Reserve-a*, at 69), Lord reaffirmed his injunction.

In doing so, Lord again laid the blame for a shutdown squarely on Reserve's shoulders. He rejected the contention that it was he, not Reserve, who jeopardized the jobs of Reserve employees. Recognizing that "the work force of Reserve would suffer immensely if the plant is shut down and they are thrown out of work" (*Reserve-a*, at 70), the company could abate its discharge. If "highly profitable" Reserve and its parent companies were intent on "seek[ing] a balancing of corporate profits against human life" (*Reserve-a*, at 70), the appropriate question for the court to answer was "[C]an a company be permitted to expose thousands of people to a known human carcinogen when they could well afford to abate the risk[?]" (*Reserve-a*, at 70).

Lord's answer was no. The court had higher responsibilities. First, it must "be concerned with those who were unable to make a real choice, particularly the children who must abide by the choice made by their parents." Second, it must be concerned about the implications of allowing "a commercial industry to require its work force to make . . . a choice that endangers their lives and the lives of their families." Finally, it must be concerned that "Reserve's discharge largely endangers the lives of thousands in other communities unrelated to the activity of the company." Given these responsibilities, Lord decided, "it becomes even more clear that the discharge must stop" (*Reserve-a*, at 70).

In concluding his opinion, Lord created a contrast of character between Reserve and himself as "the Court." Reserve was ruthlessly singleminded. According to Lord, it could afford to abate its discharge, but it chose not to do so and refused to accept responsibility for its choice. Reserve pretended to represent its employees' interests when it asked the court to save their jobs by not requiring abatement, but, Lord declared, the company actually was "using the work force at Reserve's plants as hostages. In order to free [them] the Court must permit the continued exposure of known human carcinogens to the citizens of Duluth and other North Shore communities" (*Reserve-a*, at 71). Under this great duress Lord maintained the high ground: "The Court will have no part of this . . . economic blackmail. . . . This Court cannot honor profit over human life and therefore has no other choice but abate the discharge" (*Reserve-a*, at 71).

Summary and Response

Lord framed the Reserve controversy as a dramatic contest. In this contest large corporations were attempting to profit from abusing "little guys" and corrupting the courts. They were confronted by a single judge, a champion of the community, trying to protect the "little guys" and the courts. In so framing *Reserve*'s complexities, he provided an interpretation of motives and acts that was accessible to lay as well as legal audiences. He had staked out a position that symbolized justice, making retreat almost impossible. He had taken his stand for the community and challenged the appeals court. It could support his stand or assume the burden of justifying its refusal.

On June 4, 1974, the appeals court took up Lord's challenge. Although it conceded that Reserve's dumping of taconite tailings into Lake Superior was "a monumental environmental mistake" (*Reserve-b*, at 1085), it rejected the rest of Lord's judgment. First it joined law to science. Declaring that "we are . . . governed by rules of proof, and unknowns may not be substituted for proof" (*Reserve-b*, at 1084), it anticipated that the public health case against Reserve was "simply beyond proof." For the court to recognize a threat to human health, science must show that public "exposure [to asbestos fibers is] at least comparable to [that] in occupational settings, or . . . establish principles of . . . pathology which may [predict] the occurrence of [asbestos-related] disease" (*Reserve-b*, at 1078).

The court also rejected Lord's portrayal of Reserve as hostage taker and himself as liberator. Finding "neither heroes nor villains among the present participants in this lawsuit" (*Reserve-b*, at 1085), it stayed Lord's injunction for seventy days and ordered Reserve to submit a plan for pollution abatement.[37] Praising Lord for his "innovative techniques," it expressed "confidence in his ability to assist the parties to achieve a meaningful and appropriate settlement" (*Reserve-b*, at 1086). It remanded the case for Lord's recommendations on the ordered plan.

Reactions were mixed. One observer commented that the stay permitted Reserve "to continue to pollute Lake Superior . . . for up to five years" (Court to permit, 1974, p. 1). The New York *Times* headlined its report "Judges' Decision Makes It Certain: It's Lake Inferior" (1974, p. 2); it editorially declared that "Lord continues to set an example of social conscience . . . while [Reserve] continues to put profits above the public health" (Social conscience, 1974, p. 10A; Superior, private dump? 1974, p. 14). Minnesota appealed the stay to the U.S. Supreme Court (Associated Press, 1974f, p. 10), which denied its appeal. Associate Justice William O. Douglas, Lord's "favorite," dissented (High court denies, 1974, p. 9).

The appellate courts had rejected Lord's version of the Reserve controversy. At least part of the public had accepted it. With this difference as background Lord turned to the issues on remand. Ordering Reserve not to submit proposals already rejected by Minnesota, he encouraged negotiation. He also sought to educate himself regarding potential disposal sites, inspecting some of them himself (Associated Press, 1974h, p. 33; 1974g, p. 26; Rebuffoni, 1974e, pp. 1B, 10B; 1974c, pp. 1B, 9B). Perhaps the Reserve controversy would be resolved after all.

Reserve, however, soon rekindled Lord's distrust. The company indicated that it would appeal any decision Lord might make (Rebuffoni, 1974f, p. 2B); more important, it again disobeyed court instructions. Reserve submitted a disposal plan for the Palisade Creek area near Silver Bay (Palisade), a site that Minnesota consistently had opposed. It refused to consider other options (Rebuffoni, 1974d, p. 14A; 1974h, p. 5B).

Lord observed that Reserve's plan seemed haphazard, and a company document noting that the Palisade site would make "reversion [from on-land] discharge into the lake . . . a relatively simple matter" (Rebuffoni, 1974g, p. 2B) convinced him that Reserve was repeating its deep-pipe strategy. First it would gain court approval of an unworkable plan. It would abandon the project after others discovered the plan's unfeasibility. And it would gain its true objective, delay.[38] In Lord's judgment, Reserve had "given this court more trouble than I've ever had in . . . all [other] cases put together, suffered more delay, more in accumulation of misrepresentations [and] obfuscations, than I've seen in all my legal career" (Rebuffoni, 1974g, p. 2B). On August 3, 1974, Lord rejected the Palisade plan.

Additional Memorandum After Remand

In rejecting Reserve's plan, Lord continued his dialogue with the Eighth Circuit Court of Appeals. If he had not persuaded the appeals court, neither had it persuaded him. Lord's third memorandum defended his initial judgment and warned the appeals court that it had encouraged Reserve to exploit the judicial system and obstruct justice. As Lord had predicted, Reserve had not changed. What had changed was the degree of the courts' culpability. Lord's warning renewed his challenge: to protect the community, to preserve the courts' integrity, and to conclude the Reserve controversy, the appeals court would have to choose Lord over Reserve.

Lord's warning involved three major strategies. First, by expressing concern about the limits placed on his authority, Lord warned the appeals court that it had created ambiguity about a judge's role in doing justice. Second, by describing Reserve's exploitation of judicial ambiguity, he warned that the court shared responsibility for the company's obstruction. Third, by contrasting his reasonableness to Reserve's obstruction, he justified his injunction and warned the appeals court that he would stand firm. The model of patience presented by the appeals court was mistaken; if its patience persisted, it would do so without Lord's acquiescence.

Ambiguity and authority. According to Lord, the appeals court had undermined judicial authority through ambiguity, and it had encouraged obstruction by rewarding it. Clear authority was critical in resolving *Reserve-a.* It remained unresolved because Reserve had successfully resisted the authority of government agencies and state courts. Creating ambiguity about judicial authority diminished the ability of the federal courts, as the last resort, to effect a just resolution.

The appeals court had created ambiguity in several ways. First, it had created an "uncertain" role for Lord. He had been "thrust into the midst of what appears to be a settlement procedure, absent any real power to impose a settlement" (*Reserve-a*, at 71). The appeals court had raised "some question as to how much power Congress intended to vest in the Court" (*Reserve-a*, at 74); it had ruled that Lord's injunction violated legislative prerogative, but it had not clarified the limits of judicial prerogative within which Lord should proceed.

Instead the appeals court had ordered Lord to preside over proceedings that not only presented "some problems as to [their] propriety" (*Reserve-a*, at 78)[39] but also were of uncertain dimension. As Lord observed, "There is some question among the parties and the Court as to the scope and intent of the Court of Appeals' Order. The procedure . . . is somewhat unprecedented and there are few guidelines to look to" (*Reserve-a*, at 85). Questions among the parties and the court inevitably led to appeal; ambiguity led to diminished authority and delay.

Lord's authority also was diminished by the appeals court's ambiguous interest in enforcing respect for the courts. To Lord a "finding that a litigant . . . has acted in bad faith is an extremely serious matter" (*Reserve-a*, at 84). However, although "the record is there for all to see" (*Reserve–a*, at 84), the appeals court seemed to overlook Reserve's past bad faith (*Reserve-a*, at 85). The appeals court's ambiguity undermined Lord's authority even to command the ordinary respect due judicial orders. In Lord's view Reserve stood ready to exploit the ambiguity.

Ambiguity and exploitation. Reserve's plan for on-land disposal provided one example of its readiness. According to Lord, "If the thrust of the Order of the Court of Appeals was to merely come up with a hypothetical plan . . . then defendants did exactly that. If the thrust . . . was . . . to come up with a realistic plan that might lead to a solution . . . then there may be serious question as to defendants' good faith efforts in [devising] a plan that had little or no possibility of being implemented" (*Reserve-a*, at 86).

Lord maintained that the appeals court had played an indirect part in Reserve's submission of "conceptually the same plan that was present in defendants' files since February, 1973, improperly withheld in violation of . . . discovery orders and . . . rejected in negotiating sessions" (*Reserve-a*, at 72). Earlier Lord had recounted Reserve's record of exploiting ambiguity, and the court should have foreseen that Reserve would regard its ambiguous opinion as an invitation to delay. By limiting Lord's authority rather than Reserve's opportunities for exploitation, the appeals court shared responsibility for the company's obstruction.

Lord sought to remove any doubt about obstruction in his rhetorical recreation of Reserve's "corporate shell game" (*Reserve-a*, at 72). Because the appeals court had chosen to ignore previous offenses, he offered a list of new violations. According to Lord, Reserve predicated its plan on bad-faith prior conditions,[40] then compounded its bad faith with a plan that was heedless of public health and devoid of engineering integrity. As Lord described the plan, he clearly implied that Reserve's response to ambiguity was to prolong the controversy and demonstrate contempt for the public and the courts; in appearance Reserve met the appeals court's requirements, but in substance it frustrated the court's express goals.[41]

Lord critiqued the disposal plan's engineering and technical feasibility.[42] This extended example of obstruction employed rhetorical strategies reminiscent of his May 11 memorandum, but with tactical changes. For example, in May Lord had used expert testimony to support his credibility. This time he used the testimony of Reserve's experts to impeach the company. Comparisons between the magnitude of Reserve's project and the minimal care expended on it also echoed earlier memoranda in advancing Lord's claim that Reserve's plan was an illusion.

Reserve's plan for on-land tailings disposal would contain fine taconite tailings in a natural basin uphill from Silver Bay. To supplement natural high ridges, the company would use coarse tailings to build dams up to 450 feet high, "higher than any other tailings dam now existing" (*Reserve-a*, at 79), and 7,000 feet long. The project was immense.

The project's immensity contrasted to the plan's carelessness. From Reserve experts' testimony Lord compiled an inventory of negligence. A dam engineering expert testified that Reserve's "drawings were merely conceptual," that "positions for the dams had not been finalized," and that "no test drillings or detailed geological surveys or anything of that nature had been done" (*Reserve-a*, at 78). The same expert testified that faults in foundation rock could cause dam failure and that the foundation rock was "known to be extensively faulted"; yet "[n]one of the necessary geologic field investigation has been done" (*Reserve-a*, at 80). And, although dam integrity depended on the stability of the tailings, the tailings "have not been investigated as to mineral stability" (*Reserve-a*, at 80).

This expert's testimony was supported by Reserve's executive vice president and another Reserve engineer. According to Lord, the executive "admitted that Reserve had done nothing more than eye-ball the area" (*Reserve-a*, at 78). The engineer admitted that he had "done no field work with respect to dam construction, a task he admitted would be critical"; and he "had not run any test [on] the stability of the dam construction material" (*Reserve-a*, at 78).

Shortcomings in Reserve's plan for initial construction were matched by lack of planning for long-term contingencies. During the estimated forty years of dam operation, mine operators would supervise construction and maintenance. Yet a Reserve expert had admitted that mine operators "do not always follow ideal engineering procedures," and therefore "no one could guarantee that the dams would be built according to [the engineer's] design" (*Reserve-a*, at 80). Even if construction did meet design specifications, the dams might not be safe. The same expert testified that four consecutive wet years would exceed safety specifications and "could . . . create a great risk of dam failure" (*Reserve-a*, at 80). In addition, although only "perpetual operation of control structures and water treatment plants" (*Reserve-a*, at 80) could protect against dam failure if Reserve closed its operations, the plan included none of those features.

Therefore, according to Lord, "Reserve's own officials and consultants have stated that safe dams and secure tailings containment are not possible in this region" (*Reserve-a*, at 81). Their knowledge was not new. During the federal conference Reserve's vice president had declared that tailings dams there "would represent a constant threat of leaks and rupture," exposing people to a "serious safety hazard" and "fine tailings from the air . . . over large areas" (*Reserve-a*, at 81). He also had warned that "[a]fter Reserve's mine is exhausted, surface waters would continue to erode any on-land tailings deposit until it would finally be washed into Lake Superior" (*Reserve-a*, at 81). His testimony had confirmed consultants' warnings that the Palisade plan would "pose a constant threat to life and property . . . in spite of the most conservative dam design" (*Reserve-a*, at 81).

Nevertheless, Reserve persisted in offering the Palisade plan. And, although "over 70% of larger mining operations have had tailings dam failure" (*Reserve-a*, at 81), it approached the project casually. Lord emphasized its nonchalance with examples of "bits and pieces" (Rebuffoni, 1974g, p. 2B) it added as the plan was "fashioned before the Court's very eyes" (*Reserve-a*, at 78). In spite of the danger of a dam failure that "would release millions of tons of tailings and . . . endanger residents . . . . [and] ultimately pour into Lake Superior" (*Reserve-a*, at 80), during Lord's hearings the "volume of tailings needed . . . changed from 125,000,000 tons to 376,000,000 tons"; dam slopes "ranged from 1.75:1 to . . . 6:1"; the "number of waste piles has changed from three to one to zero" (*Reserve-a*, at 79); and mine life, dam heights, and center lines had varied significantly. These examples demonstrated a tentativeness that made "adjudicating the reasonableness of this plan . . . practically impossible" (*Reserve-a*, at 79).

In Lord's judgment, Reserve's "history of ignoring or being unaware of engineering recommendations . . . weigh[ed] against Reserve's proposal" (*Reserve-a*, at 81). The company he portrayed seemed neither to understand its plan nor to care whether it would work. Lord's description illustrated his claim that Reserve had not changed. It also showed how the ambiguity created by the appeals court provided another opportunity for Reserve to achieve its real objective, delay. If the appeals court ignored Lord's warning, it would share responsibility for the consequences.

Lord's reasonableness and Reserve's obstruction. Permeating Lord's memorandum is a message to the appeals court, "overheard" by a wider audience, that "I was right." However, the rhetorical force of such a message depends on more than portrayals of others' ambiguity and obstruction. It requires a persona that embodies the reasonableness others have not displayed.

Evidence of that persona can be discerned in Lord's concern for clear definitions of authority. Clear definitions would enable him to avoid overreaching while effectively exercising his judicial power. Lord contrasted his desire for restraint, and therefore his reasonableness, to the appeals court's ambiguity. Restraint is implicit in detailed examples of statutes and precedents to which he deferred (see, e.g., *Reserve-a*, at 74-78), in references to his submission to legislative will (see, e.g., *Reserve-a*, at 83), and in avowals that any unusual actions he took had been mandated by the appeals court and were taken reluctantly (see, e.g., *Reserve-a*, at 78, 79).

The persona also can be perceived in Lord's analysis of Reserve's disposal plan. His concern for facts and reliable forecasts contrasted to Reserve's unreasonable disregard for such matters. The contrast continued in other areas as well. For example, in Lord's analysis of environmental factors, he contrasted his empirical knowledge of revegetation—he had "witnessed firsthand the fruitless efforts of the mining corporations to plant grass, shrubs, or trees in the tailings" (*Reserve-a*, at 82)—to Reserve's failure to call as witnesses company researchers engaged in ongoing revegetation experiments. It preferred the testimony of a person who "had been hired only two weeks prior to his testimony" and "had not developed a revegetation plan" (*Reserve-a*, at 82).[43]

These factors helped to create the persona of a reasonable judge. However, they were subordinate to another factor, impartiality. As Lord conceded, "repeated findings of bad faith against one side of the law suit may give the appearance of uneven justice, or bias" (*Reserve-a*, at 84). Consequently, he devoted considerable attention to establishing his efforts to cooperate with Reserve. He was a judge whose exhaustive efforts to find workable solutions were frustrated by others. He was forced reluctantly from a willingness to compromise toward a refusal to place himself, the courts, and the community in a compromising position.

For example, implicit in Lord's avowal that he was "aware of the engineering problems involved in [Reserve's] undertaking" (*Reserve-a*, at 79) was reasonable tolerance for human imperfection. Reserve, however, had met reasonable flexibility with unreasonable fluidity. After eighteen months it was "not unreasonable to expect more specificity" from Reserve; without it "adjudicating the reasonableness of this plan is practically made impossible by the fluidity of the engineering concepts" (*Reserve-a*, at 79). Lord was the moderator in this scenario. It was Reserve's immoderation that made the plan's approval unreasonable; Lord "or any other Court would be engaging in conjecture and speculation if it were to make final determinations based on such sketchy information" (*Reserve-a*, at 79).

Lord also rhetorically transformed an apparent inconsistency in his own position into an example of how Reserve's exploitation of flexibility had forced him into an inflexible position. Conceding that his previous allowance for "turn-around time" on construction could "appear to run against [my] findings that there is a potential health hazard" (*Reserve-a*, at 83), Lord explained that he formerly "was of the opinion that the fastest, most efficient solution . . . would not be through Court resolution . . . but through the good faith efforts of the parties to reach a settlement" (*Reserve-a*, at 83-84). However, Reserve's response to reasonableness was to obstruct settlement. Consequently, "we are in the same position as we were . . . several years ago, with the chance that the continued mode of discharge may be continued for several more years while this matter is decided in the appellate courts" (*Reserve-a*, at 84). Therefore Lord "felt obligated to stop these violations of law and stop a threat that the legislature and the administrative agencies had tried to protect against" (*Reserve-a*, at 84). By meeting judicial reasonableness with obstructive unreasonableness, Reserve had forced Lord to take action.

Thus Lord concluded that Reserve had acted in bad faith by presenting "a plan that in no way could help to resolve [the] dispute" (*Reserve-a*, at 85), perhaps hoping that "the plan would be rejected but enough 'good faith' would be demonstrated to allow for yet more time" (*Reserve-a*, at 86).

According to Lord, neither Reserve's intentions nor its actions had changed. Therefore he recommended that the stay of injunction be lifted and that Reserve's discharge be halted. Again he emphasized that Reserve bore the responsibility for his judgment. Reserve could have decided at any time to make good faith efforts to abate its discharge and protect its plant. However, "the decision whether or not to permanently close down the operation is clearly a management decision of Armco and Republic, not a decision of this Court. . . . If [they] choose to invest their money elsewhere at the expense of their work force . . . there is little this Court can do about this decision" (*Reserve-a*, at 87).

The courts could not control Reserve's decisions, but they were honor bound to protect the integrity of their own decisions. For five years they had countenanced obstruction that delayed compliance with the law. Lord's concluding paragraph was a reminder of the proper role of the judiciary. According to Lord, it "may be the right of a corporate entity to refuse to come into compliance with laws . . . until it is specifically ordered to. . . . However, now defendants have had their day in court in the form of this nine-month trial. . . . Due process requires that defendants be permitted the right to appeal this Court's decision. Due process does not require that defendants be permitted to violate the laws aimed at protecting the public and to continue exposing thousands of people to substantial quantities of a known human carcinogen during the several years remaining in which the appellate process continues" (*Reserve-a*, at 90-91).[44]

Summary, Response, Removal, and Aftermath

Summary. Lord's additional memorandum clearly presented a rhetorical challenge to the Eighth Circuit Court of Appeals. Rather than accepting the appeals court's judgment that there were "no villains" in the Reserve controversy Lord insisted that he had discerned the true nature of Reserve's motives and had predicted accurately the company's actions. He warned the appeals court that cooperation with the company would contaminate the structures of justice and expose community members to destruction. He presented the appeals court with a choice between judicial purity and decay. The appeals court's choice would be a test of its purity.

Response. The Eighth Circuit Court of Appeals proved itself as persistent as Lord. After ordering additional hearings, it stayed Lord's injunction for three additional months, maintaining that the alleged public health hazard had not been proved (Associated Press, 1974i, p. 29; Rebuffoni, 1974k, p. 1A). The U.S. Supreme Court was equally impervious to Lord's arguments. It rejected an appeal for an immediate halt to Reserve's dumping. Again only Justice Douglas dissented (Associated Press, 1974j, p. 16; Hill, 1974b, p. 50; Justice Department joins, 1974, p. 34; United Press International, 1974b, p. 92).

Once again the public was more receptive to Lord's arguments. Senators Gaylord Nelson and Philip Hart introduced legislation to prevent future Reserve-like controversies by requiring proof that "potentially dangerous" business activities were safe.[45] An editorial applauded the legislation, observing that it would place the "burden of proof . . . where it belongs—on the shoulders of those who stand to gain from a risk" (Try it, 1974, p. 38). The New York *Times* magazine traced the Reserve controversy from its beginnings and described the risks it involved (Greene, 1974, pp. 17, 95, 96, 98, 99, 104, 106). Minnesota's governor declared his "100 percent" support for Lord (Rebuffoni, 1974i, pp. 1A, 4A), suggesting that he was "a proper candidate for the United States Supreme Court" (Rebuffoni, 1975e, p. 1A; Wolkerstorfer, 1975e, p. 1A).

In the courts the controversy continued. Early in November, after warning Reserve not to submit another "shabby and hollow" plan for a compromise site at Milepost 7 (Associated Press, 1974k, p. 90; Rebuffoni, 1974i, pp. 1A, 4A; 1974k, pp. 4A, 10A),[46] Lord announced his intention to oversee the public safety and environmental aspects of disposal-site proposals (Rebuffoni, 1974l, pp. 1B, 2B). Reserve appealed, citing Lord's "bias, prejudice and unfounded prejudgment" and his violation of due process in joining Armco and Republic as *Reserve* defendants (Associated Press, 1974m, p. 53; 1974, p. 13B).[47]

On March 14, the appeals court again stayed Lord's injunction. Although finally conceding that the "risk to public health is of sufficient gravity to be legally cognizable" (*Reserve Mining Company v. Environmental Protection Agency* [*EPA*] [1975], at 500), affirming the joinder of Armco and Republic, and ordering Reserve to take "reasonable immediate steps" to reduce air emissions, it declined to set a deadline for ending in-lake discharges (Carman, 1975, pp. 1A, 6A; Court bids, 1975, p. 30). It speculated that the harm from "prolonged unemployment . . . may be more certain than the harm from drinking Lake Superior water or breathing Silver Bay air" (*EPA*, at 537).

The court's decision spurred Lord to further action. He convened a hearing and, complaining that the appeals court had "tied my hands, in many ways"

(Associated Press, 1975b, p. 64),[48] he urged Wendell Anderson, Minnesota's governor, to "save us two to three years of negotiation" (United Press International, 1975, p. 22) by choosing a disposal site and urged the legislature to help. He also directed Reserve and the state to report on progress toward on-land disposal (Associated Press, 1975e, p. 34; Carman, 1975, pp. 1A, 6A; Rebuffoni, 1975a, pp. 1A, 6A; Shoop, 1975, pp. 1A, 4A).

A third appeal to the Supreme Court for a two-year deadline on in-lake discharges was rejected on March 31 (Associated Press, 1975a, p. 35; 1975c, p. 34; Justice Department joins, 1974, p. 34; Weaver, 1975, p. 24). This setback for the states was followed by a setback for Lord. On April 8 the appeals court, acting on its own initiative,[49] branded Lord's "irregular" hearing "a complete nullity." It specifically denied that its decision might prolong Reserve's in-lake discharge and advised "the trial judge and counsel . . . that they must respect the letter and spirit of our opinion." Lord was instructed to "not interfere in matters . . . outside his jurisdiction" (*EPA*, at 541-542; see also Rebuffoni, 1975a, p. 1A; Wolkerstorfer, 1975a, p. 1A).[50]

An editorial noted the irony of the appeals court's ordering an end to Reserve's discharge and staying the injunction that would have ended it. It supported legislation to ensure that industry "would no longer be allowed to enjoy a financial return today for which others *might* have to pay with their lives tomorrow" (Whose risk?, 1975, p. 16). Lord also commented on the consequences of the appeals court restrictions. At a July hearing he complained that the delay in *Reserve* had brought "strangers to the proceeding" (Rebuffoni, 1975b, p. 1B) whose ignorance of court findings resulted in support for a $200 million state subsidy of Reserve and receptiveness to a "fully . . . unsatisfactory" Lax Lake plan (Rebuffoni, 1975b, pp. 1B, 2B).[51] At this point he was not sure that he could face the prospect of "going through a dark tunnel for 10 years" (Rebuffoni & Picone, 1975, pp. 1B, 2B).

Removal. However, Lord did not quit. On November 14, disturbed by new evidence that the danger of water-borne fibers had been underestimated (McCabe, 1975b, p. 4A),[52] he convened the second in a series of "irregular" hearings. He knew that, in personal terms, "there was considerable risk involved. But sometimes the stakes are so high you have to take the risk; you have to stand up and be counted. What we're talking about is the health of thousands of people . . . and I think that justifies any risks I took by stretching normal judicial procedure" (Wolkerstorfer, 1976a, p. 1A).

Lord had requested the presence of the state hearings officer, who attended only after assurances that neither Reserve nor the state objected (Rebuffoni, 1975c, p. 1A). At the hearings Lord "admonish[ed all of the parties] that you are playing with fire" (Wolkerstorfer, 1975e, p. 3A), examined witnesses, questioned the credibility of some Reserve consultants, and observed that he had "dispensed with the usual adversary proceeding here because I simply do not have time to spend listening to misrepresentations by Reserve Mining Co." (Wolkerstorfer, 1975e, p. 3A). On November 15 he ordered Reserve to pay

$100,000 for Duluth's water filtration, and on November 16 he announced a long-term filtered-water program that would cost Reserve up to $1.5 million (Wolkerstorfer, 1975c, pp. 1A, 5A).[53]

In response, Reserve complained to the appeals court that Lord had exceeded his authority and interfered with the state permit process. It asked the court to overturn his order for payment and to halt the proceedings (Wolkerstorfer, 1975d, pp. 1A, 4A). On November 20 the appeals court notified Lord that he could not act in *Reserve* until it determined whether his order was proper. The nature of Reserve's appeal had changed.

During its appeal hearing the company had made an oral request for Lord's removal, supporting its request with copies of newspaper articles (Rebuffoni, 1975d, pp. 1A, 5A). The articles reported that Lord had called the relationship between Reserve and Minnesota's governor "cozy," and that he felt that the governor's desire for a "quick and convenient" settlement overshadowed evidence that tailings dust from the Milepost 7 site would pose a health hazard. They also reported the governor's resentment of public criticism that some officials believed Lord had "orchestrated" (see, e.g., Rebuffoni, 1975b, pp. 1B, 2B; 1975c, pp. 1A, 4A; Wolkerstorfer, 1975e, pp. 1A, 3A). Minnesota's attorneys reiterated their earlier argument that Lord had shown "great patience" in the face of "withheld evidence and misrepresented facts" (Wolkerstorfer, 1975d, pp. 1A, 4A). They asked the court to consider substance rather than style (Rebuffoni, 1975d, p. 15A).

Reserve had not asked Lord to recuse himself before asking the appeals court to remove him. Judge Donald Lay had commented that only Lord seemed interested in water filtration and that while "we're fighting about procedures and who is going to pay the bill . . . nothing's being done" (Rebuffoni, 1975d, pp. 1A, 15A). Nevertheless, the appeals court in effect suspended Lord. The judge who "[s]ome environmentalists and state officials believe . . . understands better than anyone the health threat. . . . . [He] is the only public official able to fight the economic and political influence of the mining companies and [to have] the courage to take Reserve to task for its pollution" (Wolkerstorfer, 1975e, p. 1A) was temporarily off the case.

With the removal hearing scheduled for December 18 (Arguments on judge, 1975, p. 2A; Briefly, 1975, p. 2A), individuals and groups rallied to Lord. Minnesota's governor expressed his strong support (McCabe, 1975a, pp. 1A, 10A; Rebuffoni, 1975e, p. 1A; Wolkerstorfer, 1975e, p. 3A), the MPCA considered an emergency shutdown of Reserve to "show the 8th circuit court we support Judge Lord" (Wolkerstorfer, 1975f, pp. 1A, 4A), and environmental groups requested a Reserve shutdown under the governor's emergency powers. The Department of Justice urged the appeals court to keep Lord on the complex case (Rebuffoni, 1975f, p. 11B).

At the December 18 hearing Reserve accused Lord of having an "utter inability to act in . . . an objective, fair and impartial manner" and of denying its legal rights (Judge in Reserve, 1975, p. 28; Rebuffoni, 1975h, pp. 1A, 10A).

Minnesota's attorneys pointed out that Reserve had supported Lord when he was skeptical of public health claims, questioning his objectivity only after he began to rule against it. They argued that the company's complaints "should not mask [its] basic aim of avoiding its financial responsibility to . . . clean up the water it has illegally polluted" (Rebuffoni, 1975g, pp. 1A, 16A). Given the subject matter of the hearing, this testimony was expected.

What was unexpected was Lord's decision to represent himself at the hearing (Judge in Reserve, 1975, p. 28). Testifying for fifteen minutes (McCabe, 1975b, p. 1A), he repeated his judgment that Reserve was guilty of "hiding documents . . . misrepresentations . . . obfuscations and delays" (Judge in Reserve, 1975, p. 28). It also was jeopardizing evidence: Reserve's recent use of taconite wastes on icy county roads would complicate proof regarding the source of taconite fibers in the lake (Rebuffoni, 1975h, p. 10A). Although conceding that his manner sometimes resembled that of an advocate (The federal judge, 1976, p. 24), he warned the appeals court that "[w]hile these proceedings drag on . . . carcinogenic fibers continued to be dispersed. . . . If the risk becomes reality, hundreds may die" (McCabe, 1975b, p. 1A). He also renewed his complaint that limiting judicial authority delayed a just and safe resolution of *Reserve.*

Lord declared that "[n]either this judge, nor any judge, can act effectively to protect the public health absent a clear mandate and support of this court of appeals" (Rebuffoni, 1975h, p. 1A); he could not "handle this case if in every move I make I am alleged to have violated the letter or the spirit of your mandate" (Judge in Reserve, 1975, p. 28). He conceded that "it is of little importance whether or not Miles W. Lord personally presides over this case," but he maintained that "[i]t is of great importance . . . that a federal district judge be vested with full powers and full authority so that he can make the proper and expeditious determinations to insure the health of future generations" (McCabe, 1975b, p. 1A). Observing that to Reserve "the villain is the judge who exposed them for what they are" (McCabe, 1975b, pp. 1A, 4A), he asked the appeals court for its "confidence [and] faith in me." The appeals court must choose unambiguously: "The evidence is closed. I have made my judgment. It is now up to you gentlemen to do something or [the danger of Reserve's taconite tailings] can never be proved" (Judge in Reserve, 1975, p. 28).

Lord invited questions, but none were asked (McCabe, 1975b, p. 4A). There was some indication, however, that the court was not receptive to his arguments. For example, although Judge Donald Ross agreed that Reserve polluted Lake Superior, he denied that its taconite tailings were the sole source of asbestos fibers in water supplies. He also suggested that Reserve should not be ordered to pay for water filtration because filtration removed all pollutants, not just those from Reserve (Rebuffoni, 1975h, pp. 1A, 10A).

In spite of attorneys' opinions that Lord had hurt his cause by defending himself (McCabe, 1975b, p. 4A), Lord said that he felt a "great relief, a feeling of having done the right thing" (The federal judge, 1976, p. 24). In this case doing right had to be its own reward. On January 6, 1976, the appeals court ordered Duluth to return Reserve's $100,000 and ordered the Corps of Engineers to continue to provide filtered water (Wolkerstorfer, 1976a, pp. 1A, 16A).

In addition, the appeals court declined to act on Reserve's removal motion because it was oral (*Reserve Mining Company v. Lord* [*Lord*], [1976], at 188). Instead it removed Lord on its own motion, *sua sponte*. It gave as its reasons Lord's "great bias," denial of due process, and "deliberate disregard of appellate mandate" (Judge is removed, 1976, pp. 1, 9; *Lord*, at 185-186). The appeals court had recognized Lord's challenges, and his removal was its response: "It is one thing for a district judge to disagree . . . with a judgment of this court. It is quite another to openly challenge the court's ruling and attempt to discredit the integrity of the judgment in the eyes of the public" (*Lord*, at 188).

Lord's response was brief: "I have done my best to provide for the maximum protection of the public health consistent with due process, to all concerned. As of today, I can do no more" (The federal judge, 1976, p. 24). Public comment was more extensive.

Aftermath. One commentator found Lord's removal "regrettable," saying that although his style "cannot be overlooked . . . his deep concern for the health of the people . . . should not be forgotten (Lord removed, 1976, p. 8A). Another noted that because lives were at risk, Lord "deliberately [courted] stunning discipline. . . . [W]hile we can't condone Lord's rash injudicious behavior, we believe that he has forced the issue" (Now let's, 1976, p. 6A).[54] Yet another called Reserve a "scandalous example" of corporations that invested in delay rather than clean-up, observing that "[n]o one familiar with Judge Lord's . . . sometimes unorthodox judicial style would doubt that the Eighth Circuit had cause for removing him. But there are moments in the life of law when exasperation at pettifogging and delay is an understandable response. Judge Lord's indignation at Reserve's outrageous tactics has served at least to pierce the crust of public apathy and to make the public health menace real and understandable" (The Reserve scandal, 1976, p. 24).

One columnist wrote that "[t]hey might yet put it on Lord's tombstone . . . 'Here lies Miles Lord; After the polluters he went with both guns; but they are still dumping 67,000 tons' " (Klobuchar, 1976a, p. 1B). Another said that Lord's removal was as if "a player waited until after the game to complain about [a] call and the official then ruled for the player but insisted the beef had nothing to do with the ruling" (Wehrwein, 1976, p. 14A). A letter to the editor more directly proclaimed, "Rash, injudicious behavior be damned! . . . Now let's get moving! At Lord's speed—which is now" (Lofstrand, 1976, p. 14A).

Perhaps Chief Judge Edward Devitt, who had taken over *Reserve* (Judge is removed, 1976, pp. 1, 9), was listening. Although in early February a state official complained that "[t]here's just no end in sight" (Farrell, 1976, p. 13),[55] on February 22 Devitt ordered Reserve to pay the costs for north shore communities' water filtration (United Press International, 1976a, p. 23). In May he ordered the company to pay almost $850,000 in state fines for violating water discharge permits and to pay $200,000 for legal costs and as punishment for withholding documents and misrepresenting facts (Associated Press, 1976d, p. 35). Reserve appealed the next day (Associated Press, 1976e, p. 7A).

Editorial comment suggested that Devitt's orders had vindicated Lord's judgment. One columnist declared that Devitt had "fundamentally accepted" Lord's portrayal of Reserve as a "profit-conscious polluter" (Klobuchar, 1976b, p. 9A). When Reserve appealed the MPCA's rejection of Milepost 7, an editorial noted that the "higher court may have had a point about the judge's emotionalism . . . but [his] conclusions themselves continue to be persuasive" (Judge Lord was right, 1976, p. 38).

Reserve tried to focus another kind of attention on Lord. In addition to appealing Devitt's orders, it sent to the appeals court fifty-five pages of Lord's speeches and interviews critical of Reserve. States' attorneys speculated that the company hoped that renewed anger at Lord would move the court to overturn Devitt's order (Associated Press, 1976e, p. 7A). A columnist suspected that Reserve wanted "to restoke the blaze and give the [appeals court] a chance to fry Lord after it has already burned him" (Klobuchar, 1976b, p. 9A). At an appeals hearing Reserve argued that Lord might have influenced the state's rejection of Milepost 7 (Rebuffoni, 1976b, pp. 1B, 2B). But the appeals court upheld Devitt, including his July 7, 1977, deadline for Reserve to discontinue in-lake discharge.[56]

Lord's last word on *Reserve* clearly had not been spoken in his brief post-removal statement. In fact, in January Lord observed that he "expected the kind of treatment I got . . . because I am certain that you cannot pick on anyone [with] as many friends as Reserve . . . without being severely criticized." Henceforth he expected "to be reversed nine times out of 10. . . . because people are human and the Reserve case is an embarrassment to the court of appeals" (Berg and Stone, 1976, p. 8C). When the state of Minnesota appeared receptive to Milepost 7, he said that "the state of Minnesota has declared victory by giving Reserve everything it wanted, then going home" (Worth noting, 1976b, p. 7A).

In June Minnesota's governor announced that he was seeking ways to subsidize Reserve's on-land disposal. At the same time the state was objecting to the costs of improving a state prison. In a hearing on the prison matter, Lord said, "I will not listen to the argument that the state . . . cannot give humane treatment to its prisoners on the same day that the governor announces he is going to give millions of dollars to [Reserve]" (Brown, 1976, p. 17A). In September Lord's speech to the Minnesota Society of Professional Journalists included the suggestion that subsidizing Reserve would amount to paying "blackmail"; it would be outrageous for a state that "cannot afford to take proper care of the people in the mental institutions [or] properly build and run a prison." He believed, he said, "in helping the needy—not the greedy" (Dornfeld, 1976, p. 2B).

Lord never has ceased to believe that the outcome of *Reserve* was unworthy of the judicial system. He continues to predict increases in asbestos-related deaths and disease in northern Minnesota and to attribute his removal to factors including improper communication between Reserve and the Eighth Circuit Court of Appeals and some appeals judges' favoritism toward corporate litigants (Lord, 1988a; Lord, 1992). These conclusions can be disputed. What cannot be disputed is his conclusion that "I guess the rocks rolled down the hill on me in that one. Still, you can make a lot of noise when those rocks are on the way down" (McEnroe, 1985, p. 7A). Lord has been compensated for his "bruising" in *Reserve* by environmentalists' assurances that the noise he made "alert[ed] the world to the dangers of industrial pollution" (Lord, 1992).

In a dialogue with the Eighth Circuit Court of Appeals about a significant public controversy, Miles W. Lord rhetorically constructed a dramatic contest between good and evil. Through depictions of motives and actions, he simplified a complex legal case. In the drama Reserve Mining Company personified evil, and Lord, as the steadfast representative of justice, personified good. Compromise came to mean capitulation, temporizing to signify corruption. His rhetorically created polarization of the interests involved in the *Reserve* case made the contest "real and understandable" by presenting to the appeals court, the U.S. Supreme Court, and the public opportunities to choose sides. As the representative of right, Lord offered himself as the expendable instrument of justice.

By speaking plainly but dramatically, and by combining courtroom rhetoric with public comment, he suggested the larger community's legitimate role in monitoring corporations and the courts, and he invited the public to play that role. By rejecting the appeals court's attempts to modify his approach to judging, he attempted to limit the persuasive appeal of that court's version of "good judging" and to advance an alternative interpretation. Certainly Lord suggested in his *Reserve* opinions that courts do not always do justice; to members of the community who accepted his rhetorical reconstruction of events, his removal was ample proof. However, the drama of *Reserve* also offered a story of the pursuit of justice in which a judge so clearly saw what was right, and so deeply committed himself to justice and the community, that he was willing to risk himself to achieve a just community. So long as such judges existed, the community could be reassured of its underlying ethos. It had reason to continue to strive toward perfection; evil might triumph temporarily, but Lord, justice, and the community surely would win in the end.

NOTES

1. Background information relies on several books. R. V. Bartlett's *The Reserve Mining controversy* (1980) is a well-documented history of Minnesota taconite mining and Reserve. E. W. Davis's *Pioneering with taconite* (1964) is a memoir of one of the persons most responsible for developing taconite's industrial potential. Reserve's public relations firm participated in selecting F. D. Schaumberg to author

Judgment reserved (1976), and Reserve agreed to purchase copies of the work. Bastow's *This vast pollution* (1986) was written by one of the government's attorneys in the *Reserve* case. Although the works tend to corroborate each other, I have cited Bartlett most often.

2. Taconite land was protected from local property taxes (Bartlett, 1980, p. 20).

3. Beneficiation separates iron pellets from taconite ore (Bartlett, 1980, p. 20).

4. Reserve claimed that tailings would be captured in a high-density slurry, descend 900 feet to the bottom of a natural trough, and remain as inert sand. It based its assurances on studies that did not consider phenomena such as deep currents, thermoclines, and wave action. The conditions of the studies and gaps in scientific knowledge contributed to the inaccuracy of Reserve's predictions (Bartlett, 1980, pp. 21-22, 27-29).

5. State permit conditions included provisions that tailings must not affect materially the lake's aquatic life, drinking water, or appearance beyond a three-mile-square zone. The U.S. Army Corps of Engineers (COE) also issued permits, primarily concerned with the lake's navigability (Bartlett, 1980, p. 23).

6. Superior has the largest surface area of any freshwater lake, although Siberia's Lake Baikal is over four times as deep (Bartlett, 1980, pp. 41, 252n).

7. Initial production capacity was 3.75 million tons per year, rising to 6 million in 1960 and 10.7 million by 1965. Expansion depended on state permission to increase water intake and discharge. By 1968, Reserve used about 90 percent of the water taken from Lake Superior for industrial use, approximately 507 million gallons per day (Bartlett, 1980, pp. 24-26, 43).

8. The WPCA and related orders provided in part that: (1) states would conform to federal water quality-standards by June 30, 1967; (2) the Secretary of Health, Education, and Welfare (HEW), later the Secretary of the Interior (DOI), could impose standards on noncomplying states; (3) HEW could call enforcement conferences to examine evidence of violations; (4) upon finding evidence of pollution, HEW could impose a six-month deadline for ending it; and (5) if there was no response within 180 days, HEW could recommend legal action (Bartlett, 1980, pp. 32-34).

9. The Taconite Study Group consisted of representatives from the Bureau of Sport Fisheries and Wildlife, Federal Water Pollution Control Administration, Bureau of Commercial Fisheries, Bureau of Mines, and Geologic Survey. The Minnesota Department of Conservation and Pollution Control Agency, the Wisconsin Department of Natural Resources, the COE, and Reserve also were involved (Bartlett, 1980, pp. 58-59).

10. Charles H. Stoddard was the DOI Regional Coordinator for the Upper Mississippi-Western Great Lakes Area.

11. Lake Superior has a relatively small drainage basin and a single outlet to the lower Great Lakes (Bartlett, 1980, p. 42).

12. In the 1940s, Blatnik was known as one of the state legislature's "Taconite Twins" who sponsored tax bills favoring the taconite industry (Bartlett, 1980, pp. 35, 53).

13. The state stipulated holding the hearings after attempting to quash an earlier order (Bartlett, 1980, p. 83).

14. Reserve contended that the water-quality standards were unreasonable and that it should be granted a hardship variance (Bartlett, 1980, pp. 83-85).

15. The conference's legal standing was based partly on the Stoddard Report.

16. The long-running conference was chaired first by DOI's Federal Water Pollution Control Administration, then by its Federal Water Quality Administration, and finally by the new Environmental Protection Agency (EPA).

17. Reserve's hiring of former DOI Assistant Secretary Max Edwards as a lobbyist led to conflict-of-interest accusations (Bartlett, 1980, pp. 88, 261n).

18. The Court concluded that Eckman lacked authority to order a variance. He could, however, order a variance proceeding. In August 1972, it remanded the case so that Eckman could order such a proceeding.

19. The conference had secured abatement agreements from other polluters.

20. Both Armco and Republic were headed by Republican Party fund-raisers, and corporate memos reflected their belief that party contacts would greatly influence abatement decisions (Farrell, 1974a, p. 18; Greene, 1974, p. 98).

21. Reserve cited cost as a prohibitive factor. However, the conference had determined that abatement would decrease profits by only 0.6 percent and would maintain a rate of return of almost 20 percent.

22. Plaintiff intervenors included Wisconsin and Michigan; the cities of Duluth and Superior; and the Environmental Defense Fund, Michigan Student Environmental Confederation, Minnesota Environmental Law Institute, Northern Environmental Council, and Save Lake Superior Association. Minnesota and the MPCA were involuntarily joined when Lord granted Reserve's motion to enjoin permit revocation hearings (Bartlett, 1980, p. 111). Initial defendant intervenors were Minnesota's Lake and St. Louis counties; the villages of Babbitt, Beaver Bay, and Silver Bay; the town of Babbitt; the Duluth Area and Silver Bay Chambers of Commerce; the Range Municipalities and Civic Associations; Northeastern Minnesota Development Association; and Lax Lake Property Owners Association (*United States of America v. Reserve Mining Company* [1972], at 411). Lord joined Armco and Republic as defendants. His first joinder order was overturned by the Court of Appeals, which said that he had "abused [his] discretion" (*Armco Steel Corporation v. United States of America* [1974], at 691). His second order stood.

23. The Duluth Water Quality Laboratory and the MPCA began to study the similarity between cummingtonite-grunerite and asbestos after employees heard of it at a conference. A Save Lake Superior Association speaker had mentioned it only because in conversation the day before her speech a geologist had commented that Reserve's ore resembled photographs of fibers linked to increased stomach cancer among Japanese who ate rice ground in a process that used asbestos (Bartlett, 1980, pp. 119-123).

24. See Bartlett, pp. 119-160, for an extended discussion. Briefly: (1) A variety of analyses showed that cummingtonite-grunerite and amosite asbestos had many identical properties. Reserve witnesses argued that other properties clearly differentiated the minerals. (2) Safety thresholds were among several disputes generated by the second question. For example, the fiber level in Silver Bay's air met the federal workplace standard, and Reserve maintained that its emissions were safe. The government contested the standard's safety, indicating that it might prevent asbestosis but did not protect against cancer. Safety issues were complicated by the fact that scientists did not understand how asbestos produced disease. (3) Most of the evidence relating to ingestion was inferential. High rates of gastrointestinal cancers among asbestos workers could not be attributed to inhalation or ingestion alone; fibers might have been swallowed after inhalation. (4) The significance of "no

dead bodies" was disputed. Reserve claimed that it meant safe operations. The government countered that disease was detectable only fifteen to forty-five years after exposure. Neither conclusion was scientifically incontestable.

25. In January Lord had ruled that there was a prima facie case that on-land disposal was technologically and economically feasible. This ruling shifted the burden of proof to Reserve; it would not prevail unless it proved that on-land disposal was impossible and that its discharge was safe.

26. The cost of filtration systems was estimated to be $10 million (Estimate, 1974, p. 28).

27. Once Lord had made this finding, subsequent references to Reserve's economic condition included Armco and Republic unless otherwise specified.

28. Given Lord's admitted difficulty with organization, this section may have benefited from law clerks' attention.

29. The findings were as follows: (1) "[C]ummingtonite-grunerite and amosite are similar and in some cases identical" (*Reserve-a*, at 32). (2) In Reserve's air and water discharges "there are fibers within the cummingtonite-grunerite range . . . and within this number are fibers that have the identical morphology, crystallography, and chemistry as amosite asbestos" (*Reserve-a*, at 33). (3) "[T]he average daily discharge is about 67,000 short tons per day" (*Reserve-a*, at 33). (4) "[C]ummingtonite-grunerite . . . can be traced to Reserve's discharge" (*Reserve-a*, at 36). (5) "[A] number of physical phenomena . . . preclude [the density current] from being effective" (*Reserve-a*, at 36).

30. Although the nature of the issues ensured that numbers would be used, their abundance in the first two sections—there were well over 200—indicates that Lord used them for rhetorical as well as practical reasons.

31. A micron is one-millionths of a meter. Reserve's fibers actually varied in length from approximately 2 microns to 45 microns.

32. In this second section Lord cited approximately forty specific studies, and he referred collectively to many more.

33. See Bartlett (1980), pp. 154-157, on the weakness of scientific studies in relation to *Reserve*.

34. "Parenchymal" relates to specific organ tissue rather than supporting or connective tissue.

35. Other evidence also was characterized as obstructive. For example, Lord objected to some of Reserve's economic exhibits because they contradicted company documents and executives' testimony. Lord saw "no point in . . . an exhibit which seeks only to undermine testimony . . . confirmed by Republic's own data" (*Reserve-a*, at 63).

36. Lord concluded that "throughout the case, the defendants have failed to come forward with the best evidence available" (*Reserve-a*, at 63).

37. Reserve had 25 days to submit its plan, plaintiffs had twenty days to comment, and Lord had fifteen days to recommend whether to continue the stay. In the remaining ten days the appeals court would decide whether Reserve's "good faith efforts" to end pollution would warrant extending the stay (*Reserve-b*, at 1085-1086).

38. Lord suspected that Reserve hoped November elections would make state officials more receptive to its settlement demands.

39. According to Lord, the law required state agencies to decide the issues the appeals court remanded to him. He rejected Reserve's position that he could order the state to grant permits; the court was not empowered to "thrust itself in the midst of state administrative proceedings" (*Reserve-a*, at 73). When Lord based his later hearings on public health issues on his belief that the law "grants broad sweeping powers to the courts in [public health] matters" (*Reserve-a*, at 74), Reserve apparently reversed its position; it objected to the hearings and asked for Lord's removal.

40. According to Lord, Reserve showed bad faith by conditioning its Palisade plan on later approval by its board of directors and shareholders. Asking Lord to approve an unauthorized plan was bad faith because "if [Reserve was] serious . . . they would . . . [state] firmly that this is the plan they will initiate if permitted to do so"; otherwise "no plan at all has been submitted, but merely more talk, more evidence, more delay" (*Reserve-a*, at 72). Reserve also showed its bad faith by seeking to shift responsibility for harm to victims. First its attorneys made the "incredible" assertion that the appeals court had determined definitively that tailings were not hazardous. Knowing that "[n]o private individual could muster sufficient resources to duplicate the evidence in this case," Reserve was trying to erase the evidence from the record to ensure that any "representatives of those whose deaths resulted from Reserve's discharge would effectively be precluded from receiving compensation" (*Reserve-a*, at 72). Second, Reserve's insistence that Lord order the issuance of disposal permits was "equally troublesome." It was "untenable" and "absurd" to assume that he would usurp the state's power to protect the environment and citizens in order for Reserve "to use the Palisades area as a receptacle for its wastes" (*Reserve-a*, at 74). Third, Lord noted that, although his injunction was based partly on Reserve's noncompliance with state water-quality regulations, Reserve's plan "in essence . . . is seeking a variance from this regulation" (*Reserve-a*, at 83). He labeled "ironic" Reserve's intention to "put baghouse [fabric] filters on everything but the most offending aspect of their operation" (*Reserve-a*, at 79), thereby violating his order as well as state air-quality law. Citing statutes and regulations, Lord accused Reserve of "misstat[ing] the factual history of this proceeding" (*Reserve-a*, at 74), misstating the law, and manipulating a state official (*Reserve-a*, at 77) to acquire permits that "there is no basis in fact to believe . . . will be granted. In fact, it appears that [they] will not be granted" (*Reserve-a*, at 73).

41. The appeals court had said that Lord's recommendations should depend on "whether [Reserve has] evidenced good faith efforts and a reasonable plan . . . to abate the pollution of air and water, taking into account the views expressed in this opinion" (*Reserve-b*, at 1085, n. 14). Fulfilling this charge was difficult because of divergent interpretations of which "view expressed" was controlling. For example, if the controlling view was that "settlement . . . represents a necessary and desirable goal" (*Reserve-b*, at 1086), Lord was mandated to encourage negotiations without enjoining Reserve's discharge. If the controlling view was that the "stay . . . rests upon [Reserve's] good faith preparation and implementation of an acceptable plan" (*Reserve-b*, at 1085), Lord had broader latitude. He interpreted his charge as instructing him to make findings on the following: (1) the engineering and technical feasibility of the on-land disposal plan, (2) the plan's environmental soundness, (3)

the plan's compliance with air- and water-quality laws, (4) Reserve's good faith in presenting the plan, and (5) whether the stay should be continued.

42. In a short discussion, Lord found that the plan was not environmentally sound (*Reserve-a*, at 82). His rhetorical approach to ecological implications also was brief, largely consisting of a straightforward enumeration of the area's characteristics (*Reserve-a*, at 82). Although brevity may reflect disinterest, disinterest would be inconsistent with Lord's overall stance. It seems more likely that he thought other issues would carry more weight in appellate decisions.

43. Lord also used empirical evidence to assess the Palisade's uniqueness. He had "walked and seen the area myself" (*Reserve-a*, at 82) and studied the findings of long-term research. In contrast, Reserve offered the testimony of "a local school teacher, a Reserve Mining Co. welder, and an employee of a [defendant] county . . . dependent upon Reserve for its tax base" (*Reserve-a*, at 83).

44. Prior to making this statement Lord reiterated his analysis of environmental law. The appeals court had found that his injunction violated legislative prerogatives, but Lord insisted that the law compelled him to protect public health. In fact, he viewed the injunction as increasingly urgent. New information indicated that current water filtration might be ineffective, that Duluth's filtration system would not be operating for several years, and that Reserve was not proposing to use fabric filters to remove fibers from Silver Bay's air.

45. The senators also were responding to concerns about pesticides and plastics manufacturing.

46. The site was midway between the Palisade area and the town of Babbit. On Reserve's railroad it was seven miles from Silver Bay (Bartlett, 1980, p. 172).

47. The appeals in *Reserve* were numerous. Only a few are mentioned here to convey a sense of the controversy's complexity.

48. The appeals court declared that the disposal site decision "does not fall within the jurisdiction of the federal courts" (*EPA*, at 539), that Reserve could "close its operation . . . without fear of substantial fines and penalties," and that "Minnesota and Reserve [should] exercise a zeal equivalent to that displayed in this litigation to arrive at an . . . on-land disposal site and thus permit [Reserve] . . . to remain in production" (*EPA*, at 540). It also suggested that court-appointed experts should advise the court if new evidence suggested the need to reevaluate dangers to public health (*EPA*, at 540).

49. The appeals court had ordered transcripts of the hearing after reading news reports.

50. Perhaps to emphasize his ambiguous position, Lord suggested that court-appointed experts concerned about elevated fiber concentrations in Lake Superior report directly to the appeals court (Wolkerstorfer, 1975b, p. 30B).

51. Silver Bay and Duluth had new mayors, the Eighth District had a new congressperson, the MPCA had a new executive director, and Reserve had a new president and executive vice president.

52. After storms increased turbidity in Lake Superior, the National Water Quality Laboratory found that fiber ingestion during the increase would equal a year of drinking unfiltered water.

53. Water filtration decisions presumably were within Lord's jurisdiction. Filtration had continuing problems of ineffectiveness, uncertain funding, and delays in commitments to permanent filtration systems (see, e.g., Bartlett, 1980, pp. 176-178).

One of the factors precipitating Lord's hearings was the COE's decision to stop supplying filtered water (Judge is removed, 1976, pp. 1, 9).

54. On the same page was a cartoon of Lord as a knight with a broken sword and the "8th Circuit Court of Appeals" as a dragon with Reserve riding on its back and holding its reins.

55. The COE was seeking $5.7 million for water filtration, the federal government petitioned to have Reserve pay for temporary filtration until a permanent system was built, and the state asked for fines of $40.2 million against Reserve. The EPA and Council on Environmental Quality criticized Milepost 7 because "fugitive [air] emissions" would be as bad as or worse than in-lake discharge (Farrell, 1976, p. 13). The controversy seemed far from over.

56. Reserve continued to appeal in Minnesota state courts on the grounds that the MPCA and Minnesota Department of Natural Resources were biased against Milepost 7. State courts ultimately decided in favor of Milepost 7 (Merritt, 1990, p. 12A).

6

The Wages of Corporate Sin

I should have put 'em in jail.
Miles W. Lord, "60 Minutes"

In 1976 Miles Lord had endured a painful experience when the Eighth Circuit Court of Appeals removed him from the *Reserve* case (Berg and Stone, 1976, p. 8C; Judge is removed, 1976, p. 1; Wehrwein, 1976, p. 14A). In 1984 he was about to suffer another extraordinary judicial trial. A Special Investigative Committee of the Judicial Council[1] would hold a public hearing on his judicial fitness. For the Council to hear the complaint of a disgruntled defendant was extremely unusual. To hear the complaint publicly was without precedent (Marcotty, 1984d, p. 12B; Mintz, 1985, p. 233-234). But Lord had asked for it—literally. Under the Judicial Conduct and Disability Act, accused judges had the option of secret or public hearings. As he had in the *Reserve* case, Lord chose to face his accusers openly.

Lord's appearance was not the only echo of *Reserve*. Once again a corporation was claiming abuse. Once again Lord said that he acted to save lives. Once again opinion was divided as to who was the villain in the scenario. Business people disagreed as to whether Lord was a "mine loose in the channel" or a "friendly buoy to keep corporations from going up on more dangerous shores" (Oslund, 1984, p. 4A). Attorneys disagreed as to whether Lord had shown "the courage to pursue the truth" (Kaszaba, 1984, p. 4B) or brought "the courts into disrepute" (George, 1984, p. 4A). Only editorialists seemed to agree: Lord's "fireball rhetoric" (Carr, 1984, p. 5) was a species of "beautiful anger" (McCarthy, 1984, p. 10A). Once again time and money figured prominently in the controversy. And once again the underlying cause was a small thing with huge consequences. This time it was a nickel-size, badge-shaped "30 cent piece of plastic" (Oberdorfer, 1985, p. 1A) intended to prevent pregnancies (Mintz, 1985, pp. 27-28; News Services, 1989, p. 8A). This time it was the Dalkon Shield.[2]

BACKGROUND

In the 1960s, oral contraceptives (the Pill) had fomented a "sexual revolution." Millions of women welcomed a pill that freed them from the fear of pregnancy. However, by the late 1960s mounting reports of strokes, blood clotting, and other medical problems resulting from the pill inspired a search for alternatives. A ready-made market of women accustomed to controlling their reproductive lives awaited an easy, safe, and reliable contraceptive (Oberdorfer, 1985, p. 10A).

One potential alternative was intrauterine contraception, the centuries-old practice of introducing foreign materials into a woman's uterus. U.S. doctors had renounced intrauterine devices (IUDs) because of high rates of perforation, pregnancy, and infection; but Japanese women were using a polyethylene IUD with success and safety, and American manufacturers began to follow the Japanese lead (Mintz, 1985, pp. 23-26).

The Dalkon Shield (Shield) was developed by Dr. Hugh J. Davis of Johns Hopkins University School of Medicine and Irwin S. Lerner, an electrical engineer.[3] Davis's earlier IUD, the Incon, was rejected by the Ortho Pharmaceutical Corporation as ineffective and unsafe,[4] but he worked on a new design. After Lerner designed "fins" to solve expulsion problems, he and Davis agreed to sell their new device. Lerner obtained a patent,[5] Davis increased his interest in Lerner's hospital supply laboratory, and the business was renamed Dalkon Corporation (Mintz, 1985, pp. 25-28; Oberdorfer, 1985, p. 10A).

In 1969 Davis's foreword for Barbara Seaman's *The Doctors' Case Against the Pill* emphasized the Pill's dangers and the Shield's advantages. Davis also announced successful tests of a Shield for women who had never had children and so could not tolerate other IUDs. In early 1970 Seaman commended the Shield in *Good Housekeeping* magazine, and Davis testified against the Pill in a Senate hearing. In February's *American Journal of Obstetrics and Gynecology* Davis reported that Johns Hopkins's Shield tests had found exceptional tolerance, a 2.3 percent expulsion rate, and a 1.1 percent pregnancy rate.[6] None of these publications revealed Davis's financial interest in the IUD. In late 1969 the Dalkon Corporation began marketing the Shield. Sales totaled 27,000 (Oberdorfer, 1985, p. 10A).

Also in late 1969, Dr. Thad J. Earl read of the Shield's success in never pregnant women and visited Johns Hopkins to learn how to insert it. By March 1970, he was a Shield investor, and in May he suggested to an A. H. Robins Company (Robins) salesperson that Robins purchase the device. Approximately three weeks later, Robins was ready to make a deal (Mintz, 1985, pp. 29-42).

A family-owned conglomerate selling products ranging from cough syrup to flea collars, Robins was run by E. Claiborne Robins, Sr., and E. Claiborne Robins, Jr.[7] Known for his philanthropy, political connections, and aggressive marketing, Robins, Sr., disdained product research. No product-liability claim ever had been filed against Robins's pharmaceutical products. Furthermore, Food and Drug Administration (FDA) regulations required tests for drugs but not for devices.[8]

Product testing seemed indicated. Test data supplied to Robins reflected twice the pregnancy rate and 190 more "drop-outs" than Davis's publicity claimed. A Robins researcher questioned the stability of the IUD and its "tail," and a product-planning director questioned concealment of the drug effect of copper sulfate added to the Shield after Davis's tests (Oberdorfer, 1985, p. 10A). Nevertheless, Robins concentrated on market research. On June 12, 1970, the company bought the Shield's patent rights and hired Davis, Lerner, and Earl as consultants. On June 23 it began plans to market its first-ever obstetrics-gynecology-related product (Mintz, 1985, pp. 43-66; Perry and Dawson, 1985, pp. 24-51).

Robins's marketing strategy was characteristically aggressive. Hundreds of salespersons underwent training to sell the Shield to general practitioners as well as gynecologists (Oberdorfer, 1985, p. 10A).[9] Davis's 1970 article and another Shield report were distributed to doctors. English- and Spanish-language editions of a Davis textbook comparing the Shield favorably with competing IUDs were distributed internationally. Davis's comparisons were repeated in multipage advertising in medical journals and at medical conventions.

Brochures in doctors' waiting rooms encouraged women to request the Shield. Robins's public relations firm also placed articles in magazines such as *Ladies' Home Journal, Family Circle*, and *Mademoiselle*; worked with Seaman on the IUD portion of her 1971 *Free and Female: The Sex Life of the Contemporary Woman*; distributed favorable information through television programmers and U.S. and foreign newspaper writers; and sent letters to editors, purportedly from Shield users. By January 1971, the Shield captured over 50 percent of the IUD market; by January 1972, over 830,000 Shields had been sold and inserted (Dawson, 1984a, p. 4A; Mintz, 1985, pp. 67-96; Zack, 1984b, p. 5B).

Developing Problems

By 1974, domestic sales reached 2.8 million. International sales totaled 1.7 million (Marcotty, 1984b, p. 5B). But problems were emerging. Clinical studies confirmed a 5 percent pregnancy rate.[10] They also confirmed doctors' complaints. In one Shield study over one-fourth had to be removed for medical reasons, and doctors protested patients' pain. Although the Shield's antiexpulsion "fins" folded down when the IUD was inserted, one doctor wrote that insertion was "the most traumatic manipulation ever perpetrated upon womanhood" (Oberdorfer, 1985, p. 11A). The fin-folding design made removal even more painful.[11] Then the FDA ruled that the copper in G. D. Searle & Company's Cu-7 IUD made it subject to drug-testing guidelines. Study results and copper made the Shield vulnerable.

Robins's advertising, however, continued to claim excellent user tolerance and a 1.1 percent pregnancy rate. The company denied that the IUD's copper sulfate had contraceptive properties. It denied that Shield users experienced problems, suggesting that pain or pregnancy resulted only when doctors incorrectly inserted the IUD. It refused to fund further studies; instead it sought favorable data from selected doctors. It also ignored FDA requests for more information (Mintz, 1985, pp. 97-127; Zack, 1984c, p. 1B).

Problems with pregnancies, pain, and expulsion were serious. However, when Robins purchased the Shield it was warned of a more serious potential problem—the IUD's tail. Because the Shield's fins resisted removal, its tail was stronger than the monofilament string on other IUDs (Oberdorfer, 1985, p. 10A). Nylon monofilaments were encased in a nylon sheath that extended through the vagina and cervix into the bacteria-free uterus. Bacteria in spaces between the monofilaments could be wicked toward the Shield, bypassing the cervical mucus that protects the uterus.[12] The danger of infection increased with pregnancy as the uterus expanded and enveloped more of the tail (Oberdorfer, 1985, pp. 10A, 11A).

Several factors intensified the hazards. First, nylon deteriorated in the body, increasing the infection potential. Second, the sheath could be damaged during manufacture. Third, if a tail broke, surgery was needed to remove the IUD. Fourth, Robins deleted the Dalkon Corporation's recommendation to replace Shields after two years; it interfered with sales. Finally, Robins recommended leaving the Shield in place if pregnancy occurred, claiming that a woman's "bag of water would gently push the (shield) aside" (Marcotty, 1984f, p. 5B; Oberdorfer, 1985, p. 11A).

The hazards produced severe effects. Women developed pelvic inflammatory disease (PID), sudden, painful, acute infections of the fallopian tubes and ovaries. For nonpregnant women the consequences included abscesses in their reproductive organs that could be treated with antibiotics and surgical draining, more serious abscesses that led to sterility or removal of reproductive organs, and the infection's spread to other organs (Walsh, 1984, p. 1). For pregnant women they also included miscarriages; spontaneous septic abortions; premature deliveries; and babies born with cerebral palsy, mental retardation, hydrocephalia, or dead (Dawson, 1984a, p. 4A; Furst, Peterson, and Gonzales, 1984, pp. 1A, 7A; Marcotty, 1984f, p. 1B; Mintz, 1985, p. 241; Walsh, 1984, p. 1).

Withdrawing the Dalkon Shield

The Food and Drug Administration seemed to overlook early Dalkon Shield suits and a University of Arizona doctor's reports of Shield-related deaths. However, after the doctor announced that he would publish his findings, Robins reported to the FDA twenty-three septic abortions, four of them fatal to women. It also held a conference with twelve doctors, five of them from its paid advisory panel. Robins asked them whether the Shield posed a greater infection risk than did other IUDs. Working with company data that excluded a number of PID cases and all references to wicking, the doctors divided; five said yes, five said no, and two abstained (Mintz, 1985, pp. 152-162).

By late1973, Robins acknowledged thirty-six spontaneous abortions and five deaths. In April 1974 it sought FDA approval of a letter informing doctors of septic abortions, advising Shield removal from pregnant women, and asking doctors to inform patients that pregnancy might warrant a therapeutic abortion. The FDA found the warning inadequate; it did not advise removing the Shield from women with PID symptoms. Nevertheless, Robins mailed the notice to 120,000 doctors in May.[13] Two weeks later FDA officials asked Robins to halt Shield distribution pending investigation. Robins refused; attorneys feared that product withdrawal would weaken its legal position in forty-seven pending lawsuits.

At the end of May the Planned Parenthood Federation of America alerted patients to the Shield's risks, and the Center for Disease Control reported the results of a survey linking the Shield to a much greater proportion of pregnancy complications, PID, and other infections than competing IUDs. On June 15 the Arizona doctor's promised article appeared in the *American Journal of Obstetrics and Gynecology*.

Two FDA committees recommended that Robins be required to recall the Shield. On June 26, however, the FDA Commissioner agreed to voluntary suspension of IUD sales. U.S. sales ceased in August 1974, international sales in May 1975, but Robins was not required to recall the IUD. By the end of 1974, reported deaths reached 7, septic abortions 110 (Dowie and Johnston, 1976, p. 49; Mintz, 1985, pp. 163-172; Oberdorfer, 1985, p. 12A; Plague of problems, 1974, p. 35).

THE DALKON SHIELD SUITS

Strategy

The first "relatively unsophisticated" Shield suits were filed in 1972 (Tuttle, 1982, p. 2503). Fifty percent of the complaints involved uterine perforation, 35 percent involved PID, and about 10 percent involved pregnancies. Robins determined not to settle any suit and to appeal unfavorable verdicts to the highest possible court. It hoped to discourage potential plaintiffs and garner trial expertise for an anticipated ten years of lawsuits (Engelmayer and Wagman, 1985, pp. 79-80; Tuttle, 1982, p. 2503; Zack, 1984a, p. 5A).

Robins's legal strategy relied on two assertions, that doctors were incompetent and that the company had no relationship with patients. It contended that doctors perforated uteri by "simply shov[ing] the device through the uterine wall," and caused PID by "inserting the device in a contaminated field" (Tuttle, 1982, p. 2503). It also claimed that its only responsibility was to doctors, and that obligation was met by the instructions and warnings in Shield packaging (Tuttle, 1982, pp. 2503-2504). Robins assisted women's suits against doctors, supplying witnesses and exhibits in return for agreements not to sue the company (Engelmayer and Wagman, 1985, pp. 77-78, 82).

This strategy initially succeeded. Robins avoided a number of lawsuits, and in losing cases its damages generally fell short of $10,000 (Tuttle, 1982, p. 2504). However, after a plaintiff attorney's survey of doctors revealed the use of spermicidal foam in Davis's study, Robins realized that its strategy increased the likelihood that trial discovery would reveal irregularities in the research on which it based advertising claims. Then, following the discovery of references to contradictory sets of test data, Robins became vulnerable to charges of deceiving doctors, the FDA, and IUD users. Suits became more sophisticated, complaining of defective design, insufficient testing, inadequate warnings, and fraud (Tuttle, 1982, p. 2504).

As lawsuits multiplied and a jury assessed punitive damages for the first time, Robins hired an outside law firm and changed its strategy. Although the new attorneys preferred settling to trying a case, intimidation was even better. Intimidation tactics included refusing to negotiate with attorneys who could not afford long trials; seeking to disbar attorneys who solicited Shield cases; settling only if attorneys agreed not to work on other Shield cases; asking "dirty questions" about plaintiffs' sexual activities (e.g., frequency of intercourse, whether they had intercourse during menstruation, the number and identity of sex partners, and how often and with whom they engaged in oral or anal sex); and prolonging proceedings.[14] Cases were dropped, potential plaintiffs were discouraged, and plaintiff expertise was lost as a result of these tactics (Engelmayer and Wagman, 1985, pp. 82-98).

The legal strategy also included separating Shield liability cases; intimidation worked only if plaintiffs were dependent on their individual resources. Matters of discovery and punitive damages were exceptions, however (Engelmayer and Wagman, 1985, pp. 98-100). Consolidated pretrial discovery and punitive damage claims would reduce Robins's exposure to major discovery orders and damages, and increase the predictability of individual cases.

Consolidated Pretrial Discovery

The Judicial Panel on Multidistrict Litigation consolidated pretrial discovery and assigned it to Judge Frank Theis of Kansas.[15] Discovery began in 1976. Robins responded to an order to produce all material "which pertains in any way to the Dalkon Shield" (Mintz, 1985, pp. 221) with more than 60,000 documents. Depositions and argument continued until 1980,[16] and the proceedings had the effect Robins desired. Although in individual suits plaintiffs' attorneys often requested additional discovery, their requests usually were denied (Engelmayer and Wagman, 1985, pp. 100-102; Mintz, 1985, pp. 221-222; Tuttle, 1982, p. 2504). Then Robins appeared before Lord, the judge who declared that the "whole object is to get at the truth" (Mintz, 1985, p. 229).

VIRGINIA CAVALIERS MEET THE MINNESOTA HUMANIST

After a Supreme Court decision permitting attorney advertising, two Minnesota attorneys offered their services to women injured by the Shield. A number of women responded. Some suits settled, but progress on others was slow. Robins was seeking the lawyers' disbarment, and their self-defense interfered with their Shield cases. As delay kept the cases on the court calendar, judges divided responsibility for them.[17] The lawyers referred their clients to a law firm that had considerable resources and, now, more than 300 Shield cases. Unfortunately for Robins, one of the firm's lawyers had a reputation for "bulldog-like tenacity" (Siler, 1988, p. 8), and twenty-one Shield cases were assigned to Lord (Engelmayer and Wagman, 1985, pp. 83-84, 131).

Consolidation and Collision

By December of 1983, three Shield suits had been tried in Minnesota. One had lasted four months, and a second was entering its third month. Predicting that without consolidation "the ladies will be dead and gone before their cases get litigated" (Engelmayer and Wagman, 1985, p. 133), Lord tried to streamline his proceedings. He proposed to hear the cases in four stages. A large jury would consider whether the Shield might have caused injuries. If so, the jury would divide to consider whether the Shield had caused specific injuries in individual cases. If the answer was yes, a full jury trial would determine whether Robins had known of the Shield's risks and provided adequate warnings.

On December 9 the plaintiffs' attorneys agreed to consolidation. At Lord's request they chose lead attorneys, selecting the lawyers who had won a recent $1.75 million jury award (Anderson, 1984b, p. 8A). Robins first agreed, then objected to consolidation, asking for time to prepare and to transfer cases. Lord denied both requests; some cases had been filed in 1980, and transfer would put them at the end of another jurisdiction's calendar. He set January 3, 1984, as the trial date.

Lord's streamlining proposal involved admitting all of the evidence admitted in other Minnesota trials, with Robins having the right to appeal. He also wanted both sides to eliminate extraneous claims, evidence, and argument.[18] If the first jury decided that the Shield could not have caused injuries, the plaintiffs would forfeit their liability claims. However, Lord would require Robins executives to testify at the trial (Engelmayer and Wagman, 1985, pp. 131-146).

On December 20 Alexander Slaughter, Robins's lead attorney, appeared for the first time.[19] He informed Lord that Robins had not decided whether its executives would appear. On January 5 Charles Socha of Denver, another of Robins's seventeen pretrial attorneys, appeared.[20] Yet another attorney told Lord that Robins executives would neither testify at trial nor be deposed. Four days later Lord granted the plaintiffs' request for videotaped depositions; one way or another the executives would participate in the trial. The trial date was moved to January 23 to accommodate the depositions.

One of Lord's cases settled before the first pretrial hearing. In December a Minnesota jury decided in favor of a Shield plaintiff; another did the same on January 12. On January 13 Robins settled twelve more of Lord's cases. Ten days before trial, eight cases remained. The plaintiffs moved to preclude arguments on the issue of negligence, contending that the issue had been decided by the four Minnesota juries who had found Robins negligent. Lord, the judge who "has a thing about wanting to find out facts" (Engelmayer and Wagman, 1985, p. 159), deferred a decision (Engelmayer and Wagman, pp. 146-160).

Plaintiffs' attorneys went to Richmond to obtain depositions from Robins executives.[21] The depositions dragged on, with frequent telephone calls asking Lord to rule on objections. When witnesses could not remember their discussions of the Shield, Lord ordered Robins to submit the minutes of its board of directors to the plaintiffs. Robins gave them to Lord instead. Finally, with both sides' agreement,[22] Lord flew to Richmond to be on hand to rule on objections. The trial date was moved to February 1.

In Richmond Lord took an active part in the depositions. Then he learned from his law clerks that, in Minnesota, Robins had objected to submitting Shield reports mentioned in the directors' minutes.[23] He convened a hearing and, over Robins's objections, ruled that a list of the reports must be submitted. He also requested the presence of Robins's insurance carrier so that he could rule on a request for documents concerning denial of Shield coverage. At that point Robins challenged Lord's authority to act in Virginia. Lord ended the hearing and, after further depositions the next day, returned to Minnesota.

In Minnesota Robins's multiple attorneys complicated pretrial proceedings. One Robins attorney objected to agreements reached with another, new attorneys required court briefings, and attorneys who had prepared motions could not be identified. To rationalize procedures, Lord required that court reporters record all telephone discussions, that attorneys sign documents they helped to prepare, and that out-of-state attorneys swear an oath of ethical practice and submit to the Minnesota State Board on Ethical Practices' jurisdiction.[24] After Lord said that he would excuse all oathless attorneys, Robins dropped its objections.

Discovery and the War of Attrition

Two more cases settled; six remained. A jury was selected on February 1, but the trial was delayed. Discovery issues remained, including decisions on the submission of insurance documents concerning denial of Shield coverage. Lord ordered the insurance materials brought to Minnesota. Without notice, Robins obtained a Virginia judge's order transferring the documents to its insurance carrier.[25] Thus challenged, Lord distributed a draft of his discovery order and appointed two special masters to oversee further discovery.

Robins objected, claiming that the Kansas consolidated pretrial proceedings had closed discovery. Lord telephoned Theis, who confirmed that his orders did not foreclose further discovery. Then Lord sent the special masters to Richmond (Engelmayer and Wagman, 1985, pp. 194-211).

On February 8, 1984, Lord issued his discovery order (*Dean v. A. H. Robins Co., Inc.* [*Dean*], [1984]). He began with a review of "the exceptional events" (*Dean*, at 22) that preceded the order. They included depositions during which Robins executives had "difficulties in answering even the most basic of questions due to lack of recollection" (*Dean*, at 22), and "a nudge by an attorney could—and did—silence the deponent" (*Dean*, at 23). They also included the discovery of board of directors' minutes showing that Robins, Sr.'s, and Robins, Jr.'s, "detailed knowledge of the corporation's affairs" conflicted with their claims of "limited participation in the concerns of the company" (*Dean*, at 22).

Lord observed that Robins consistently "appears to accept the court's orders without objection and then fails to abide by them, or recoils at the slightest hint of a new directive and asks for additional time" (*Dean*, at 23); it caused further delay by "obscuring the responsibility of its attorneys so that it is impossible to determine at any given moment who is accountable for representations made to the court" (*Dean*, at 23). Lord declared that these tactics strengthened accusations that Robins' strategy was "to wage a 'war of attrition': prolonging and protracting the litigation so as to wear down its opponents" (*Dean*, at 23).

Lord rejected Robins's claims that further discovery was "oppressive" (*Dean*, at 24-25). Instead, noting that "[t]here are more than 3,000 lawsuits pending," he suggested that his order would "aid the resolution of all of these outstanding cases, and it is not so drastic an undertaking when considering the massive scope of the litigation" (*Dean*, at 25). The order required Robins to produce a variety of documents relating to the Shield's characteristics, safety, and insurance history (*Dean*, at 25-26).[26] Lord refused to grant a stay.

The special masters began their work. Confronted by Robins's on-the-scene objections, they responded that they could not grant stays of a court order. So on February 9 Robins appealed Lord's order to an Eighth Circuit Court of Appeals judge, requesting a stay until the full court heard its appeal. It also asked for Lord's removal, complaining of his "unprecedented degree of hostility" (Anderson, 1984a, p. 1B). Later the same day the appeals judge refused a stay, noting that Lord's order protected privileged documents and appeared consistent with his judicial power. The full court would not hear Robins's appeal until February 16; in the meantime the special masters could proceed.

When Lord appeared in court the next day, he was accompanied by a federal magistrate. Lord would not be involved in Shield cases "while looking over [my] shoulder at a recusal petition" (Engelmayer and Wagman, 1985, p. 214), so the magistrate would supervise discovery until the court of appeals made its decision on discovery.

In Richmond the special masters' work was difficult. Although Robins had not located or cataloged any documents, it was deciding unilaterally which documents it would produce. On February 16 the federal magistrate responded with an order: the special masters were to supervise document production closely because "not a single document has been produced [but] this court has been involved in a day-to-day and hour-by-hour process of definition, of redefinition, of defining and redefining, further redefinition, and of discussion as to the propriety of production, the methods of production . . . of examination, [of] who should be allowed to view, and many other technical hindrances" (Engelmayer and Wagman, 1985, pp. 216-217).

When the full appeals court heard Robins's discovery appeal, it urged settlement and pressed the federal magistrate to declare a mistrial. He did so on February 22. On February 23 the court denied Robins's appeal, ordering the company to produce its documents within fifteen days. Lord thereupon denied Robins's recusal motion, resumed responsibility for the Shield cases, and ordered that document cataloging be completed for his review within ten days. Not one document had been produced.

Robins immediately began to negotiate settlement. It agreed quickly to pay a reported $4.6 million to the plaintiffs (Anderson, 1984b, p. 8A), but it balked at other conditions. Among the demands it rejected were requirements that Robins executives agree to the settlement in open court, that Lord approve the settlement, that discovery continue, and that Robins agree to an order not to destroy documents. Four plaintiffs settled; two agreed to risk their settlements by withholding agreement while discovery proceeded.

On February 27 Robins delivered a check but rejected all other settlement conditions. The remaining plaintiffs refused to budge. Negotiations ended. Lord expressed disappointment; he had looked forward to addressing some "remarks" to the Robins executives who were to sign the agreement. After informal discussion of his planned remarks, Lord granted the plaintiffs' motion for a nondestruct order. He ordered Robins not to destroy the documents he earlier had ordered them to produce: the special masters had found 100,000 documents that had not been submitted in multidistrict litigation.

On February 28 Robins capitulated, agreeing to most of the plaintiffs' terms.[27] The plaintiffs' attorneys stated for the record that Robins's president, E. C. Robins, Jr.; its senior vice president for research and development, C. Lunsford; and its vice president and general counsel, W. A. Forrest, Jr., would agree to the settlement in open court as a condition of final settlement. The signing was scheduled for ten o'clock the following morning (Engelmayer and Wagman, 1985, pp. 212-226).

Lord's Last Chance

On February 29 Lord would have his last chance to influence Dalkon Shield cases. After Robins hired his son-in-law's law firm to represent it in Minnesota, Lord disqualified himself from hearing additional cases (Oberdorfer, 1984a, p. 8A). A number of events made this last chance important. Outside the courtroom, the U.S. Senate was considering the Uniform Products Liability Act. The bill provided retroactively that only the first person whose complaint against a product was resolved in court could recover punitive damages—even if a manufacturer consciously chose not to modify or recall a defective product. In courts around the country Shield cases had been on the calendars for twelve years. There had been 36 trials and 6,900 settlements in which Robins had promised to pay approximately $200 million (Zack, 1984a, pp. 1A, 5A). More than 3,300 cases were pending. In addition, the courts could anticipate legal actions regarding the nearly 7,000 settled cases; as plaintiffs attempted to enforce their settlements, Robins argued that they were not binding. Claiming that its management was not aware of the terms agreed to by attorneys, the company refused to pay (Engelmayer and Wagman, 1985, p. 219).

Lord had reason to fear for the progress of Shield cases. His own attempts to streamline litigation had resulted in three months of eighteen-to-twenty-hour days, seventeen pretrial hearings, seven motions, sixty-five pleadings, ten written orders, many oral orders, 1,260 pages of hearings transcripts, 5,721 pages of deposition transcripts, and a request for his removal (Engelmayer and Wagman, 1985, pp. 147, 220-221); and other courts had complained of Robins's "shell game tactics" (Mintz, 1985, p. 292, note 6).

But Lord would not waste his one last chance. His efforts to find a legal remedy had been exhausted, so he would try a different approach. He would appeal on a personal level to Robins, Jr., who protested his ignorance of problems with the Shield; to Forrest, who neither warned his wife about the IUD's dangers nor asked whether her hysterectomy was related to the Shield she wore (Engelmayer and Wagman, 1985, pp. 232-240; Mintz, 1985, pp. 108-112); and to Lunsford, who supervised the medical department but claimed not to know of safety concerns that prompted warning letters to doctors (Engelmayer and Wagman, pp. 240-245). He would approach them as human beings who had erred but who could atone for their errors and redeem themselves by saving others. There were risks involved in the approach, but it might work. And Lord was determined to do "exactly the right thing" (Oslund, 1984, p. 4A).

So on February 29 Lord entered the courtroom. He witnessed each executive signing the settlement. He asked each man whether he had read and understood the agreement and signed it of his own free will. All said yes. Lord directed his clerk to distribute a document to the men, asking them "to take time to read it and not leave this courtroom until you have read it" (Transcript of *Gardiner v. Robins* [*Robins*], [1984] [Further pretrial proceedings], at 12). The document was Lord's 1981 speech to the Minnesota Council of Churches, "The Church's Claim on the Corporate Conscience: Toward a Redefinition of Sin." In it Lord had discussed his philosophy regarding corporate wrongdoing, saying, "It has been said that the corporation has no soul, it has no heart, it has no conscience, and yet its acts are the composite of the individual acts of many people" (Mintz, 1985, pp. 255-256).[28]

When the executives were through reading the documents, Lord distributed his personal appeal to them. After they read his appeal, Lord began to ask them questions about their testimony. Robins's attorney objected; Lord's appeal had impugned the executives' integrity. Lord reminded him that the appeal was not in the record; only the judge, the executives, and their attorneys knew its contents. Nevertheless, the attorney charged that Lord was abusing his discretion and requested that he end the proceedings; if he did not, the attorney would appeal his actions.

Lord perceived a danger that his actions would be distorted on appeal (*Robins*, at 25). He therefore decided to clarify the record; he would read his appeal into it. Then Lord intoned, "Mr. Robins, Mr. Forrest and Dr. Lunsford. After months of reflection, study, and cogitation, and no small amount of prayer, I have concluded it perfectly appropriate to make to you this statement, which will constitute my plea to you to seek new horizons in corporate consciousness and a new sense of personal responsibility for the activities of those who work under you in the name of the A. H. Robins Company. It is not enough to say, 'I did not know,' 'It was not me,' 'Look elsewhere' " (*Robins*, at 25-26).[29]

THE ROBINS OPINION

As in *Reserve*, Lord witnessed what he perceived to be a clear and immediate danger to the public, to the courts, and to the cause of justice. He also uncovered obstruction and duplicity; Robins, like Reserve, had concealed documents that could protect the people from danger and the courts from unknowing abetment of injustice. Unlike in *Reserve*, Lord recognized limits on his judicial power to end the peril. But he also recognized a judicial obligation to pursue justice in whatever ways were open to him. The similarities and differences in the rhetorical situations of *Reserve* and the Shield cases are mirrored in the similarities and differences in the rhetoric Lord produced.

The differences between Lord's appeal to the Robins executives and his *Reserve-a* memoranda are significant. First, the appeal to the executives was delivered orally. This had not been Lord's plan, but in writing an appeal that could be read relatively quickly he had written one that was short enough to deliver orally in ten minutes (Anderson, 1984b, p. 1A). Consequently, Lord's appeal and his *Reserve-a* memoranda contrasted sharply in length. Second, Lord's appeal to the Robins executives did not constitute a legal decision that he presumed would become a part of case law. As a result, it lacked the formal citations and explicit orders of the *Reserve-a* memoranda.

A third difference was that the appeal did not follow a trial. Therefore it lacked the references to sworn testimony and exhibits that had supported Lord's arguments in *Reserve-a*. Fourth, the appeal to the Robins executives was framed as an appeal to specific persons. Although the specificity of its intended audience did not prevent it from appealing to others, specificity did result in the inclusion of accusations and appeals targeted even more directly than those in *Reserve-a*.[30]

Lord's appeal resembled his *Reserve-a* opinion in that an essential element of both was to fix responsibility for harm firmly on the blameworthy party. Establishing guilt had a positive purpose; it clarified the remedies that would be effective and just. However, in fixing blame the appeal to the Robins executives revealed a perspective significantly different from that in *Reserve-a*.

In *Reserve-a* Lord had stripped away a corporate veil to expose Reserve Mining Company as a fiction, the empty personification of two steel corporations holding hostage the lives, health, and livelihoods of workers and the public. The corporation was to blame for the harm, and changing its actions would remedy the harm. In the appeal to the Robins executives Lord went further. An important element of his message was that the legal fiction of a corporate person was sterile in matters of justice. To obtain justice it was necessary to acknowledge that corporations were human constructs and to hold accountable the humans who constructed them. Only by reaching a human individual's sense of control over and responsibility for corporate acts—by activating "free will"—could the conduct of corporations be corrected and justice be served.

The difference is crucial. In making his argument that "the accumulation of corporate wrongs is . . . a manifestation of individual sin" (*Robins*, at 26), Lord intended to ensure that the Robins executives would "never again testify in any Court that they knew nothing about the dangers inherent in the Dalkon Shield" (*Robins*, at 25). This was a quasi-legal purpose. However, Lord also hoped that his message "burns its mark into your souls" (*Robins*, at 16). This was a hope that transcended law.

In spite of these differences, Lord's appeal to the Robins executives can be understood as a judicial opinion. It contains the conclusions of a judge regarding issues of fact, law, and justice that emerged in a case over which he presided, even if he presided only over pretrial proceedings. In this sense the appeal constituted Lord's *Robins* opinion. Both the differences and similarities in the *Robins* and *Reserve-a* opinions will be explored here.

The Judicial Persona

The *Robins* opinion presented unusual obstacles to Lord's rhetorical development of judicial persona. In his *Reserve-a* opinion, Lord had developed his persona deliberately, moving from dispassionate explication of facts bolstered by expert authority to a careful meting out of criticism, and from there to an impassioned judgment of motives and actions. Although justice was the *Reserve-a* judge's desired end, law came first.

In the *Robins* opinion Lord made judgments beyond the law. Over years of litigation, legal judgments had failed to influence Robins's conduct. In Lord's view, something more was needed. His "something more" was an appeal to the moral dimension of justice: "I must therefore resort to moral persuasion and a personal appeal to each of you" (*Robins*, at 39). In his appeal, Lord adopted the persona of a moral as well as a legal arbiter, hoping to alter the men's perceptions of their own acts. By law Lord could not touch them; by appealing to justice he hoped to do so.

The conventional judge. In expanding his judicial persona, however, Lord could not the ignore the characteristics of conventional judges. These characteristics supported judicial credibility and helped to substantiate judges' presumed access to higher law. Therefore, in abbreviated arguments reminiscent of his *Reserve-a* opinion, Lord claimed conventional characteristics.

Lord claimed the quality of restraint. In judging the executives, he was "specifically directing and limiting my remarks to that which I have learned and observed in these consolidated cases before me" (*Robins*, at 28). The boundary of his judgment was fixed by his knowledge; he was impartial until he confronted evidence of wrongdoing. Lord's judgment of lawyers also was based on the conduct he observed: "[L]ocal law firms do not come under any of the strictures of that which I have said. As far as I have been able to know and has been reported to me, they have acted honorably" (*Robins*, at 36).

Lord's restraint was companion to reasonableness. He made judgments only when facts supported them. The deeds he discussed were "not matters about which I speculate. They are matters contained in the evidence that has gone before me in the briefs of counsel, in the admissions and in the documents" (*Robins*, at 39). And, in spite of the damning nature of the facts, Lord still observed the legal rights of the damned: "I haven't disclosed anything about them except my conclusion" (*Robins*, at 39).

Restraint and reasonableness were marks of the conventional judge. So was mainstream thought. The resemblance of Lord's views to the views of other judges was another proof of his propriety. Other judges had pressed for consolidation. Not only had the "multi district litigation panel of the Federal District Court found these cases to have sufficient similarity on issues of law and fact to warrant their reference to a single Judge" (*Robins*, at 36), but "Judge Gerald Heaney of the Court of Appeals . . . recently urged Judges in Minnesota to work together to devise a coordinated system for dealing with all of their Dalkon Shield cases" (*Robins*, at 37). Lord was not alone; his opinion that Shield cases must be viewed as one was the conventional legal wisdom shared by conventional judges.

Neither did the content of Lord's judgment break new ground. Judge Frank Theis, who had presided over consolidated pretrial discovery, had reached similar conclusions. He had discovered that "it is not at all unusual for the hard questions posed in Dalkon Shield cases to be unanswerable by anyone from Robins" (*Robins*, at 34). Other judges had found that Robins impeded the search for truth.

Lord had come to just conclusions based on documented facts through fair procedures. If more evidence of his restraint was needed, his recognition of the limits to judicial power supplied it. Lord had identified wrongdoing and knew how to correct it, but he would not overstep his legitimate bounds: "If this were a case in equity, I would order that your company make an effort to locate each and every woman who still wears this device, and to recall your product. I would order you now to take to the Food and Drug Administration a correct and proper report. . . . If I did that, they would order you to recall" (*Robins*, at 38). But, he acknowledged, "I do not have the power to order you to do this" (*Robins*, at 39). Instead he made an "appeal."

Thus Lord sought to establish his credentials as a conventional judge. These credentials formed the foundation on which he could build a broader authority. Judicial responsibility transcends specific cases; judges are obligated to the courts and to the reason for law—justice. Therefore Lord stepped from the realm of law into the realm of justice. He was a judge of higher as well as human law.

The moral judge. In the realm of justice Lord needed sources of rhetorical authority beyond written law. He went to the top, suggesting that he received divine as well as legal guidance. It was only "[a]fter months of reflection, study and cogitation, and no small amount of prayer [that] I have concluded it perfectly appropriate to make to you this statement" (*Robins*, at 25). Reflection, study, and cogitation were the marks of a conventional judge; prayer introduced a more profound kind of judgment.

However, claims of religious connections were not Lord's primary means for developing his persona as moral judge. In fact, only two other such references appear in his appeal (*Robins*, at 26, 40). Instead of relying on declarations of divinity to establish his persona, he largely relied on language with a familiar religious resonance to sustain the note of a "higher" judge.

In the *Robins* opinion the "meek and the poor" (*Robins*, at 36) formed "legions" of victims (*Robins*, at 27) whose "wombs" (*Robins*, at 31) were destroyed by Robins's "actions and omissions" (*Robins*, at 37). Their lives were ruined if they dared "raise their voices" (*Robins*, at 28) against injustice. The "poor and downtrodden" (*Robins*, at 29) were punished for their wrongdoing, but the Robinses sought Congress's help in "forgiving you for punitive damages" (*Robins*, at 25-26). True forgiveness could come only with an "admission of guilt, a certain contrition, an acknowledgment of wrongdoing and a resolution to take a new course" (*Robins*, at 32). Lord reminded the Robinses that "confession is good for the soul" (*Robins*, at 32); and because they surely "have hearts and souls and consciences," they should "confess to your Maker and beg forgiveness" (*Robins*, at 40). The men who were the "corporate conscience" (*Robins*, at 40) could change their course and the course of their company.

Lord combined claims to the conventional attributes of a courtroom judge with language redolent of religion to create the persona of a moral judge. This persona was essential to the effectiveness of his judicial rhetoric; in the Shield cases sin was a crime against justice.

The Sinners

Lord declared that corporate wrongs manifested individual sin, and he attempted to create a persona that would legitimize his judging such sin. The rhetorical force of his persona supported the moral force of his judgment. An essential element of that judgment was fixing the blame on the those who sinned. Lord identified the sinners.

The first words of Lord's appeal were "Mr. Robins Jr., Mr. Forrest and Dr. Lunsford" (*Robins*, at 25). The use of the names was strategic. Although a corporation was the legal defendant, individuals determined what the corporation did, and the individuals could be identified. Robins, Forrest, and Lunsford were the sinners. Repetition emphasized their culpability in corporate sin: "Dr. Lunsford" was named five times (*Robins*, at 25, 26, 31 32, 33); "Mr. Robins" was named six times (*Robins*, at 25, 26, 31, 32, 33); and "Mr. Forrest" was named seven times (*Robins*, at 25, 27, 29, 31, 32, 33). Robins also was identified as the representative of the "Robins family," and reference to the "Robins mentality" (*Robins*, at 26) underscored his influence on the corporation. Other personal references and pronouns amplified the accusatory effect of calling out the mens' names. The terms "you three men" (*Robins*, at 30, 31), "you men personally" (*Robins*, at 30), "you gentlemen" (*Robins*, at 33), "you three gentlemen" (*Robins*, at 38), "gentlemen" (*Robins*, at 27, 29, 32, 39, 40), and "you, the men in charge" (*Robins*, at 40) were only some of the references. Lord also used the plural pronoun "you" sixty-four times, the singular "you" eight times, the plural "your" forty-eight times, the singular "your" six times, and "yourselves" once to amplify his accusations.

Lord rhetorically closed the escape route to the men who had said " 'I did not know,' 'It was not me,' 'Look elsewhere' . . . in refusing to acknowledge your responsibility and pretending to the world that the chief officers and directors . . . have no responsibility for the company's acts and omissions" (*Robins*, at 26). Lord held them responsible for everything. The corporation's acts were the concrete reflection of their character; the calling of their names was the rhetorical reflection of their responsibility.

The Sins

By naming the three men responsible for the acts of the Robins company, Lord set the stage for a rehearsal of their sins. All were guilty of the corporation's transgressions, but each had guilt of a specific nature. Robins provided the underlying motivation and the manifest model for corporate conduct; he had "been heard to boast many times that . . . the prosperity of this company is a direct result of its having been in the Robins family for three generations, the stamp of the Robins family is upon it, the corporation is built in the image of the Robins mentality" (*Robins*, at 26). Like a god, Robins had fashioned a legal "person" in his image and likeness; he was responsible for the wreckage his hubris had wrought.

Lunsford "violated every ethical precept to which every doctor under your supervision must pledge as he gives the oath of Hippocrates and assumes the mantle of one who would cure" (*Robins*, at 26-27). He had special responsibility for the betrayal of women who had turned to the corporation for help. Forrest was guilty of offending justice. As a lawyer he had knowledge of law and justice, and he had the duty to "counsel and guide [his client] along a course which will comport with the legal and moral and ethical principles which must bind us all. You have not brought honor to your profession, Mr. Forrest" (*Robins*, at 27). Forrest was particularly responsible for the company's subversion of the law and the courts.[31]

Sins against women. Lord marked rhetorically the special areas of each man's sin. Each contributed to the more general sins of the corporation. The dimensions of their guilt were drawn in an enumeration of those sins. Sins against women were the source of their downfall. They caused women to give "a part of their womanhood . . . [or] . . . their lives so that you might prosper" (*Robins*, at 27). They "invaded their bodies by the millions and caused them injuries by the thousands" (*Robins*, at 28); "planted in the bodies of these women instruments of death, mutilation, and of disease" (*Robins*, at 28); and "allow women, tens of thousands of them, to wear this device, a deadly depth charge in their wombs, ready to explode at any time" (*Robins*, at 31). By emphasizing the bodily harm that was done and the number of women who were harmed, Lord sustained his judgment that the men's sins were mortal, stemming from conscious, deliberate acts rather than mistake. Their sins of physical cruelty were compounded by sins that inflicted emotional and social pain.

When women complained to the courts, Robins "attacked their characters, you inquired into their sexual practices and . . . . exposed these women and ruined families and reputations and careers" (*Robins*, at 28). Women paid with their family and community relationships for their right to seek justice. Once they paid that price, another was exacted; Robins would "force women of little means to withstand the onslaught of your well financed nationwide team of attorneys, and to default if they cannot keep up with the pace" (*Robins*, at 36). Having paid twice, they still might be denied their right to redress. Lord's description of the relentlessness of the sins, aiming for the destruction of social personhood after destroying womanhood, underscored the aggravated nature as well as the gravity of the transgressions.

These indeed were grievous sins. But another set of sins added urgency to Lord's judgment; they were sins against the courts.

Sins against the courts. Lord's indictment of Robins for endangering women's lives resembled his indictment of Reserve. In addition, as he had in *Reserve*, in the Shield cases Lord witnessed an attempt to implicate the courts in wrongdoing. As the "sheer number of claims" (*Robins*, at 34) strained court resources, Robins's legal strategy posed a grave danger. The courts were "burdened" and "clog[ged]" (*Robins*, at 34) as a result of Robins's deliberate decision to "segment and fragment litigation of these cases nationwide" and its "dilatory tactics" that "consum[ed] vast amounts of judicial and jury time" (*Robins*, at 34). In addition to preventing courts from achieving justice for Shield plaintiffs, Robins's strategy delayed or prevented others from having their day in court.

Not content with devouring the courts' time, Robins attempted to deprive them of expertise by demanding that "cases be transferred to other jurisdictions and to other judges unfamiliar with the cases" (*Robins*, at 35). This tactic used time—the cases would "wait at the bottom of the calendar for additional months and years before they could have their day in Court" (*Robins*, at 35-36)—but more important it prevented judges from gaining the knowledge and trial records that could help them administer justice: "Your company settles those cases in which it finds itself in an uncomfortable position, a handy device for avoiding any proceeding which would give continuity or cohesiveness to this nationwide problem" (*Robins*, at 34). What made a position uncomfortable was a judge who "catches on to what's going on"; when a judge caught on, Robins would "settle the case and flee the jurisdiction" (*Robins*, at 36). By describing Robins's legal strategy in these terms, Lord offered an image of Robins as controlling the courts, using and discarding them at will. They became a weapon in the sinners' arsenal rather than a force for justice. As Reserve had done, Robins was corrupting the courts.

This was not the only resemblance to Reserve in Lord's depiction. Lord, a judge who had "caught on" and refused to be controlled, had discovered the depth of the company's perfidy. His pursuit of the truth gave lie to the company's protestations of innocence when it revealed that Robins had withheld documents: "the Multi District Litigation Unit was only given about a third of the documents, and the most relevant documents are in the hands of [Robins] lawyers" (*Robins*, at 37). These documents contained evidence of the sin that Lord was condemning. In the *Reserve* case Lord had branded the bad faith of concealment "an extremely serious matter" (*Reserve-a*, at 84). It was perhaps an even graver matter in the Shield cases: in the *Reserve* case the "dead bodies" were missing; in the Shield cases they could be counted.

Lord recognized an obligation in justice if not in law to speak out in these circumstances. Robins once again was employing its "system [of] evasion and avoidance" (*Robins*, at 35) to escape a difficult case. Noting that "[i]f a Judge were to wait until all the cases were over before he spoke out on the evils he sees inherent in the system and in the trial tactics, then no one would ever speak out" (*Robins*, at 37), Lord spoke out. He enacted the moral decision he asked the Robins executives to make; at risk to himself, he took personal responsibility for ending the evil he saw.

Lord's decision and the appeal he made constituted a warning to courts as well as to the Robins executives. As in *Reserve*, the courts were being corrupted. Their decisions had abetted Robins's segmentation of litigation, its "callous legal tactics" (*Robins*, at 36), and its concealment of documents. Lord observed that "[t]here is a time when measures must be taken . . . to see that fair play and ethical standards apply to the disposition of all the cases that are to come to the future regardless of what might have happened in the past" (*Robins*, at 37-38). He named the sinners, identified the sins, and by word and example demonstrated what must be done to rectify the evil. To ignore his message was to share in the responsibility for the consequences. It was time to broaden the scope of the courts' justice, to focus on human reality rather than on legal artificialities.

A Study in Contrasts

As he had in *Reserve-a*, Lord used contrasts to increase the persuasiveness of his depiction of sinners and their sins confronting women and the courts. He contrasted Robins's power to the meanness of its motives and to the plaintiffs' weakness. He contrasted Robins's hardship claim to its actual condition, and its claim of clemency to the criteria for mercy. Through these contrasts he gave added dimension to his drama of good against evil.

Robins against women. Lord's contrasting descriptions of Robins and women made the rhetorically created image of Robins's abuse more compelling. Robins was great in size and power. It was a "gigantic multi-national corporation" (*Robins*, at 26). Through its "monstrous mischief" (*Robins*, at 29) it caused a "nationwide problem" (*Robins*, at 34) with "catastrophic" results

(*Robins*, at 27). Robins had wrought a "disaster of the highest magnitude" (*Robins*, at 38), and when called to account it defended itself with a "well financed nationwide team of attorneys" (*Robins*, at 36). This powerful corporate body was ruled by a small mind. It focused only on the "bottom line" (*Robins*, at 40) and attempted to evade responsibility for the basest of motives: admitting responsibility "would hurt your balance sheet" (*Robins*, at 31).

In contrast to Robins's great power, Lord described the women in large terms only in their number: "9,000 women have made claims. . . . [a]nd there stand behind legions more who have been injured but who have not sought relief" (*Robins*, at 27). These women had been "invaded . . . by the millions and [injured] by the thousands" (*Robins*, at 28); there were "tens of thousands of them" (*Robins*, at 31) who brought "more than 3,000 Dalkon Shield cases" (*Robins*, at 34). Repetition of their numbers—"thousands of cases" (*Robins*, at 36, 37) and "thousands of victims" (*Robins*, at 38)—told much about the enormity of Robins's power to affect women but little about the women themselves. They remained nameless, faceless victims. Anonymity emphasized their powerlessness; essentially they were marginalized beings "who seem through some strange quirk of our society's mores to be expected to suffer pain, suffering and humiliation" (*Robins*, at 27).[32]

Remonstrance against reality. Through contrast Lord portrayed Robins as having a bully's unerring instinct for identifying the most vulnerable prey and using superior strength to abuse them: "I dread to think what would have been the consequences if your victims had been men rather than women" (*Robins*, at 27). Contrast also brought into high relief another attribute of bullies, cowardice. The company that "without warning to women, invaded their bodies" (*Robins*, at 28) could dish it out but not take it. It complained that it had "suffered enough" and pleaded for the right to "survive as a competitor" (*Robins*, at 29). It attempted to use a shield of "innocent shareholders" to protect it from the "infliction" of punishment, and it enlisted others to fight its battles, "working with members of the Congress" (*Robins*, at 29) to escape punitive damages.

Lord described a different reality. Robins remained free to flourish as it destroyed women's lives. Its executives were "being enriched by millions of dollars each year," and the company "boasts of new records for sales and earnings with a profit of more than fifty-eight million" (*Robins*, at 30). Not even one settlement payment intruded on its accumulation of wealth (*Robins*, at 31); Robins used its power "to delay the payment of these claims for such a long period that the interest you earn in the interim covers the costs" (*Robins*, at 32). As contrasted to company-created fiction, Robins actually had to "pay nothing out of your pocket" (*Robins*, at 33). By contrasting this reality with Robins's protestations of pain, Lord rhetorically reinforced the image of a bully who responded to the prospect of mere discomfort with disproportionate fear and dishonest defenses. Its "life" was not in danger. The "company has not suffered, nor have you men personally," and there was "as yet no evidence that your company has suffered any penalty whatsoever" (*Robins*, at 30). And even if it were to suffer a penalty, all that it risked was money. Yet Robins argued its entitlement to a solicitude that its real-life victims had never had. Duplicity, greed, and cowardice were the components of Robins's "personality."

Repentance against reward. In addition to creating an image of Robins as self-serving and false-speaking, Lord's contrast between fictitious hardship and real prosperity served a second rhetorical purpose. The contrast supported Lord's argument that showing clemency would implicate the courts in further injustice. Lord observed that "the poor and downtrodden in this country commit crimes, they too plead that these are crimes of survival, and . . . [o]n a few occasions when these excuses are made and a contrite and remorseful defendant promises to mend his ways, courts will give heed to such a plea" (*Robins*, at 29). His observation established the criteria for clemency. Equal justice would demand that courts require of Robins the contrition and remorse demanded of individuals. Lord contrasted Robins's conduct to those criteria.

According to Lord, the Robins executives and the company showed neither contrition nor remorse. Instead, they disclaimed knowledge of and responsibility for their misdeeds. The executives "have consistently denied any knowledge of the deeds of the company you control" (*Robins*, at 33), and the company "in the face of overwhelming evidence denies its guilt" (*Robins*, at 29). Although disavowing knowledge and guilt, they continued to aggravate their offenses, "engag[ing] in the same course of wrongdoing on which you originally commenced" (*Robins*, at 30). Robins's failure to recall the Shield continued its knowing violence; "[u]nder your direction your company has in fact continued to allow women . . . to wear this device" (*Robins*, at 31). Although they pretended ignorance of their sin, its only unknown aspect was its total dimension: they were "not willing to find out" (*Robins*, at 31) how many women still used the Shield, and therefore they could not know how many women ultimately would be harmed.

Given the distance between the criterion of contrition and Robins's conduct, acceptance of its "hollow and cynical" remonstrances would be an injustice (*Robins*, at 30). It would be an injustice to the plaintiffs: until Robins was "willing to cease and desist this deception and seek out and advise victims" (*Robins*, at 30), it would continue to harm women. It also would encourage other injustices. Excusing Robins would invite other corporations to transgress: "The only lesson could be that it pays to delay compensating victims, and to intimidate, harass and shame your victims" (*Robins*, at 33).

Legal Authority against Moral Authority

Lord's final contrast was between what he would do as a judge with legal authority and what he could do as a judge with moral authority. With greater legal authority, he would order the executives to amend their actions, to identify victims and potential victims, to recall the Shield, and to submit accurate reports to the Food and Drug Administration. These actions would prevent further harm to women, enable the government to protect the public, and compensate victims for their suffering.

Lord, however, lacked the requisite legal power. Instead, the executives were "the people with the power to recall. You are the corporate conscience" (*Robins*, at 40). Therefore he resorted to a plea that was based on the moral authority he had attempted to establish earlier in his appeal. Reminding the executives that "[y]ou've got lives out there, people, women, wives, moms, and some who will never be moms" (*Robins*, at 39), he pleaded with the executives "in the name of humanity, lift your eyes above the bottom line" (*Robins*, at 40).

This final contrast brought Lord's appeal full circle. It had begun with the individual responsibility of Robins executives for what they had done and caused to be done in their names. It ended with their individual responsibility for what they would do and cause to be done in the future. Lord's "plea" was that they would commit themselves to "tracing down the victims and sparing them the agony that will surely be theirs" (*Robins*, at 40). Ultimately it was up to the executives whether they would stay in the ranks of the sinners or be redeemed.

Summary

In his appeal to Robins executives, Lord offered a judicial opinion that departed from convention in the circumstances in which it was given and in the nature of the judgments it declared. Speaking at the signing of a settlement, Lord rejected the legal fiction of a corporate "person" to place responsibility for corporate actions in real persons. The responsibility he assigned to corporate executives went beyond legal considerations. As human beings, their "hearts and souls and consciences" (*Robins*, at 40) determined what they were, would be, and would do. Expanding his judicial persona through familiar religious language, in moral rather than legal terms Lord rendered a judgment. Sin was a moral crime, and the Robins executives were guilty.

Lord's study in contrasts provided details to the moral "case" he judged, painting in broad strokes a portrait of executives whose cruel features had been masked by a corporate veil. Lord rhetorically removed the veil, exposing the inconsistencies in their acts and their protestations of innocence. With contrasts of powerful versus vulnerable, large versus small, and words versus deeds, he constructed a drama of an abusive corporation exploiting defenseless victims and corrupting the courts, similar to the drama in *Reserve-a*. The essential difference in the dramas was Lord's adding to the script the motives, acts, and accountability of the individuals who made decisions about how a corporation would act.

Lord recognized the risk that his plea would be appealed to higher courts. The explicit and implicit message to appellate courts was that in making their judgments they would bear the responsibility for whatever latitude their decisions offered Robins to continue the conduct Lord had described. Judges as well as executives were individually responsible for the harm their actions permitted. The public, too, was included in the audience. They were reminded that they, too, could choose to act or not act in their occupational as well as their personal lives. The public's added responsibility came in relation to Congress. If the public allowed laws such as those that enabled Robins to escape punishment, and if they suffered Congress to pass legislation such as the Uniform Products Liability Act, the public shared in the responsibility for the consequences of what they allowed and suffered.

The executives, the courts, and the public were left with crucial decisions to make; Lord's contrasts polarized the alternatives. Lord, who had made a decision for justice when the stakes were high in personal and professional terms, personified the right decision. His appeal to the Robins executives thus was both similar to and different from the *Reserve-a* opinion. But one essential ingredient was identical; Lord exhorted his audience to "do the right thing."

RESPONSE AND AFTERMATH

Response

Robins complains. As Lord read his appeal, the Robins executives remained "stony-faced and motionless" (Engelmayer and Wagman, 1985, p. 257) while plaintiffs wept (Anderson, 1984b, p. 8A). It did not appear that Lord was reaching his intended audience. When he finished, Robins's attorney rose to object that Lord had become the plaintiffs' advocate. Lord replied that "after reviewing thousands of documents . . . I have concluded that the plaintiffs are right and . . . my judgment [is] based on the record. . . . You don't have to argue that I am prejudiced at this point. I am" (*Robins*, at 41). He wrote "So ordered" on the settlement agreement.

As Lord's appeal was reported by journalists who had been in his courtroom, it reached another audience. For example, one columnist found that "[s]ometimes anger can be beautiful. From [Lord's] bench it can be majestic" (McCarthy, 1984, p. 10A). Robins did not agree. On March 30 it appealed Lord's "So ordered," arguing that he had no authority to approve the settlement. It did not, however, appeal his plea to the Robins executives; observers thought that the ordeal was over. It was not.

On April 24 Robins filed a complaint under the Judicial Conduct and Disability Act, accusing Lord of abusing his authority and exposing the Robins executives to public ridicule. It asked the Judicial Council to expunge Lord's appeal from court records and impose a punishment "of comparable impact to that of the speech" (Oberdorfer, 1984a, p. 1A; George, 1984, p. 1A; Mintz,

1985, pp. 232-233). Lord's appeal would be judged by yet another audience. Representing Robins was Griffin Bell, U.S. Attorney General under President Jimmy Carter and former Fifth Circuit Court of Appeals judge.

Commenting that "[w]hat's sauce for the goose is sauce for the gander" (George, 1984, p. 4A), Lord retained Ramsey Clark, who had served as President Lyndon Johnson's Attorney General. And he made sure that public attention would be focused on the controversy; he asked for a public hearing (George, 1984, p. 4A; Oberdorfer, 1984a, p. 1A). The hearing was set for July 9.

Clark contended that Robins's complaint was filed to deflect attention from its own wrongdoing (Associated Press, 1984a, p. 9B). He requested dismissal of the "cynical attack" on judicial independence (Kaszaba, 1984, p. 4B). Judge Frank Theis, who had presided over the consolidated pretrial discovery, confirmed Robins's courtroom wrongdoing. He termed Lord's lecture "mild punishment indeed" (Marcotty, 1984a, p. 1B) for having withheld documents for ten years after assuring him that they did not exist. Theis suggested that Robins, not Lord, needed discipline; the company had abused the judicial system (Marcotty, 1984b, p. 5B). Support also came from other sources. The American Civil Liberties Union declared its approval, and an editorial observed that "[i]t would be sad and perverse to find that judges must be constrained from making speeches in the cause of justice" (Miles Lord's speech, 1984, p. 22A). Lord's message had been heard and understood.

On the hearing date, the audience arrived before the performers in the continuing judicial drama. Reporters from national news media convened to cover the event (Marcotty, 1984c, p. 12A). Arriving with his four children, Lord was pleased with the turnout. Remarking that "[w]ith an audience like this I should make a speech," (Sern, 1984, p. 88), he proceeded to the front row, shaking hands as he went. Lord's appeal and Robins's conduct were famous; his words had been excerpted in newspapers and *Harper's Magazine*, and columnists had discussed it across the nation (Marcotty, 1984b, p. 1B). In the next month "60 Minutes" would couple its re-airing of a 1981 Dalkon Shield report with a story about Lord's speech (Carr, 1984, p. 5). The hearing would keep the issue alive in the media.

In the hearing room the fight between Robins and Lord went into another round. Robins insisted that Lord "is biased against corporate America"; Clark returned that Robins had begun "a test between economic power . . . and the independence of a federal judge" (A. H. Robins hauls, 1984, p. 27). When the Judicial Council asked why Robins had not appealed to the Eighth Circuit Court of Appeals, Clark provided Lord's answer: Robins meant to intimidate judges still hearing Shield cases. Bell conceded that censuring Lord might diminish judges' right to speak from the bench, but the prize was worth the cost; "if what Lord did is wrong we deserve some kind of remedy" (Bjerregaard, 1984, p. 1). Lord asserted that Robins "was feverishly settling the cases . . . to get out from underneath further discovery and . . . flee from this jurisdiction";

Bell replied affirmatively, saying Robins "paid a lot of money to get out of Judge Lord's hands" (Marcotty, 1984, p. 12B).

Although Clark admitted that the rehabilitative objective of Lord's appeal had not been accomplished—"[y]ou haven't heard them say one thing about the women today" (Marcotty, 1984, p. 12B)—media coverage of Robins's complaint fulfilled a second objective. Women were notified of the Shield's dangers through media accounts of Lord's hearing. If Lord's words had not reached them, his continuing story would. The Judicial Council shifted Robins's complaints to the Eighth Circuit Court of Appeals. There would be another hearing.

Split decision. As media accounts continued, the effects of Lord's appeal were felt outside the courtroom. In responding to a subpoena, Robins's former attorney, Roger Tuttle, also answered Lord's call for individual responsibility. In spite of Robins's attempts to prevent his testimony,[33] he revealed that in 1975 Robins had combed key officers' files and burned hundreds of Shield-related documents. The person who had ordered the destruction was William Forrest, one of the executives to whom Lord had appealed (Walsh and Schwadel, 1984, p. 13; Zack, 1984a, p. 1A; 1984b, p. 5B).

Tuttle had saved, and now produced, some of the documents. They included a memorandum suggesting Robins, Sr.'s, guilty knowledge and Davis's perjury (Associated Press, 1984c, p. 9C; Zack, 1984c, p. 4B). Robins's characterization of Tuttle's testimony as "the product of the imagination of a disgruntled former employee" (Carr, 1984, p. 4) coincided with the scheduling of a hearing on the disappearance of documents, including records of a wicking test and the minutes of a meeting during which executives prepared a chronology of the Shield. The presiding judge said that "the issue is not whether or not sanctions should be imposed, but, rather, just how severe a sanction" (Carr, 1984, p. 5; Kaszaba, 1984, p. 4B; Walsh, 1984, p. 20).

The Uniform Products Liability Act was in trouble. At Robins's urging, a Virginia senator had introduced an amendment providing retroactively for a one-time-only award of punitive damages for defective products (Carr, 1984, p. 5). In Robins's case the "punishment" would amount to $75,000; as of the summer of 1984 it would save the company approximately $233 million. The "Robins bailout bill" lost the sponsorship of a Minnesota senator after publicity surrounding Lord's appeal spurred questions about its benefit for the senator's businesses (Boschwitz backs off, 1984, pp. 1A, 4A; Sturdevant, 1984, pp. 1A, 9A). It never reached the Senate floor (Mintz, 1985, pp. 239-240).

In July other judges began prohibiting Robins's "dirty questions" and sanctioning Robins's failure to produce documents. In September the first jury hearing evidence from the "Judge Lord documents" and Tuttle's testimony returned a $4.5 million verdict against the company. Robins settled other suits when judges granted requests for the documents (Associated Press, 1984e, p. 7C; Oberdorfer, 1984b, p. 13A; Walsh, 1984, pp. 1, 20).

On September 14 the second hearing on Lord's conduct commenced with Judge Donald Lay instructing Bell and Clark to focus on Lord's "So ordered"; it had heard enough about the Shield and Lord's appeal (Oberdorfer, 1984b, p. 13A). But when the court's decisions came, the controversy rekindled.

On November 2, Robins won round one. The Eighth Circuit Court of Appeals confirmed that Lord's "So ordered" had no legal force and struck Lord's appeal from the record (Associated Press, 1984f, p. 46). Although Lord's dismissal of the cases with prejudice effectively nullified his "So ordered," the appeals court found "sufficient legal prejudice" to act (*Gardiner v. Robins* [*Gardiner*] [1984], at 1187). Lord's appeal to the Robins executives earned harsher criticism.

The court declared that Lord had "implicated the . . . liberty interests of the three officials, and the property interests of Robins" by failing to give notice of "a governmental attack on their good name, reputation, honor, and community standing" (*Gardiner*, at 1191). It rejected Lord's argument that his rebuke was based on the record, contending that without a trial the record was incomplete and could not be judged fairly. Therefore, it decided, "Judge Lord crossed the line separating permissible judicial comments from impermissible public accusations"; he had "shed the robe of the judge and . . . assumed the mantle of the advocate" (*Gardiner*, at 1192).[34] The court also took up Lord's challenge to judges to acknowledge their individual responsibilities. Although "[m]any people will champion what Judge Lord has done," they conceded, "these people overlook the proper role of a judge" (*Gardiner*, at 1194).

Once again Lord had lost the argument to judges. But once again he seemed to have affected others. Although he complained of his reprimand's chilling effect on judicial speech (Judge Lord criticizes, 1984, p. 1B; Lord, 1984), he also noted that neither Robins nor the appeals court had "seriously contested the truth of my remarks"; he maintained that "recent events have . . . indicated the validity of what I've done" (Zack, 1984d, p. 16A).

The events included Robins's $4 million advertising campaign to notify U.S. women that it would pay for removal of their Shields. Between October 29 and November 13 Robins received more than 10,800 calls (Tai, 1984, p. 7A). By April 1985, more than 4,400 Shields had been removed, and doctors continued to remove more than 100 each week (Engelmayer and Wagman, 1985, p. 299).

Although 2.8 million Shields had been sold in the United States, this "recall" was the least of Robins's potential expenses. The number of claims against the Shield had reached 11,000; 4 new claims were filed each day. Jury verdicts were increasing; although average settlements amounted to $50,000, in Colorado a $6.2 million verdict was upheld by the state's supreme court. In Kansas juries awarded $7.5 million in one case, $1.1 million in another. In Minnesota the company agreed to settle 198 cases for $38 million, six times the previous national average.[35] Only 114 federal cases remained in Minnesota, and the plaintiffs' attorneys credited Lord's "monumental and pivotal" discovery orders for revealing several "smoking guns" (Mintz, 1985, pp. 244-245; Peterson, 1984, p. 7A).

On December 26, 1984, the Judicial Council dismissed Robins's claims against Lord (Associated Press, 1984g, p. A14). Clark declared victory: "[I]n terms of both truth and justice, Lord has prevailed" (Oberdorfer, 1984d, p. 1B). Lord had prevailed in other ways as well. On December 24 Robins announced that in 1986 it would extend its recall to 1.7 million women in eighty countries where the Shield had been distributed through the U.S. Agency for International Development (Associated Press, 1985, p. 7B; Dowie and Johnston, 1976, p. 49). By the end of 1985, Robins had paid $378 million in settlements. Also in 1985 a perjury investigation of a Robins witness was initiated, and in November 1986 a federal grand jury began considering whether crimes were committed in the manufacture and sale of the Shield (Associated Press, 1986, p. 10Y). It seemed to Lord that events were progressing as they should.

Aftermath

Snatching defeat from the jaws of victory. Then in August 1985 Robins adopted a new legal strategy, the "Manville defense." Failing to win approval for consolidation of punitive damage claims, it sought a new venue. Although Robins had remained profitable in spite of the Shield controversy (Sandler, 1987, p. 20), the company declared bankruptcy. All other court actions stopped.

The bankruptcy judge found Robins much as Lord had found it, remarking that he observed "less cooperation in this case than any other case in 20 years" (Associated Press, 1987a, p. 3M). The proceedings would drag on for over four years. Even at the beginning they did not bode well for women. Although by 1985 women had claimed $12 billion in damages *excluding* punitive damages, and 320,000 additional claims were anticipated, Robins approved a $750 million fund to settle all present and future claims (Associated Press, 1987a, p. 3M; United Press International, 1987, p. 3M).

After eighteen months Robins had yet to file a reorganization plan. Then, in February 1987, it received an estimated $2 billion purchase offer. Brokers began to discuss trade in Shield claims, Robins's stock rose, and stockholders held out for a better deal (Parsons, 1987, p. 7B; Sandler, 1987, p. 20; United Press International, 1987, p. 3M). The company submitted plans for a $1.75 billion settlement fund. In one attorney's words the plan put "the fox . . . in charge of the chicken coop" (Parsons, 1987, p. 7B); Robins was to administer it and would receive any money remaining after settlements were paid. Women would be paid $100 to settle immediately; if they could prove injury they would receive between $300 and $2,000 (Parsons, 1987, p. 7B).

Stockholders' patience paid off. In July Robins was offered a $2.6 billion merger that would pay Robins, Sr., and Robins, Jr., $300 million. Although the father and son were not satisfied (A. H. Robins chiefs, 1987, p. 11B), they were better off than Shield victims. The amount set aside for women remained the same—$1.75 billion to settle 320,000 claims (Robins plans, 1987, p. 9B; A. H. Robins chiefs, 1987, p. 11B).[36]

In December 1987 the bankruptcy court increased the Shield fund to $2.475 billion. Victims' attorneys had estimated that reasonable compensation for damages would require $7.2 billion; Robins had argued for $1.6 billion. Although a Shield claimants' attorney observed that "women have been waiting and waiting and waiting, and they deserve to have this thing resolved expeditiously" (Associated Press, 1987c, p. 5B), Robins announced its intention to settle the claims over seven years. It estimated that 85 percent of the claimants would receive $5,000 or less (Associated Press, 1987c, pp. 5B, 9B). Then Robins reopened bids.

After a month of bidding, with offers climbing to over $2.92 billion and a January 6 court deadline approaching, on January 2, 1988, Robins announced that it would merge with a French pharmaceutical company that would allow the Robins name to endure (Associated Press, 1988a, pp. 5B, 6B). Both Shield claimants and Robins stockholders declared their opposition to the merger, the claimants because the merger plan would take seven years to establish a settlement fund (Associated Press, 1988b, p. 2A), the stockholders because they were not convinced that it was "the highest and best offer" (Associated Press, 1988c, p. 2D). Stockholders need not have feared. On January 20 Robins made another announcement; it was accepting American Home Products Corporation's $3.1 billion bid (Associated Press, 1988d, p. 3D).

The new plan called for a $2.38 billion trust fund for Shield claimants. Robins, Sr., and Robins, Jr., would pay $5 million to the fund. However, this agreement was not a sign that Lord's words had reached them; their "contributions" would buy immunity from all further claims (Robins top 2, 1988, p. 2D). As a Robins witness was indicted on eight counts of perjury and obstruction of justice (Shenon, 1988, p. 1; IUD witness, 1988, p. 1A), groups of Shield victims denounced the plan, opposing both Robins and a committee of other Shield claimants' attorneys.

The women's grievances included the plan's provisions for shareholders to receive almost three times the value of their stock at the time of Robins's bankruptcy declaration, for the Robins family to receive almost $600 million, for other creditors to receive full payment, and for Robins's officers' and insurer's immunity from lawsuits. They complained that Shield victims were slated to receive only 35 to 55 cents on the dollar, and they were not told when they would receive it. This, they declared, was contrary to bankruptcy law, which provided that shareholders could be paid nothing until all creditors had been paid. Victims were left to "shoulder all the uncertainties of the plan while all other parties profit from the business deal" (Lewin, 1988, p. 34Y; Associated Press, 1989, p. 13A; Dalkon claimants, 1988, p. 2D).

The groups' attempts to enlist other Shield victims were made more difficult because Robins refused to disclose the list of claimants who would vote on the reorganization plan (Lewin, 1988, p. 34Y). On July 26 the plan was approved by the bankruptcy court (Appelman, 1988, p. 9C). One year later, 20,000 dissatisfied Shield claimants lost their appeal to the Fourth Circuit Court of Appeals (Associated Press, 1989, p. 13A). Five hundred seriously injured women appealed to the U.S. Supreme Court, claiming that immunizing the Robins executives was illegal. They were opposed by other claimants who feared that their victory would collapse the entire reorganization plan (Decision to fight, 1989, p. 8A; Gladwell, 1989, p. 12A). They lost their appeal in November 1989 (News Services, 1989, pp. 1A, 8A).

Four months later 100,000 U.S. Shield users received their first explanation of how their claims would be paid. The Shield trust fund provided for a payment of $725 without documentation; a payment of up to $5,500 if women submitted medical proof of injuries; a larger, unspecified settlement if they agreed to a thorough medical review; or a deferred claim if they wished to collect more evidence of their injuries (Dalkon Shield victims, 1990, p. 13A). Fund administrators would not disclose the upper limit for any claim. By August 1990, the trust fund was earning $500,000 in interest per day. Most of the payments made were for $725. One hundred ninety-five thousand Shield claimants had survived screening; 81,000 of them, many of them the most seriously injured, had not been paid. A fund of $2.3 billion remained ($2.3 billion, 1990, p. 1D). Perhaps one day it would be returned to Robins. Lord's reaction to the situation was predictable. He declared: "I would have decided the cases exactly the opposite way. The lesson taught . . . is that it pays to make profit by injuring people. If they had been my cases, every claimant would be paid and the Robins people would be left relatively penniless" (News Services, 1989, p. 8A).

Lord confronted a complex rhetorical situation as he addressed the executives of A. H. Robins Company. By expressing his opinion on a matter of public controversy he would violate the conventions of U.S. courts of law, in which judges are given great latitude in speech to litigants after a trial but are constrained from explicitly judging litigants in the absence of a trial. There would be no other Shield trial over which he would preside. *As a judge*, if Lord did not speak out now regarding what he perceived to be a grave injustice perpetrated by one of the litigants in his courtroom, he never would speak out.

Lord confronted tension between the principles of justice and the integrity of the courts. In his view, if he did nothing to influence the Dalkon Shield situation, he would *be* an unworthy judge; if he commented on the cases from the bench, he could be *perceived* as an unworthy judge. His credibility depended on his inventing an expanded judicial persona that would reconcile the tension in the rhetorical situation.

Lord attempted to reconcile the tension by incorporating human law with higher law in his persona. Referring to the characteristics of his deliberations, decisions, and actions that coincided with expectations of a conventional judge, he couched his opinion in the language of religion, weaving into his rhetoric the implicit sanction of the sources of higher law. Through those references and that language he constructed a persona with a wider range of judicial authority than ordinarily is granted a U.S. judge. Within that range Lord could be a moral judge whose respect for human law compelled him to constrain a "right" and "natural" condemnation of wrongdoers and deliver a "plea" to redeemable human beings. The recognized risk inherent in his action added to the persuasiveness of his persona. He became a moral example by speaking and therefore performed a legitimate judicial function by speaking.

Lord's persona interacted with his drama of individuals, dehumanized by great power, inflicting injury and injustice on fellows they no longer recognized as their own kind. His enactment of the argument that the strong are obligated to protect the weak, even at cost to themselves, gave added rhetorical force to his depiction of the evil that denying human obligation entails.

Lord simplified a complex legal case to an even greater extent than he had in *Reserve*. The individual was the prize in the dramatic battle between good and evil, and the individual controlled the outcome of the battle. On this level the Dalkon Shield cases were accessible to all audiences, and Lord's decision to speak emphasized the accessibility by providing an example that the "right" decision could be made.

Lord's appeal challenged all of his audiences to reject the artificiality of their offices and occupations to make morally right decisions. Thus it offered a version of a "good" judge who protected the principles underlying law by expanding the purview of those who administered law and justice. A. H. Robins's charges against Lord offered a unique rhetorical opportunity. In the context of his appeal they became an additional proof of his contention that corporations may corrupt those who run them. Lord became the exemplar of the opposite. In spite of his exalted position he made himself publicly accountable for his actions, continuing the drama of individual responsibility he had begun in his courtroom. He offered to the public as well as to the courts another opportunity to participate in a contest between good and evil. His demonstration that his actions matched his words imbued his words with greater moral authority. Lord upheld his persona as he invited the courts and the public to judge the judge. The invitation to the community to participate in the reconstitution of the concept of a good judge provided the occasion for renewed involvement and commitment in the creation of a just community.

NOTES

1. The Judicial Council consisted of circuit court and district court judges, in this case Eighth Circuit Appeals Judges Donald Lay, Myron Bright, and Richard Arnold; and District Court Judges Albert Schatz of Nebraska and Howard Sachs of Missouri (George, 1984, p. 1A; Kaszaba, 1984, p. 4B). Robins's was the only judicial conduct complaint not dismissed to that date (Oberdorfer, 1984a, p. 8A).

2. The background relies heavily on Mintz's (1985) *At any cost: Corporate greed, women, and the Dalkon Shield.*

3. Lerner started Lerner Laboratories in 1964 with a partner, attorney Robert E. Cohn.

4. Ortho discovered that the IUD Davis codeveloped was expelled frequently and in one case led to intestinal herniation and uterine perforation (Mintz, 1985, p. 27).

5. Lerner's sole-inventor status allowed Davis to avoid a potential obligation to share profits with Johns Hopkins (Mintz, 1985, p. 28).

6. Shield tests did not meet research standards requiring 1,000 to 1,200 women to use IUDs for one year. In Davis's test 640 women averaged five and one-half months' use. One-third used the Shield for only three months; only eight used it for an entire year. Davis did not account for between 45 to 235 dropouts. Nevertheless, Davis's textbook compared the results favorably to the Population Council's trials of competing IUDs (Mintz, 1985, pp. 34-36; Oberdorfer, 1985, p. 11A).

7. A stockholders' proxy statement said that the Robins father and son "may be considered as control persons of the Company" (Mintz, 1985, p. 51).

8. Legislation requiring testing of medical devices was passed in 1976 (Mintz, 1985, p. 115).

9. Robins never had a gynecologist on its staff, but market researchers had advised against marketing to general practitioners and osteopaths because even gynecologists had problems inserting the Shield. However, limiting the target market greatly reduced sales potential (Mintz, 1985, pp. 66, 71-72).

10. That rate earlier had been projected by an analysis of Davis's data that reflected several problems. None of the studies met a 10 to 15 percent dropout rate standard. Because dropouts may reflect problems, actual pregnancy, discomfort, and infection rates may have been underestimated. There were no studies of Shields for never pregnant women or of design changes made after Robins's purchase (Mintz, 1985, pp. 79-88; 104-108). For private patients, Davis had omitted patient consent and recommended concurrent spermicidal foam use (Dowie and Johnston, 1976, pp. 37-38).

11. The Dalkon Corporation advised doctors to use painkillers during insertion and removal. Robins deleted the recommendation in marketing, and brochures claimed that women would not need it. Dalkon Corporation recommendations that Shield users also use spermicidal foam were deleted until mid-1972 (Mintz, 1985, pp. 98-103).

12. A quality-control employee who conducted his own wicking experiments and urged heat-sealing for the Shield's tail was fired (Mintz, 1985, pp. 138-145).

13. In 1980 Robins sent a second notice advising doctors to remove Shields after six years (Engelmayer and Wagman, 1985, p. 235).

14. For examples of delaying tactics, see Engelmayer and Wagman, 1985, pp. 93-96.

15. Kansas, the geographic center of the United States, had the largest number of pending Shield cases. Its calendar was less crowded than those in other districts, and it already had tried a Shield case (Engelmayer and Wagman, 1985, p. 100).

16. In 1981 and 1982 discovery was reopened temporarily when evidence emerged that Robins had withheld documents.

17. Shield cases originally were assigned to one judge. He asked for help after one trial lasted almost four months in spite of his denying discovery (Engelmayer and Wagman, 1985, p. 131).

18. For example, Lord wanted plaintiffs to give up some liability issues and "lectures" on anatomy. Robins was to eliminate "dirty questions" unless it showed their relevance and that it had warned women of "dangerous" sexual activities. Both sides were to present their cases within five days and stipulate as to experts' credentials. Lord also told the plaintiffs to be ready to settle (Engelmayer and Wagman, 1985, pp. 137-147).

19. William Forrest was Robins's general counsel. Mays, Valentine, Davenport, and Moore of Richmond dealt with Shield settlements. McGuire, Woods, and Battle of Richmond, whose former partner was on Robins's board of directors, handled litigation. Slaughter, a McGuire partner, coordinated up to 150 firms on Shield cases.

20. Robins imported attorneys to handle motions and appearances. For example, Socha appeared several times. Slaughter and Socha have been described as a "good guy, bad guy" team. Socha's role was to provoke judges to make intemperate remarks. The remarks later would be used to support appeals on the grounds of bias (Engelmayer and Wagman, 1985, pp. 158-159). Attorneys for Robins's insurance carrier also attended many of the hearings.

21. The depositions were in Richmond because the elder Robins's doctor said that cold weather would stress his heart. They were held at the Robins facility because the doctor also considered the courtroom atmosphere dangerous to his health. The deposition site led to suspicions of Robins's use of electronic equipment to listen to plaintiffs' confidential discussions and to send surreptitious instructions to deponents (Englemayer and Wagman, 1985, pp. 166-167, 189-190).

22. Judges have authority to act only in their own jurisdiction unless they are assigned elsewhere or have the consent of all litigating parties.

23. The minutes had revealed that the Robins father and son received regular reports on Shield litigation. References to the reports were excised from the minutes submitted in consolidated pretrial discovery (Engelmayer and Wagman, 1985, pp. 163-164).

24. Minnesota's Ethical Practices rules prohibit attorneys from agreeing not to handle similar cases as a condition of settlement (*Dean*, at 24).

25. Once the documents were under the insurance carrier's control, they were no longer subject to Lord's orders.

26. The order contained more specific provisions; e.g., authors, recipients, and possession or control were specified, and documents for which privilege was claimed were separated from others.

27. In return, plaintiffs agreed not to oppose a motion to vacate judgment in two other Shield suits.

28. This speech met mixed reviews. One columnist praised its "closely reasoned summary of gut philosophy" (Wehrwein, 1981b, p. 12A). Another, an advertising company's public relations director, accused Lord of promoting communism and called him a "billygoat" whose "sweeping and silly" speech should excuse corporations from his courtroom (Cohen, 1981, p. 8A).

29. Lord sought advice on his address from three other judges (Mintz, 1985, p. 231).

30. To consider the appeal private communication probably is to err. Although Lord anticipated that the executives would read it, he also had "given thought to publishing [it] at some future date" (*Robins*, at 13). In any event, its delivery in open court made it public.

31. A special place in hell might be reserved for Forrest; his profession was that to which Lord belonged, and Lord's accusation implicitly compared Forrest's actions with his own.

32. The point was made earlier but less elegantly in *Mother Jones*. Writers asked, "[W]ould it have taken 17 deaths and hundreds of painful operations on male genitalia before a new variety of condom, say, was taken off the market?" (Dowie and Johnston, 1976, p. 47).

33. Robins had threatened Tuttle with disbarment after his article on the Shield defense appeared in the *Oklahoma Bar Journal* (Dawson, 1984b, p. 9B). Now it obtained a temporary restraining order and applied for a permanent injunction to prevent him from testifying, accused him of violating attorney-client privilege, and again threatened disbarment (Mintz, 1985, pp. 237-238). Tuttle testified that when Congress was considering a bill to impose criminal liability on officers for corporate actions, Robins was refusing to submit records to the FDA. According to Tuttle, he had told the medical research director that he "should be on your knees praying to your God or mine that you're not in that position, because you'd be doing hard time if the truth were ever known" (Dawson, 1984a, p. 1A; Zack, 1984b, p. 5B).

34. The appeals court cited its finding in *Reserve* that "[w]hen the judge joins sides, the public as well as the litigants become overawed, frightened, and confused" (*Gardiner* [1984], at 1193).

35. The average included settlements of $10,000 to $15,000 in the years before evidence of the Shield's role in PID had been developed (Peterson, 1984, p. 7A).

36. In October 1987 Robins, Jr., was held in criminal contempt and fined $10,000; he had refused to recover part of $6.8 million in improper postbankruptcy payments to Robins executives. Doubtless Lord would have appreciated the bankruptcy judge's comment that "[h]e's got to suffer the consequences" (Judge holds Robins, 1987, p. 2M).

7

Arms, the Judge, and the Man

That was a good speech.
Miles W. Lord

The *Reserve-a* and *Robins* opinions displayed the hallmarks of a "realist" judge. Lord's concern for how the law and litigants operated in the world outside of the courtroom, his thirst for "facts" and acknowledgment of experience, and his emphasis on justice over procedure emerged in his plain speaking, dramatic language, and public comment. His rhetoric invited the interest and understanding of lay audiences, and it exposed the man as well as the judge. Active insistence on equality under law, including equality of access, and "deconstruction" of corporate claims to legal and social privilege were recurring themes in his judicial speech.

Lord's appeal to executives of the A. H. Robins Company seemed representative of some of the dilemmas posed by judicial realism. Although Lord said that he "was talking to the courts" in that appeal, trying to convince them that "[w]e can't go on piece by piece, every judge being fooled, every judge going over the same territory . . . trying this over and over" (Lord, 1988b), the appellate court had rejected his message. As had been true for realist judges before him, Lord's realism resulted in the censure of the legal community.

Nevertheless, the hearing on Lord's judicial fitness and the appellate court's rebuke had enabled him to declare victory of a sort. Although they were personally painful and professionally harmful (Anderson, 1984, p. 10A; Carr, 1990, p. 28), they were rhetorically effective. They focused public attention on Robins's misconduct, helped to spur the recall of IUDs, and roused public support for Lord's enactment of a "good" judge. The community was considering its relationship to the courts. In "realistic" terms, these were estimable outcomes. Perhaps as a result of these outcomes, the *Robins* opinion seemed to mark a point of departure in Lord's judicial rhetoric.

Although the controversial appeal was a response to a specific rhetorical situation, its themes had been sounded in Lord's earlier rhetoric. The appeal also, however, involved the rhetorical extension of previous invention. Lord's analysis of the causes and cure for collective misconduct had altered; the individual replaced the institution as the source of and solution to wrongdoing. In the peculiar circumstances of the appeal Lord's tone had intensified; judgment had overtaken explication. Lord's ability to use controversy as an educational tool—to "perform" his judicial opinions for public edification—had yielded results beyond his expectations (Carr, 1984, p. 5). In Lord's view, he had "hit his stride as a judge" (McEnroe, 1985, p. 6A). Eight months after the *Robins* appeal, another Lord "speech" seemed to reveal the "good" judge toward which Lord had been striding.

In November 1984 Lord sentenced two felons. His sentencing remarks placed him and a significant public issue on the pages of newspapers and magazines once more. Again his plain speaking generated public debate and prompted complaints to the Judicial Council. As on previous occasions, public opinion was divided as to the propriety and import of his remarks. Some agreed with an observer who declared that "Lord restored the honor of the legal profession" (Panzer, 1985, p. 15A); others tended to the view of a columnist who characterized Lord's remarks as "rantings" (Berkowitz, 1985, p. 36). This time the response of the appellate court was that Lord had done nothing wrong. On its face, judicial approval of Lord's remarks seemed contradictory; the distance between the courtroom and the issues Lord discussed appeared to be much greater than that which had existed in his censured opinions. To understand Lord's remarks and the appellate court's response to them, we must return to the scene of Lord's first actions in the Dalkon Shield cases.

BACKGROUND

U.S. against the Sperry Corporation

December 9, 1983, was a significant date in the rhetorical history of Miles Lord. Immediately preceding the presentation of his proposal for consolidating the Dalkon Shield trials—an event that started him on the road to his *Robins* opinion—he engaged in a "heated" exchange with attorneys for the U.S. government and Sperry Corporation (Sperry). The attorneys had asked Lord to approve a plea bargain concerning three felonies. Sperry had agreed to admit its culpability and pay a $30,000 fine[1] if the government dropped the charges. The felonious conduct had sprung from Sperry's reluctance to suffer the consequences of its mistakes. The company had underestimated the costs of developing a computer system that would target MX missiles, and it considered its losses unacceptable. It recouped the losses by falsifying employee timecards, charging MX costs to a computer-launch system for Minuteman missiles. Sperry had been caught, and the government had decided that prosecution would dissuade other defense contractors from cheating on their bills.

On December 9, the government was satisfied that knowledge of Sperry's criminal charges and $30,000 penalty would effect "a change in attitude in the [defense] industry" (Engelmayer and Wagman, 1985, p. 127) and deter future defense overcharges.[2] All the attorneys wanted was a judge to approve the plea bargain. In the search for an available judge, the attorneys chanced upon Miles Lord.

Ordinarily approval might have come quickly. But not this time. When Lord heard the plea-bargain provisions, he was struck by an irony. Recently antiwar protesters had been arrested for demonstrating outside Sperry's plant. They had gone to jail. Yet Sperry was to be excused for its crimes by agreeing to return a minuscule part of the $1.4 billion that it earned from the government. To Lord the scales of justice seemed unbalanced. If the protesters were going to jail, the people who had directed Sperry's crime should receive equal treatment. The prospect of serving jail time might catch defense contractors' attention in a way that a $30,000 fine would not.

Lord "got mad but busy" (Lord, 1990). He ordered a presentence investigation, instructing a federal probation officer to find the individuals responsible for Sperry's misconduct. The government was not inclined to cooperate. Only Lord's threat of contempt citations convinced the U.S. attorneys to submit their case files. Even with those files the probation officer could not identify individuals who could be called to account. But he did find something that made the $30,000 fine seem even less proportionate to the crime; the government's original claim against Sperry was for $3.6 million, not the $325,000 on which the plea bargain was based (Berkowitz, 1985, p. 35).

Outraged, Lord demanded to know why Sperry had not been prosecuted for the misappropriated millions. The $3 million discrepancy was a "disagreement over bookkeeping procedures" (Berkowitz, 1985, p. 35), replied the government. Disgusted, Lord released the audit report to the public; they might be interested in the extent to which bookkeeping disagreements affected defense costs. But that was all that he could do. Complaining that "[i]t hasn't come to my attention that any individual has been punished" with demotion or firing, if not prosecution (Serrill, 1984, p. 88), Lord approved the plea bargain (Berkowitz, 1985, pp. 35-36; Engelmayer and Wagman, 1985, pp. 126-129, 135, 136; McEnroe, 1985, p. 7A; Oberdorfer, 1984c, p. 10A).

U.S. against Katt and LaForge

Approximately six months after Lord's search for Sperry felons, two spurious employees entered a Sperry plant. Toting briefcases, Barbara Katt and John LaForge walked with workers on the seven o'clock shift past the company's security guards. No one asked to see the badges that Sperry employees were required to display. No one asked what the couple wanted during their twenty-minute "tour" of the plant. And no one questioned Katt as she studied the specifications for a computer in an assembly room. Katt and LaForge were looking for computer prototypes described in Sperry's shareholder reports, and Katt had found them. The computers were to be used in U.S. Army fighter aircraft and U.S. Navy nuclear submarines. Katt and LaForge were determined to interfere with that use.

None of the twenty assembly-room workers intervened when Katt and LaForge extracted a banner from their briefcases, draping the message "Violence Ends Where Love Begins" across a table. No one intervened when they poured baby bottles of blood onto the computer equipment. Only when they took hammers from their briefcases and applied them to the computer equipment did their actions attract attention. Assuring the now attentive workers that "all we're going to do is beat up on computers" (Lord, 1990), they smashed the machines. While waiting for the security guards called by the workers, Katt and LaForge explained what they had done. The blood they had poured symbolized the blood that would be shed if the computers were put to their intended uses. With their hammers they had destroyed weapons of mass destruction and had tried to save lives. What they had done was a good thing.

Sperry viewed the hammering in a different way; its spokesperson announced that Katt and LaForge had wrecked equipment worth $36,000. The couple went to jail, and not for the first time; they had protested weapons before. Their crime was investigated by the FBI, and Katt and LaForge were charged with the felony of destroying government property. If convicted they might serve ten-year prison sentences and pay $5,000 fines. Conviction seemed certain; not only had the couple acted openly and explained their actions to twenty workers, they also had discussed with reporters their motives for assaulting the machines.

In trial Katt and LaForge caused problems for their attorneys; as one of their lawyers commented, "It is their case . . . they wanted it that way from the start" (*U. S. v. LaForge* [*LaForge*], Cr. 4-84-66 [D. Minn. Nov. 8, 1984] [sentencing transcript], at 5). Their way meant pleading justification as their defense, explaining their motivation (*LaForge*, at 6) and showing documentary film footage of Hiroshima after the atom bomb fell (*LaForge*, at 10). They maintained that the government's development of the weapons Sperry worked on was a violation of international treaties against genocide. Therefore it was unconstitutional.[3] In many courtrooms Katt's and LaForge's evidence might not have been admitted. But this time, like the government and Sperry, the protesters had chanced upon Miles Lord.

The defendants' evidence was admitted, but the jury was unmoved. Katt and LaForge were found guilty of destroying U.S. government property. All that was left was hearing and serving their sentences.

At the sentencing hearing, both Katt and LaForge made presentence statements. Katt claimed that in her "act of disarmament . . . I have found a lifeline to hope, the resurrection of hope from a living death" (*LaForge*, at 7). LaForge declared that "after letting go of the hammers and the baby bottles . . . we were filled with the feeling of inner peace that Aristotle referred to simply as 'justice' " (*LaForge*, at 13). However, another aspect of their statements ordinarily was more relevant to sentencing; both declared that they neither would be rehabilitated nor make restitution to Sperry (*LaForge*, at 8, 10). They were willing to lose freedom in the cause of disarmament.

But that is not what happened. Faced with unrepentant felons, Lord imposed six-month suspended sentences. As one columnist noted, "He didn't jail the trespassers because if he did he couldn't have made his speech" (Klobuchar, 1984, p. 3B). And make a speech Lord did, pronouncing an opinion in which he has continued to take pride (C. Johnson, 1985, p. 1B; Lord, 1988).

THE SENTENCING OPINION

The Rhetorical Situation

Some aspects of the situation in which Lord sentenced the protesters seemed familiar. The power of mighty institutions, the U.S. government and the Sperry Corporation, was arrayed against two individuals. The powerless parties insisted that life-or-death issues were involved; Lord agreed. The specter of injustice shadowed the impending imprisonment of two people charged with a $36,000 crime against government property after a corporation had been excused for a $325,000 or, in Lord's view, a $3.6 million crime against the government. The resources for rhetorical invention in the instant situation included ingredients Lord had encountered earlier, and he exploited those resources once more. In important ways, however, Lord's sentencing remarks departed from previous patterns, and the departures seemed to reveal as much of Lord the man as they did of Lord the judge.

The Audience for Judicial Speech

To a greater extent than in any other opinion examined in this study, the community emerged as the intended audience in *LaForge*. Lord's previous opinions had invited the public to "overhear" judicial discussion. Accessibility of language, polarization of issues, and dramatization of opposing actors had enabled nonlawyers to understand Lord's evidence, to criticize his analyses of motives and actions, and to comprehend the judicial dialogue that followed his opinions. The opinions had prepared and rhetorically sanctioned the public to form their own judgments about disputes that reached the courts, about the disputants, and about the relationship of the courts' actions to the goal of justice. An informed public potentially could influence the disputants who came to court and the laws that ruled the judges. They also could renew their commitment to the courts, as represented by Lord, as arbiters of justice under law. In essence, Lord had invited the public into the courtroom to prepare them to speak on behalf of justice outside of it.

The *LaForge* opinion was different. Although Lord addressed legal matters and the legal community, he also raised issues that the courts could not resolve and demanded responses that the courts could not give. His inclusion of these issues invited the community's more direct participation in his rhetorical act.

Lord emphasized his preoccupation with the public audience through the placement of community concerns in his *LaForge* opinion. Judicial references in its initial four paragraphs were indirect, and their indirectness underscored the community-grounded nature of the issues Lord addressed. For example, although he characterized Katt's and LaForge's claim of justification as an "allegation" (*LaForge*, at 14), suggested that the defendants had "made a plausible argument" regarding international law (*LaForge*, at 14), and noted that he was responsible for deciding their punishment (*LaForge*, at 14), he muted the legal implications of his language. The judicial resonance his words was attenuated by their association with nonlegal references, such as the "military madness" Katt and LaForge alleged and Lord's "own personal view" of what should be done (*LaForge*, at 14). Lord's acknowledgment that "*we* must ask *ourselves*" (*LaForge*, at 14; italics added) for answers to the questions raised in the opinion also had a leveling effect. Lord joined the community as he asked the community to join him.

Lord's next nine paragraphs constituted a more direct appeal to the community. In these paragraphs, and again in the middle of the opinion, his rhetorical questions addressed essentially moral and political issues. Although these issues impinged on Katt's and LaForge's sentences, the protesters and their individual circumstances were absent from these paragraphs. The rhetorical questions invited the audience to join in Lord's broader contemplation of the moral and political, as contrasted to legal, context in which he made his sentencing decisions. Lord's contemplative questions included: "Can it be that those of us who build weapons to kill are engaged in a more sanctified endeavor than those who by their acts attempt to counsel moderation and mediation as an alternative method of settling international disputes? . . . Why do we condemn and hang individual killers, while extolling the virtues of warmongers? . . . How can we even entertain the thought that all people on one side of an imaginary line must die? . . . How many people in this democracy have seriously contemplated the futility of committing national suicide in order to punish our adversaries?" (*LaForge*, at 15). As a judge, Lord could make no greater claim to providing expert and authoritative answers than could any other competent and compassionate citizen. These were questions for the community, not for the courts.

Lord further highlighted the nonjudicial nature of his questions by locating the source of responses outside the courts. Answers could be found in citizens' "great lack of faith in our democracy, our body politic, our people, and our institutions" (*LaForge*, at 16). Faith in underlying principles was the foundation for all democratic authority, not just for judicial authority; it was a distinctly political quality. Faith also embraced a moral dimension, and Lord suggested that its absence led to political immorality. That absence would transform Armageddon into a "semi-religious celebration" (*LaForge*, at 16): "[W]hen the bombs go off, Christ won't have to come to earth—we will all, believers and non-believers alike, meet him halfway" (*LaForge*, at 16).

Lord's introduction, approximately one-third of his sentencing address, provided a distinctly nonlegal framework for his judicial decisions. Although judges and lawyers were included in his audience, they were included as citizens, not as legal experts. The community clearly was preferred in the *LaForge* opinion.

The "Fatal Fascination" of Opposing Terms

In his initial remarks Lord suggested the extralegal character of his message by associating echoes of legal language with clearly nonlegal terms. In his questions to the community, oppositional language strengthened the extralegal message. In addition, the wording of the questions created through contradiction the image of a society held in thrall by an unholy alliance of arms and ideals, in danger of condemning itself to death through its preoccupation with the means of destruction.

Consider the question "Can it be that those of us who build weapons to kill are engaged in a more sanctified endeavor than those who by their acts attempt to counsel moderation and mediation as an alternative method of settling international disputes?" (*LaForge*, at 14). In this question Lord created contradiction by pairing opposing terms. He incited internal conflict by the pairing of "build" and "kill," words that "mean the opposite." The conflict escalated with his association of "kill" and "sanctified." Coupling "build" with "kill" had introduced intellectual discordance; uniting "kill" and "sanctified" implicated the spirit as well as the mind. Similar contradictions appeared throughout Lord's rhetorical questions, for example: "What is so *sacred* about a *bomb*, so *romantic* about a *missile*" (*LaForge*, at 14-15; italics added); "extolling the *virtues* of *warmongers*" (*LaForge*, at 15; italics added); "we can see the *outgoing* [*weaponry*] as a *national virtue*" (*LaForge*, at 16; italics added); and "something *sanctified* about . . . *national suicide*" (*LaForge*, at 17;

italics added). In Lord's strategic questions, the pairing of sacred and profane terms suggested moral as well as intellectual degeneration. This degeneration led to the ultimate idolatry, "a system which finds its humanness . . . sublimated to . . . the worship of the bomb" (*LaForge*, at 19).

Lord depicted the Strangeloveian state of society as a kind of enthrallment. A "fatal fascination . . . attracts us to the thought of mass destruction of our brethren" (*LaForge*, at 15), to the idea that "all people on one side of an imaginary line must die" (*LaForge*, at 15), and to the need "to punish our adversaries" (*LaForge*, at 15) and "protect ourselves from the spread of foreign ideologies" (*LaForge*, at 16). This view led to a generalized absorption with death. The "ungodly" cynicism (*LaForge*, at 15) of this rhetorically created society linked national ideals to superiority in arms and transformed good into evil. Violence begat violence, and the society that found virtue in weapons directed against others came to accept the death of its own people; the cause of destroying others presaged a willingness to commit futile "national suicide" (*LaForge*, at 15) and to "die at our own hands" (*LaForge*, at 16).

These were grave issues indeed, and well worth bringing to public attention. However, introducing them in the beginning paragraphs of a judicial opinion created rhetorical obstacles for the judge. Perhaps the first and most pressing obstacle was the challenge they posed to Lord's development of a judicial persona. Because the issues were beyond the courts' capacity to resolve, there was a risk that a judge would be perceived as an irrelevant actor in the greater political and moral drama at hand.

Judicial Persona

Lord could not follow the model of the *Robins* appeal, in which he expanded his persona to the dimensions of the issues; even Lord had limits. His introductory enumeration of grave societal issues had placed his judicial decisions within a much larger context. The magnitude of the society's ills emphasized his decisions' smaller scale. Adequate expansion being impossible, Lord fashioned a judicial persona to match the modesty of his decisions. He strategically contracted the power and authority of his rhetorical role to become a judge bound by rules. In doing so he offered a model for individual action against almost insurmountable odds.

When Lord introduced his judicial persona in the seventeenth paragraph of the *LaForge* opinion, he noted that "it is a very difficult job for a Federal Judge to . . . punish two individuals who are charged with having caused damage to the property of a corporation" (*LaForge*, at 16). The job was difficult because the rules made the situation unjust. Lord underscored the injustice and the ascendancy of rules by reviewing Sperry's transgressions and his judicial impotence when he was confronted by those transgressions. His former impotence was matched in the current situation; the rules obligated him to punish those who had destroyed Sperry's property after they had required him not to punish Sperry (*LaForge*, at 16-17). In spite of the injustice, Lord must comply. His apparent compliance with the rules he depicted as unjust emphasized the strict limits within which his constrained judicial persona operated.

However, Lord identified one source of limited power that enabled this persona to withstand the defense industry's "powerful pressure on a judge in my position" (*LaForge*, at 18): judicial independence. Independence was a fragile defense against the combined force of arms manufacturers and the government, but it nevertheless empowered Lord not to sentence the protesters to ten years in prison: "A judge sitting here—as I do—is not called upon to do that which is politically expedient or popular, but is called upon to exercise his calm and deliberate judgment" (*LaForge*, at 19). In spite of his limited scope, a constrained but independent Lord could take a modest step "to accomplish and accommodate and vindicate the rights of the people . . . and the rights of those people who are the subject matter of such actions" (*LaForge*, at 19). If Lord could not do justice, he still could move toward it.

Given the forces at work in a troubled society and the uneven contest between justice and the rules, at first this constrained judicial persona might appear a pathetic character. Bound by rules, he might seem to add to rather than ameliorate the problems he described. The persona functioned well, however, as a rhetorical device; it provided Lord with the means for amplifying the significance of the modest actions he could perform as a judge.

The constrained persona identified Lord with the protesters; that is, his judicial attributes were fused with those of decent, vulnerable "little guys" working on behalf of others, dedicating the whole of their modest means to overcoming tremendous opposition. In these circumstances, the significance of small acts increases. Consequently, when Lord, constrained by rules and facing "powerful pressure," made a decision not to do the expedient thing, not to "sentence these defendants to a 10-year period of imprisonment [as] some judges might be disposed to do" (*LaForge*, at 19), his act took on a dimension it would have lacked had his judicial persona been more powerful. Within the confines of a constrained persona, Lord's decision was courageous.

To demonstrate persuasive courage, a person must face risk. In this regard Lord's prior reputation and present circumstances contributed to the rhetorical force of his judicial persona. When he observed that he would "anxiously await the protestations of those who complain of my attempts to correct the imbalance that now exists" in the justice system (*LaForge*, at 19), his observation had special meaning. It had been less than a week since the Eighth Circuit Court of Appeals had rebuked him, and he still awaited the Judicial Council's disposition of Robins's complaint against his judicial fitness. Therefore the risk Lord faced was both real and substantial, and his willingness to take a new risk contributed both to the credibility of his persona and the significance of his acts.

As a result of the risk it entailed, Lord's "small" effort in pronouncing the protesters' sentences "to take the sting out of the bomb, attempt in some way to force the Government . . . to remove the halo—which it seems to hold over any device which can kill—and, instead, to place thereon a shroud" (*LaForge*, at 18-19) seemed not only relevant but more important. As he had in the Dalkon Shield cases, in *LaForge* Lord enacted an argument. The message embedded in his constrained judicial persona was that one person, no matter how limited his or her resources, can make a difference. Lord's working for justice in a small way was superior to doing nothing; in the context of "powerful pressure," the modest act of a constrained judge gained significance by virtue of the constraints.

Contrasts in the Courts

In his rhetorical construction of the larger context for his judicial decisions, Lord had presented his perspective on the community's political and moral course; fatal contradictions in ideals and actions were leading toward catastrophe. In his constrained judicial persona, Lord had integrated the political limitations and existential liberty of activists who tried to correct the community's destructive course; his persona implied that individual insight and action could contribute to collective redemption. Two elements of a dramatic scenario, certain danger and potential rescue, were in place. However, a significant rhetorical obstacle remained. The danger and the rescue were in different places. The actor was separated from the scene.

The urgent issues Lord had described were in the community. The judicial persona he had created was bound to the courtroom by the tight grip of rules. The issues had to be moved into the courtroom to enable the judge to act. Lord's strategy for connecting the larger context to the courts was to depict the conflict in the courtroom as a reflection of the contradictions in the community. In this depiction he was on familiar rhetorical ground. In the community those who supported the building of weapons threatened the "fundamental concepts" of democracy (*LaForge*, at 15) and oppressed those who counseled mediation. In the courtroom those who built weapons attempted to implicate the courts in the corruption and oppression.

As he had in his *Reserve-a* and *Robins* opinions, in *LaForge* Lord used contrasts to develop his courtroom drama. In his introduction he had issued a general indictment of mighty institutional forces, arms manufacturers and the U.S. government. In the body of his opinion he particularized his complaints, and in that process contrasted Sperry's resources, wrongs, and punishments with those of the protesters. The contrasts demonstrated the similarity of the courtroom situation to the community context.

Crime. In the community, powerful "warmongers" perverted nationalism in order to harm the people and their government. In the courtroom, Sperry performed a similar role. Its resources were enormous, and it used those resources to compound its crimes by corrupting the government. Sperry's great wealth made its crime possible: "wrongfully and feloniously juggling the books" (*LaForge*, at 17), the company had "embezzled" (*LaForge*, at 16) and "stole[n]" $3,600,000 (*LaForge*, at 21). In contrast, Katt had "no assets" (*LaForge*, at 17), and LaForge owned only "a 1968 Volkswagen, a guitar, a sleeping bag, and $200 in cash" (*LaForge*, at 18). The severity of their crime matched the extent of their wealth; they "had caused damage to the property of a corporation in the amount of $33,000" (*LaForge*, at 16). The protesters' capacity for crime was 1/100 of Sperry's capacity. However, unlike Sperry, the protesters were to pay more dearly for their crime.

In spite of Sperry's greater crime, the company had faced negligible punishment. Possessing sufficient power to negotiate on equal terms with the government, and perhaps receiving "special treatment because of the nature of their work" (*LaForge*, at 17), the company had escaped charges that would have reflected the scope of its crime: "it did not occur to anyone in the office of the Attorney General of the United States that the actions of these men constituted a criminal conspiracy for which they might be punished and imprisoned" (*LaForge*, at 17). Instead, money generated by arms production had changed hands; Sperry had only to "pay back a mere 10 percent" (*LaForge*, at 17). There was no charge, no jury, no criminal conviction, and no sentence. Sperry was protected by its victim rather than prosecuted.

In contrast, the government seemed anxious to prosecute Sperry's injury at the hands of the protesters. Although Katt and LaForge had struck at "the property of a corporation" (*LaForge*, at 16)—and a criminal corporation at that—the government charged and prosecuted them with the crime of destroying government property. They faced the prospect of "a 10-year period of imprisonment" (*LaForge*, at 19) as well as restitution. Two individuals acting in the open and accepting responsibility for their acts had been considered more dangerous and blameworthy than a group of people who concealed their identities and used corporate influence to escape accountability. In Lord's view, this was a perversion of justice that paralleled the perversion of ideals occurring in the community.

Injustice. The protesters were "struck down as enemies of the people" (*LaForge*, at 18) for having tried to save "friend and enemy alike" (*LaForge*, at 14). As they pondered their potential sentences, Sperry pursued its course of corruption. As part of the arms industry, it influenced Congressional "pork barreling . . . to obtain more such [arms] contracts" (*LaForge*, at 18) and "exerted a powerful pressure on a judge" (*LaForge*, at 18). A known criminal, it had been let loose to subvert the legislative and judicial branches of a government charged with protecting and serving the public. The government preferred to protect the public from two individuals who had tried to save lives by means of a crime that was not "subversive, traitorous, treacherous, or treasonous" (*LaForge*, at 18); those individuals might not be let loose for ten years.

In Lord's view, these cumulative contrasts revealed a greater underlying, malignant contrast: there was "one type of justice for the rich and a lesser type for the poor, one standard for the mighty and another for the meek, and a system which finds its humanness and objectivity is sublimated to military madness" (*LaForge*, at 19). This was the ground upon which the intellectual and moral degeneration of the community met the subject matter of judicial decisions to be made in the courtroom. The protesters had been prosecuted to the full extent of the law because they fought against the "effort to commit national suicide" caused by the community's degeneration.

In the courtroom Lord rejected "military madness"; he sentenced the protesters to probation. Yet he believed that, in spite of his willingness to act, he had not been able to prevent the courts' complicity in an injustice. The protesters had been convicted and were being sentenced because they had destroyed military property valued at $33,000; individuals who had engaged in more serious crimes, who had conspired criminally and embezzled more than 100 times that amount in the production of military property, never would be punished. Lord had extended himself to the limit of his authority as an independent judge under the rule of law to remedy injustice and derail the forces that were leading the community toward self-destruction. But in the contest between good and evil, it was not enough. In this contest there should be no middle ground, yet Lord had been forced to stand on such ground, ameliorating but not eliminating injustice. However, he had done as much as he could do: his "duty is done, my conscience is clear" (*LaForge*, at 21). Others would have to carry on.

SUMMARY

In his *LaForge* opinion Lord had spoken plainly about injustice in the courtroom as a reflection of injustice in the community. As in earlier opinions, he was the symbol of the forces of good; in his judicial role he remained the champion of the "little guys." He was the guardian of the courts' function as an arena in which the powerless could meet the powerful on equal terms, even if the former were armed only with principles and personal courage and the latter were strengthened by material wealth and political influence. Lord's use of contrasts to dramatize the fundamental conflicts underlying the immediate legal dispute remained an essential element of his rhetorical effort; the picture of conflict was incomplete without a depiction of its wider implications. The accessibility of Lord's language, the simplification and polarization of issues, and the controversial nature of both the issues addressed and Lord's manner of addressing them once more were features of the opinion that increased the likelihood that Lord's rhetoric would become an educational tool in the school of democracy. It would spark public debate about a significant issue, and through debate the community would be better able to perfect itself.

The *LaForge* opinion, however, also reflected an important shift in Lord's rhetorical emphasis. In *LaForge* Lord emphasized that courtroom controversy was a *reflection* of the unequal struggle between forces of evil and good. The courtroom was not the scene of a direct and decisive confrontation between those forces; that confrontation took place in the community.

Lord's litany of self-examining interrogatories—"we must ask ourselves," "those of us who build weapons," "Why are we so fascinated?" (*LaForge*, at 14), "Why do we condemn?" "What is that fatal fascination which attracts us?" "How can we entertain?" "[I]f we be so ungodly cynical?" "[H]ave we given thought?" "What is the myopia that possesses us?" and "[H]ave we so little faith?" (*LaForge*, at 15)—indicted the community's motives and actions. In the confrontation between good and evil, the public, not just Sperry and the government, was culpable. It had cooperated in the perversion of its values that led to the occasion for Lord's rhetoric, to his sentencing of arms protesters. In spite of Lord's acting in his "own small way" to mitigate injustice, the greater effect of the *LaForge* opinion's plea to the public audience was to remand the fight for justice to the theater of politics. Lord's message had outstripped the authority of a judge to deliver it. That seemed to be the direction in which he had been striding—toward public responsibility for the issues that came to the courts.

RESPONSE

Lord's judicial experience during the Vietnam War had led him to a strong belief in reconciliation rather than armed conflict. After hearing many cases against draft resisters, he had come to the conclusion that "the kids were right first, and then the public, and last the judges. . . . [Eventually] they didn't serve a lot of time coming out of my court" (Klobuchar, 1974b, p. 6B). When Katt in her presentence statement observed that protest actions like hers would "do nothing unless the judges, prosecutors, elected officials and corporate heads open their minds and their hearts" (*LaForge*, p. 7), her words coincided with Lord's own opinion (Oslund, 1984, p. 6A). Lord availed himself of the opportunity presented by the protesters' case to comment on an issue that troubled him deeply. If the public would listen, it would be "better than if Ellen Goodman said it" (Lord, personal interview, 1988b).

The public listened, and its reactions confirmed Lord's controversiality (Zack, 1985a, p. 2B). Admirers claimed that it had taken a "fearless judge" to "examine seriously the values that compelled [the protesters] to break the law" (Lawrence, 1985, p. 15A); that Lord's departure from most judges' inclination "too often [to] take revenge on those who question the state" had resulted in "a wise sentence and a courageous one" (Panzer, 1985, p. 15A); and that Lord's "clarity [of conscience] has assured [him] continued respect" (McCarthy, 1985, p. 14A). Others welcomed Lord's opinion but deplored his sentencing decision, noting that the "[j]udge gave [the protesters] probation they didn't deserve [but he] also gave the world a juicy sermon . . . which it probably did deserve" (Klobuchar, 1984, p. 1B) and that "opposition to warfare was admirable . . . but no justification for computer bashing" (An institution, 1985, p. 14A). Still others condemned both Lord's opinion and the sentence. One noted that he "spoke with much indignation but little wisdom," delivering an opinion that "should be stricken from the record before its damage spreads" (The danger, 1984, p. 30A). Another complained that Lord "is charged with enforcing the law, not making national security policy," and that in his vendetta against Sperry he was "$33,000 down, $3,567,000 to go" (Berkowitz, 1985, p. 36).

The *LaForge* opinion also generated two complaints to the Judicial Council. On January 24, 1985, the anonymous first complaint was dismissed. The Eighth Circuit Court of Appeals declared that "[d]isenchanted litigants . . . should not be able to attempt to influence a federal judge . . . through the threat of disciplinary sanction" (C. Johnson, 1985, p. 1B). Lord characterized the dismissal as an "emancipation proclamation," although he insisted that it would not change his approach to judicial opinions: "I'll just say what I have to say" (C. Johnson, 1985, p. 1B). The second complaint, brought by the Washington Legal Foundation, was not dismissed until after Lord had announced his intention to retire. He characterized this complaint, and its dismissal in June of 1985, as something of a capstone to his career; the conservative law center's complaint proved that his judicial tenure had been a success (Zack, 1985c, p. 22A).

The *LaForge* opinion could be termed a success in the sense that it provided an opportunity to confirm judges' right to speak from the bench. However, in terms of public attitudes and government actions concerning the arms race or the treatment accorded the powerful as compared with the powerless, Lord seemed to have expressed accurately the limits of his opinion: "I know it will be futile— to [try to] remove the halo—which [the government] seems to hold over any device which can kill—and, instead, to place thereon a shroud, the shroud of death, destruction, mutilation, disease and debilitation" (*LaForge*, at 19).

EPILOGUE

In spite of his realization that "it's hard for most people to give up being a judge [and] [t]here's something very satisfying about being able to boss lawyers around" (Klobuchar, 1983a, p. 2B), from time to time over the years Lord had contemplated retiring from the bench to return to politics or to the practice of law (Berg and Stone, 1976, p. 9C; Dornfeld and Rebuffoni, 1975, pp. 1B, 2B; Klobuchar, 1983a, pp. 1B, 2B). After Robins's complaint to the Judicial Council, however, talk of retirement halted abruptly.

As far as Lord was concerned, Robins had nothing to complain about. In fact, his appeal to Robins's executives had been milder than he originally had planned; he had deleted the part that said "'E. C. Robins, you miserable old S. O. B., above the gates of your mansion it should read, 'This mansion was built on the ruined and mangled bodies of American womanhood'" (McAuliffe, 1986, pp. 3B, 12B). As he awaited the Judicial Council's decision on Robins's complaint, Lord made a decision of his own: if the Council determined that he had transgressed, then "I will sit here until I'm senile. They'll have to send a committee to invite me off to the funny farm" (Lord, 1984). Although the "worst of the damage [was] done as soon as the complaint [was] filed [and frightened] every . . . judge who is running for . . . the Supreme Court—which means 99 percent of them" (Anderson, 1984, p. 10A), Lord was determined to do his part to resist the complaint's chilling effect upon judicial speech.

The Retiring Judge

When the Judicial Council dismissed Robins's complaint, Lord declared victory (Oberdorfer, 1984d, p. 1B) and retirement again seemed possible. Then came his *LaForge* opinion and more complaints to the Judicial Council. It seemed that the "quiet time to go" (McEnroe, 1985, p. 6A) for which Lord was waiting might never come. While the Judicial Council considered the latest complaints, Lord continued to make decisions, including rulings against wolf trapping (Rebuffoni, 1985, p. 1A), cutoffs of Social Security disability payments (Associated Press, 1985a, p. 13B; Parsons, 1984, p. 1A), and restrictions on Aid to Families with Dependent Children (Judge Lord orders change, 1985, p. 21A). Finally the Judicial Council dismissed the *LaForge* complaints, and Lord announced that he would retire. On July 1 he would become a senior judge with a reduced work load, and he and Maxine Lord planned to smell the roses and go fishing (Lord to stay, 1985, p. 6D; McEnroe, 1985, pp. 1A, 6A, 7A). On September 11, 1985, Lord retired from his senior judgeship as well (Lord announces, 1985, p. 3B).

Although a columnist commented that Lord's retirement was a favor to "the appeals judges who have tried to cope with [him] the past 20 years" (Klobuchar, 1985, p. 1B), the Eighth Circuit Court of Appeals could not resist a "parting shot." Almost two years after Lord's retirement, in April 1987, it reprimanded him for having allowed a jury to celebrate his sixty-fifth birthday by presenting him with cakes inscribed "the world's greatest judge" (Parry, 1987, pp. 1B, 2B). Nevertheless, the judge who had been labeled President Ronald Reagan's "Exhibit X, to be avoided at all peril" (Klobuchar, 1982, p. 1C) proved hard to replace; confirmation of his successor, a former president of the Minnesota Bar Association, was delayed for almost two years because he "was not conservative enough" (Phelps, 1987, p. 3A; Assuming the robes, 1987, p. 3B).

Lord's retirement attracted almost as much attention as had his opinions. Many comments related to his character, decisions, and actions. He was "hammy, gutsy . . . and morally right" (Klobuchar, 1985, p. 1B). A newspaper editor characterized him as an "incisive" judge who was applauded "not merely because he seemed to champion the powerless [but because] he was often right" (An institution, 1985, p. 14A). A Republican Senator noted that "[e]very single human is important to Miles Lord" (Furst, 1985, p. 3B), and a law professor named Lord to "the Order of the Little Child . . . who says, 'The Emperor has no clothes' " (McAuliffe, 1986, p. 12B). These comments were reminiscent of the earlier accolades of business people who had applauded Lord for "decid[ing] to be himself, even on the bench" and for having "the guts to stand up" (Oslund, 1984, pp. 4A, 6A). But the comment that most seemed to capture the direction in which Lord had headed throughout his judicial career was that of a trial lawyer who said that "Lord is proof that one man can make a difference" (Zack, 1985a, p. 2B).

In the midst of these comments on Lord's character, his opinions were not forgotten. One editorial praised him as the epitome of a "dedicated, plain-spoken, hard-working public servant" (An institution, 1985, p. 14A), and George McGovern observed that "[w]e don't have enough people in public life who speak as straight as Miles Lord" (Furst, 1985, p. 3B). Lord's writing and speaking days were not over; he contributed commentary to a local newspaper (Lord, 1986, p. 23A) and received "20 to 25 requests for speeches a week" (Zack, 1985b, p. 3B). On the day of his retirement he delivered a speech to energy cooperative members in Albuquerque, New Mexico (Miles Lord leaves, 1985, p. 3B), and after his retirement his audiences ranged from employment managers (Hage, 1985, pp. 7B, 11B) and University of Minnesota students (Tubert, 1986, pp. 3B, 8B) to Minnesota Democratic-Farmer-Labor Party convention delegates.

The Unretiring Lawyer

However, speaking and writing were not enough to consume Lord's energies; he went back to law. Representing striking workers (Diaz, 1985, pp. 1A, 4A; Klobuchar, 1986, p. 1B); fired faculty (Armour, 1989, pp. 1, 3); a missing Marine; and people injured by bursting gas pipelines, breast implants, and ice-cleaning machines (Hopfensperger, 1991, pp. 1A, 6A; Oberdorfer, 1987, pp. 1A, 10A), he has continued to spark controversy.

The judge who once was called "one of the best tipsters in town" (Carr, 1990, p. 25) has become a lawyer known for his advertising (Wascoe, 1987, p. 3M). The judge who once used controversial opinions to educate the public has become a lawyer who has hired medical experts to address public meetings (Oberdorfer, 1987, p. 11A), used full-page advertisements in the yellow pages of the telephone book, and taken to the radio and television airwaves.

To those who protest that advertising is inappropriate for a former federal judge, Lord points out that former judges who join corporate law firms are considered "perfectly respectable" (Carr, 1990, p. 25). But he "like[s] being on the side of some poor devil who's down and out" (Carr, 1990, p. 26), so for him courting "the wealthy and the affluent, the businesses and the bankers . . . on the golf courses, on the jetliner vacations, at the fancy private clubs, in the handball courts" makes no sense: "You wouldn't see many of my clients there" (Oberdorfer, 1987, p. 11A). His friend Eugene McCarthy agrees, saying that "[i]t's not as if he sold his name to some corporation, so I don't have any problem with . . . the fact that he advertises on TV" (Carr, 1990, p. 26). Lord has maintained that "if somebody does not let the people know they should hire a lawyer, then the people will not get what they have coming" (Oberdorfer, 1987, p. 11A). Lord is determined to get for the people what they have coming. Thus, to him, his law practice "is entirely consistent with everything I've ever done" (Carr, 1990, p. 24). Perhaps so.

NOTES

1. Sperry also agreed to pay $650,000 in damages and $167,000 in interest. Lord did not consider damages and interest as punishment because Sperry could deduct them from its taxes (Engelmayer and Wagman, 1985, p. 127).

2. The maximum fine for each felony charge was $10,000. Engelmayer and Wagman suggest that the government had the capacity to raise Sperry's fine if it desired. They describe a similar case against General Electric Company in which a U.S. attorney believed that the company should pay at least $1 million in fines. The attorney therefore identified 100 falsified time cards and charged one felony count for each card (Engelmayer and Wagman, 1985, p. 127).

3. In his presentence statement LaForge said that "the Government itself has chosen to ignore and . . . violate its own Constitution in this case. At Article 6, Number 2 of the United States Constitution, it is made flatly clear that international law supersedes all State and Constitutional rules. . . . We have banned not only the wanton burning of innocent people, but we have banned the planning of such an act, by adopting the principles of Nuremberg. . . . I wish your Honor to do what little you can to prevent an unimaginable crime, by declaring the relevancy of Article 6" (*LaForge*, at 10-12).

8

Judicial Rhetoric and the Community

> Miles Lord made footprints that still mark the social landscape of the state and the nation.
>
> David Carr, *Heaven Can Wait*

The rhetoric of Miles Welton Lord attempted to engage and persuade multiple audiences, offering all of them opportunities to reinvent a "just" community. His judicial opinions captured the attention of the media and through the media reached a public audience. They were noted, quoted, and considered by the community in public debates about significant controversies, and they sparked discussion about the relationship between the courts and the community in unifying a public divided by those controversies. Clearly, as a lower-court judge, Lord attempted to influence public perceptions of what life is like under the rule of law.

In legal terms, some of Lord's opinions are those of a "losing" judge; appellate courts rejected their conclusions. Even so, his opinions carried his arguments forward in time and outward in space. Even after Lord had left the debate, those who had been engaged by his rhetoric entered it, reinterpreting the principles and values he espoused and in some instances formulating the new rules he had suggested.

Lord's example suggests the importance of examining the rhetoric of lower-court judges to learn how their judicial opinions construct stories of justice. By identifying the rhetorical strategies that appeal to multiple audiences we may make those strategies available to others, and, more important, we may understand more fully the trial courts' role in helping to shape perceptions of courts and communities and contributing to public discourse.

THE PUBLIC AS AUDIENCE: USING A SHARED LANGUAGE

The empirical audience for judicial opinions may be drawn from at least five groups: the parties to legal disputes, attorneys, judges, governmental bodies, and the public may read the opinions.[1] Although factors such as community controversy and schools of judicial thought[2] may affect the likelihood of the public forming a significant part of the audience, any judge who wishes to influence the public through argument as well as through the exercise of authority (Perelman, 1980, p. 14) must approach judicial opinions with J. B. White's "equal reader, equal speaker" (1984, pp. 281-282) in mind. Speaking a language that recognizes and integrates the citizen as equal in the process of judging is difficult; the obstacles it presents can be overcome only with consistent rhetorical effort.

Lord began the effort to engage the public audience at a fundamental point: effective speaker-audience interaction requires a shared language. In judicial opinions, the need for a common language presents multilayered rhetorical obstacles. On the one hand, judicial opinions *must* speak to lawyers; to be understood and accepted as legal authority they must use language that complies with legal convention. If lawyers cannot understand the legal "instruction" contained within opinions, they cannot mold their professional actions to the legal models presented by judges.

On the other hand, legal language is notorious for perplexing terminology and complex sentence structures that confuse laypersons. In effect if not intention, technical language may exclude the larger community from participation in the judgments expressed in judicial opinions. The difficulty of apprehending what is *said* may impede understanding what is *meant*. In addition, opinions that emphasize the differences between legal and common language also emphasize judicial detachment from everyday life. To the citizen they are the equivalent of a judicial "trust me." Because controversy generally signals the absence of trust, technical language will not be persuasive.

Therefore, if controversial judicial opinions seek community adherence to the values and rules they espouse, they must use language that is accessible to the public. Lord's controversial opinions provide examples of accessible language. They encourage comprehension and community participation by linking technical terms with ordinary language and by using "plain" but "entertaining" words to "[shorten] the distance between judges and mortals" (G. E. White, 1976, p. 232). By deemphasizing differences in the languages of lawyers and laypersons, they suggest active, reciprocal relationships between the courts and the community, between law and justice, and between justice and life.

Plain Language

Although Lord's controversial judicial opinions avoid technical terms, they do use legal words and phrases. As we have seen, some technical language is necessary to append an opinion to a body of law. The most conventional of the controversial opinions examined here provides instructive examples of language strategies that diminish difficulties in translation from the courts to the community and increase accessibility and appeal to a nonlegal audience. *Reserve-a* illustrates the rhetorical obstacles a judge confronts in writing a relatively conventional opinion with unconventional attention to the audience of ordinary citizens.

The *Reserve-a* opinion contains more than sixty words and phrases that have specific legal meanings and/or are closely associated with legal speech. Some of these terms are used repeatedly.[3] The problems presented by vocabulary are compounded by two additional characteristics of conventional judicial opinions, quotations from statutes and case citations.

Legal terms and speech habits limit the effectiveness of judicial argument by impeding audience understanding. Quotations from statutes and regulations disrupt argument by interrupting a judge's voice. Statutes speak in a distant voice; they may be authoritative, but they are tedious rather than persuasive, and they are more comprehensive than comprehensible.[4] If the voice of the statutes is mistaken for the voice of the judge, argument to the public may be lost for want of readers willing to decode it. Case citations disrupt the development of judicial arguments in another way. Although they may provide technical support for assertions, they also direct attention away from the present discussion and toward authorities outside of the opinion. Their implicit instruction is to "look it up."

The *Reserve-a* opinion illustrates several factors that can be exploited to mitigate the public's potential difficulties with such necessary legal language. In some instances drawing on parallels in legal and ordinary meanings obviates the need to define legal terms. For example, the public audience may not understand the technical nuances of the terms *complaint*, *nuisance*, and *stay* in a judicial opinion. Everyday experience of those words, however, makes them meaningful in an essential way; the essential similarities serve as bridges to understanding. Mass media have made other legal terms relatively familiar to citizens who never have been in court. For example, words such as *plaintiff*, *defendant*, and *injunction* are understood in a general way by people who have read newspapers, listened to radio or television news broadcasts, or watched popular entertainment programs such as "Perry Mason" or "L. A. Law."

Where such linkages between everyday and legal terms do not ameliorate language difficulties, judges must turn to other definitional strategies. The challenge is to make the terms understandable to the public without providing unnecessary vocabulary lessons to the legal audience. The *Reserve-a* opinion demonstrates one of the most useful strategies to ease comprehension while respecting convention: contextual definition.

For example, in the *Reserve-a* opinion Lord discusses his reasons for naming Armco Steel Corporation and Republic Steel Corporation as defendants in the lawsuit. In doing so he uses several terms and phrases that will be familiar to the legal audience but might be foreign or confusing to the public audience, such as "interposition of corporate entity" and "agency or instrumentality." For the public audience Lord clarifies the words' meanings through substitution and family metaphor. He interchanges "interposition of corporate entity" with "independent corporate identity," "an independent decision making entity," "separate entity," and "separate corporate entity" (*Reserve-a*, at 27-29). For the nonlawyer, this substitution or interchange isolates the important defining characteristics of entity that may be interposed. The opposing characteristics that define Reserve, "agency or instrumentality" are clarified by discussing the company as being the "personification" of Armco and Republic, its being "dominated by its parents," "being used as a shield to protect the parents," and having its decisions made by its "parents" (*Reserve-a*, at 27-29).

Such contextual definition is rhetorically efficient. Substitution and metaphor serve the rhetorical purposes of legal distinction and emphatic repetition for the legal audience. For the public audience, they establish denotational meaning and suggest connotational evaluations. In the instance of Reserve's agency, the image of parents manipulating and exploiting a dependent whom they deny the right of self-control evokes negative evaluation as well as understanding; comprehension of meaning implies an accompanying judgment of motive.

Legal issues and terms may not be the only ones that are unfamiliar to a general audience. In *Reserve-a* Lord does not assume that the public audience already is or should be knowledgeable about a wide range of technical matters. Instead he assumes that they are capable of understanding and making judgments about a wide range of matters when they are provided with sufficient information adequately explained (Perelman and Olbrechts-Tyteca, 1971, p. 37). In addition to defining scientific and legal terms, he also clarifies what may seem relatively familiar financial terms, e.g.,"a 90 per cent return on owners' equity" means that "for every dollar . . . initially invested . . . they get back ninety cents each year" (*Reserve-a*, at 19). His efforts to universalize language—to make his meaning plain—may expand the potential membership of his audience and thereby increase the likelihood that the community will act on its capacity to make reasoned judgments about controversial issues that have reached his court. The same would hold true for other legal speakers.

Another area of concern for judges who wish to render opinions in "plain" language is the conflict between maintaining a persuasive judicial voice and the need to cite statutes and regulations. In this area Lord's rhetoric demonstrates the usefulness of footnotes as a strategy to avoid complex legal language and long interruptions of a judge's voice. For example, in the *Reserve-a* opinion Lord must refer to the provisions of Minnesota's Water Pollution Control Act, or WPC 15, to explain accusations made against Reserve. In the text of the opinion he summarizes the substance of the provisions in 9 easily understood lines: "Basically WPC 15(a)(4) is a non-degradation regulation requiring that waters of a quality better than the established standards be maintained at high quality. WPC 15(c)(2) prohibits industrial discharges which cause nuisance conditions. WPC 15(c)(6) requires that secondary treatment or its equivalent be applied to all non-biodegradable industrial wastes" (*Reserve-a*, at 24). The provisions themselves are relegated to a footnote. That note requires 101 lines of reduced-size type.

This footnoting strategy accomplishes several rhetorical objectives. First and most obvious is an overall reduction in the opinion's length, which increases the odds that the opinion will be read. Second, footnoting decreases the proportion of the opinion that is presented in a voice other than Lord's. As a result, the opinion gains in coherence and potential persuasiveness. Third, separation of the various legal voices facilitates comparison that works to Lord's advantage. Nonlawyers who read the footnoted provisions will note immediately that Lord's explanations are considerably shorter and more comprehensible than the law itself. The competence and directness implied by his concise summaries increase his credibility. Finally, Lord's simplified explanations encourage readers who are not lawyers to trust in their capacity to understand "basic" arguments. By favoring essence over detail, the explanations imply that accessible general principles are more important than legalistic particulars. The underlying message is that the community is competent to judge; it can have a legitimate role in resolving the issues discussed in the opinion.

Citations of authorities present a more intractable rhetorical problem. Because the authorities to which they refer usually are unknown to the public, their rhetorical effect may be negative rather than neutral. At best, references to authorities may disrupt argument directed to a general audience and so decrease its persuasiveness. At worst, they may signal the community's exclusion from the argument. However, the legal audience recognizes the citations *as* argument, and thus citations may not be omitted from opinions unless judges are willing to relinquish their legal audience.

An extreme example of the problem can be seen in the *Reserve-a* opinion at page 27.[5] In one paragraph Lord presents three sentences of argument. Each sentence is followed by citations of precedent authority. Approximately 38 percent of the paragraph is devoted to citations. It is clear that Lord has not abandoned appeals to a legal audience and that he has not solved all of the problems inherent in addressing multiple audiences. His strategy for dealing with the difficulty is not unique; it is to concentrate citations within specific areas of his opinion. In the *Reserve-a* opinion almost all references to previous opinions are contained within fifteen of the opinion's approximately seventy-five pages (pp. 25-29, 44-45, 55-59, 76-77, 83). This solution to the citation problem is imperfect, but it does reduce the number of times the public may be reminded of their ignorance of law and, disempowered, be tempted to abandon the opinion.

Thus, although legal language presents obstacles to judges who wish to address the larger community, it does not present insuperable obstacles. Judges do not confront an either-or choice that forces them to abandon the legal audience to speak to the public. In their opinions they may avail themselves of strategies that can help to bridge comprehension gaps caused by specialized vocabulary and other conventions of legal language.

However, bridging the comprehension gap is only the first step in writing a judicial opinion that invites the public's participation in reconstituting a community under the "rule of law." Once comprehension has been achieved, community-minded judges also must use language that can engage the public's imagination and enable them to envision the just community they are asked to create.

Entertaining Language

"Entertaining" language is not language that diverts attention from the serious matters discussed in judicial opinions. It is language that is hospitable to the human as well as institutional dimensions of law. By animating its subject matter, such language exposes the law's human origins and implications, making room for community participation in matters of justice.

Legal language often is short on such animation. Certainty is the ultimate goal of judicial decisions. The language used to justify them often mirrors that goal, seeking to eliminate ambiguity through words with fixed meanings that defy imagination. However, controversy concedes uncertainty, and in an uncertain situation imagination is required to envision satisfactory resolution. In the midst of controversy entertaining language may enable judges to put words together in unexpected ways to win acceptance for new formulations of a just community or to resuscitate old formulations by breathing new life into familiar principles.

The language strategies that contribute to animated judicial opinions are not esoteric. What seems unusual is their use in law. Lord's controversial judicial opinions offer a number of examples of seemingly simple strategies that enliven his opinions and sharpen his vision for readers. Verbs encourage images as well as convey denotational meaning: density currents *peel off* rather than separate (*Reserve-a*, at 36), and engineers *eye-ball* rather than examine cursorily (*Reserve-a*, at 78); executives *extricate* rather than defend themselves (*Robins*, at 27), and IUDs are *planted* rather than inserted (*Robins*, at 28); profits are *boosted* rather than raised, and books are *juggled* rather than altered (*LaForge*, at 17).

Adjectives, alliteration, and assonance are strategies used to suggest attributes of people, objects, and actions. A "midnight phone call" results in changed testimony (*Reserve-a*, at 68), and efforts to grow plants are "fruitless" (*Reserve-a*, at 82). A defective IUD constitutes a "deadly depth charge" *(Robins*, at 31) with which a corporation inflicts "monstrous mischief" (*Robins*, at 29). And bombs are "sacred," missiles are "romantic" (*LaForge*, at 15). Labels such as "corporate shell game" (*Reserve-a*, at 72), "a captive lot" of workers (*Reserve-a* at 43), and "hostages" (*Reserve-a*, at 72) also imply the qualities of human beings and their conduct.

Such language is arresting. It produces verbal and visual images that invigorate argument and create connotation. Metaphor, analogy, and description extend the images, increasing their strength. For example, in the *Reserve-a* opinion metaphor "evaporates" objections to Lord's injunction against the mining company's dumping of taconite tailings: "[T]he specter of tremendous economic hardship . . . is just that—a specter. As do other specters, this disappears in the light of the facts and reason. It is simply not there" (*Reserve-a*, at 88). In *Robins* analogy illustrates and dramatizes the injustice inherent in corporate personhood:

> If one poor young man were by some act of his, without authority or consent, to inflict such damage upon one woman, he would be jailed for a good portion of the rest of his life. And yet your company, without warning to women, invaded their bodies by the millions and caused them injuries by the thousands. And when the time came for these women to make their claims against your company, you attacked their characters . . . and ruined families and reputations and careers in order to intimidate those who would raise their voices against you. You introduced issues that had no relationship whatsoever to the fact that you planted in the bodies of these women instruments of death, mutilation, and of disease. . . . [But your] company has not suffered, nor have you men personally. You are collectively being enriched by millions of dollars each year."
>
> *Robins*, at 28-30

In the *LaForge* opinion a description of Sperry's activities and the government's response to them sets the stage for Lord's statement of what he perceives to be the underlying wrong in the situation:

> I am here called upon to punish two individuals who are charged with having caused damage to the property of a corporation in the amount of $33,000. It is this self-same corporation which only a few months ago was before me, accused of having wrongfully embezzled from the United States Government the sum of $3,600,000. The employees of this company succeeded in boosting corporate profits by wrongfully and feloniously juggling the books. Since these individuals were all employees of a corporation, it appears that it did not occur to anyone . . . that the actions of these men constituted a criminal conspiracy for which they might be punished and imprisoned. . . . Could it be that these men—

> who are working to build weapons of mass destruction—receive special treatment because of the nature of their work?
>
> *LaForge*, at 16-17

These rhetorical strategies, along with parallelism, antithesis, personification, and other strategies, assist Lord in creating what K. K. Campbell calls "virtual experience" (1982, pp. 8-9), an audience's sense of having "been there" in their minds. This sense of shared experience is an essential part of creating community. It is a sense that cannot be acquired through judicial opinions that rely upon conventional legal language that seeks to omit the emotional and physical vicissitudes of human life in the name of rationality. It is the sharing of experience through language that can prepare the members of an audience to identify with one another—to create the "set of shared relations, attitudes, and meanings" (J. B. White, 1985, p. 42) that constitute a community.

Through language that is comprehensible and that has the capacity to capture the attention and imagination of a public audience, judicial opinions may reach beyond the legal community to influence the larger community regarding matters of justice. In the case of controversial opinions, however, the task is made harder by divisions of interest that exist, and the difficulty may be exacerbated by judicial decisions that attempt to declare a "winner." In his controversial opinions Lord confronts the obstacles to community posed by division, and a review and evaluation of his rhetorical strategies of unification may yield insight into approaches that may be useful in overcoming those obstacles.

UNITY FROM DIVISION

Each of the controversial opinions examined here involves issues that threaten to divide communities. The *Reserve-a* case involves a multilayered controversy in which a confrontation between industry and the environment seems likely to force people to choose between their jobs and their health. *Robins* focuses upon the responsibility of a corporation for the products it makes and sells. *LaForge* centers on the government's treatment of individuals and corporations that have affected the government's property and agreed or disagreed with its public policy.

All of these cases require that the law be applied to conflict in order to produce justice. A fundamental requirement or principle of justice is, according to Ch. Perelman and L. Olbrechts-Tyteca, to "giv[e] identical treatment to beings or situations of the same kind" (1971, p. 218). J. B. White agrees with this foundational principle, saying that justice "establishes an essential equality between people" that requires "extending imaginative sympathy to those differently situated from ourselves" (1984, p. 274). In rhetorical terms, this requirement of justice has the advantage of not only being accepted by legal scholars and practitioners but also of fitting the larger community's intuitive understanding of justice. It therefore may form an appealing rhetorical base on which to construct justifications and from which to address multiple audiences.

In terms of Lord's controversial opinions, the widely accepted fundamental rule of essential equality also enriches the rhetorical possibilities of perhaps the most salient feature in each of the controversies examined: each involves a corporation. As Lord points out in his speech to the Minnesota Council of Churches, the law grants corporations the status of artificial personhood. Itself illustrating the role of imagination in law, the construct of corporate personhood becomes a crucial element in Lord's judicial rhetoric because it supplies him with the ready-made ingredients of drama. Although the drama has many variations, in Lord's "sympathetic imagining," at the root of the drama can be found what U.S. Supreme Court Justice Brandeis called "the curse of bigness," the idea that "with their complex combination of creativity and limited intellect, human beings could create institutions that were too big for them . . . to control" (Strum, 1984, p. 340).

The rhetorical issues embedded in "bigness" become clear when the fundamental rule of essential equality meets the construct of corporate personhood, when controversies arise from collisions between human and corporate interests. If human beings and corporations both are persons, comparisons between them must be direct. In rhetoric about law they must be treated alike; to recognize distinctions would be unjust. Furthermore, their "alikeness" will be based upon the human model; the opposite analogy would strain the purposes of law.

Direct comparisons and assumptions of alikeness produce rhetorically useful results. In imagining corporate and human "persons," in every case the corporate person will be the larger, more powerful entity. In human terms, large size and power are equated with independence, self-assurance, and potential danger for others. Smaller size and powerlessness imply dependence, vulnerability, and the need for protection. These prior associations of attributes are important in dramatic terms.

Although in uncontrolled conflict the larger, more powerful "person" may have the advantage, in stories about justice the smaller, more vulnerable person may win the audience's sympathy. The human person is a "natural" underdog, and in almost any contest corporate and human competitors may seem mismatched. Therefore the intervention of a judge-referee may seem particularly appropriate, and the human scale of the fundamental principle of justice may seem particularly apt. These factors increase the potential for transforming rhetoric that seems to divide the community into unifying discourse.

Reserve

For example, in his *Reserve-a* opinion, Lord speaks of the mining company as if it actually were a person. That is, he endows Reserve with parents, a personality, motives, and acts. On the basis of Reserve's motives and acts, the artificial person may be judged. And, in keeping with the requirement of justice, it may be accorded no greater or lesser consideration than would be accorded any other individual.

The application of the requirement of justice assists Lord in making of the mining company a symbol of deliberate division. Lord repeatedly emphasizes the company's wealth and power, but initially these differences are morally neutral. They merely increase Reserve's capacity beyond that of a human individual to act effectively, whether for good or for ill. What transforms wealth and power into divisive characteristics is Reserve's will; Lord consistently portrays Reserve as using its greater capacity to act as a tool for isolating itself from the community. The company seeks to exempt itself from the laws that govern everyone else: Reserve has "suggested that the Court order . . . state and federal agencies to . . . immunize [its] operations from ever complying with future environmental regulations" (*Reserve-a,* at 20); Reserve has been "directly asked by the Court if [it] would . . . implement a program . . . consistent with applicable state and federal regulations. . . . The answer to the question . . . was no" (*Reserve-a,* at 69); Reserve has "tried to argue that [Minnesota's air pollution law] should not be applied as to [it]" (*Reserve-a,* at 83); Reserve has "refus[ed] . . . to cooperate with the Court" (*Reserve-a,* at 60). This self-exemption from the rules violates the requirement of justice. Reserve is claiming the right to be treated differently, to place itself outside of the agreements that regulate the rest of the community's relationships.

Lord suggests strongly that Reserve's self-exemption is based upon a perception that power justifies differential treatment: "If a local food processor was injecting a known human carcinogen into the food it processes there would be no question that any regulatory authority which did not order it stopped would be in dereliction of its duty. In this case, however, we are . . . dealing with . . . a mammoth industry. . . . Should the size of the polluter involved be the determinative factor in the Court's decision as to whether or not to protect the exposed population?" (*Reserve-a,* at 69-70). If size is the determinative factor, clearly individuals never will merit the treatment accorded Reserve.

Reserve also estranges itself from the community by its deliberate refusal to recognize reciprocal responsibilities. Although the company demands loyalty and special consideration for its economic interests, it does not acknowledge others' vital interests or their entitlement to consideration: "It [is Reserve's] choice whether [it] would make the investment or abandon t[its] employees" (*Reserve-a,* at 20), and the company seems to prefer abandonment. Reserve has tried to "extract the last dollar of profit, even at the risk of injury to thousands" (*Reserve-a,* at 69); the company both "require[s] its work force to make . . . a choice that endangers their lives and the lives of their families" (*Reserve-a*, at 70) and "us[es] the work force at [its] plants as hostages" (*Reserve-a*, at 71).

The failure to reconcile the corporate person with the community is not the result of misunderstanding or neglect. Consistent efforts to accommodate Reserve are rebuffed consistently: Lord has "exhaust[ed] every possibility . . . [to] alleviate the health threat without a disruption of operations" (*Reserve-a*, at 20-21). The harm in Reserve's divisiveness is compounded by the fact that the company is not satisfied with separating itself from the community; it also seeks to divide community members from each other. It demands that it be "allow[ed] to . . . continuously and indefinitely [expose people downstream] to a known human carcinogen in order that the people in Silver Bay can continue working" (*Reserve-a*, at 17); it asks that some community members sacrifice their physical well-being for the economic well-being of others.

Reserve's attempts to coerce preferential treatment from the courts and its demands for exemption from the rules that bind the community demonstrate the profound potential for injury created by violations of the requirement of justice. Reserve's insistence upon its own superiority to the community threatens the relationship between the people and their protectors. At the same time that the company insists that "[i]n order to free [Reserve's workers] the Court must permit the continued exposure of known human carcinogens to citizens of Duluth and other North Shore communities" (*Reserve-a*, at 71), the company "attempt[s] to limit the . . . effect of this Court's findings to protect against future liability if everybody's worst fears are realized and . . . people . . . contract fatal diseases" (*Reserve-a*, at 72). Seeking to augment its own power at every turn, the company wants others in the community to stand alone, separated from one another's support and the court's protection.

In Lord's judicial opinion, Reserve Mining Company symbolizes division as a result of its acts. Initially separated from the people by morally neutral characteristics of wealth and power, the corporation uses its wealth and exerts its power in the pursuit of disunity. Its assumption of inequality has caused individuals to be abandoned, injured, forced to make dangerous choices, held as hostages, exposed to carcinogens, and deprived of compensation for their injuries. It has sought to divide itself from the community's rules, to separate its well being from that of community members, to alienate community members from one another, and to deprive the community of the protection of the courts. Regardless of community actions, Reserve is determined to remain aloof from their concerns; the community cannot cooperate with Reserve, it must submit to it.

Reserve's usefulness as a symbol of division is enhanced by the rhetorical construction of a scenario in which the community *cannot* join the company and maintain its just character. Because neither cooperation nor submission can bind the community with Reserve in an equal partnership, the choice is between justice and Reserve. Only one route to unity with honor remains open: the community must reject Reserve.

The rhetorical path to Reserve's rejection may seem divisive in the sense that unity among some members of the community is achieved only by eliminating another member. That is not the case, however. Although the community cannot join Reserve and remain unified, Reserve can join the community. All that is required of the company is that it abandon its claims to special status: "[i]f [Reserve] decide[s] to comply with state and federal law [it] . . . can continue [its] profitable operations in Minnesota" (*Reserve-a*, at 87). What is meant by rejecting Reserve is rejecting the assumption of inequality that Reserve represents. The requirement of justice becomes the foundation for unity: all persons, including Reserve, are alike, and they must treat one another as equals.

Robins

The conflict that gives rise to the *Robins* opinion is similar in several ways to that which led to the *Reserve-a* opinion. A powerful corporation, in this case "gigantic" and "multi-national" (*Robins*, at 26), again is embroiled in controversies regarding the harm to individuals it is alleged to have done. Again the corporation's wealth and power are well beyond those of the individuals it confronts, as evidenced by its ability to finance a "nationwide team of attorneys" (*Robins*, at 36) to defend it from individuals. And again the corporation has resisted modifications in its conduct over a period of years. However, these parallels in situation do not lead to an analysis of division and outline for unity identical to those in *Reserve-a*. In *Robins* it is pretense rather than power that is at the root of injustice, and the fact that the pretense is legal complicates the obstacles in the rhetorical way to unity. And although in *Robins* as in *Reserve-a* the concentration of wealth and power in the corporation magnifies the effects of its acts, in *Robins* unlike *Reserve-a* it is the separation of human from human rather than corporation from human that is the focus of rhetorical attention.

In *Reserve-a* the corporate person is a character in the judicial drama. To achieve unity it is necessary to establish the individual's equality with the corporate character and to treat the corporate and human persons alike. In *Robins* the corporate person is not a character but a mask that hides character. The fiction of corporate personhood divides actual persons—persons who supply a corporation with its motives and are responsible for a corporation's acts—from the community and makes those persons impervious to the requirement of justice.

Lord demonstrates the division of actual persons from their responsibility for corporate acts in his accusatory linking of executives with the acts for which they disclaim their culpability. His initial rejection of claims that " 'I did not know,' 'It was not me,' 'Look elsewhere' " (*Robins*, at 26) begins a litany of the division of persons from their acts. The actual persons who direct the A. H. Robins Company "pretend to the world that [they] . . . have no responsibility for the company's acts and omissions" (*Robins*, at 26), are "not willing to find out" how many women are wearing an intrauterine contraceptive device (*Robins*, at 31), and "consistently den[y] any knowledge of the deeds of the company you control" (*Robins*, at 33). In separating themselves from their acts these persons isolate themselves from the community. They attempt to put themselves beyond the reach of a sense of personal responsibility as well as beyond the reach of the requirement of justice.

Many of the acts from which Robins executives separate themselves have their parallels in Reserve's divisive acts. Some are designed to divide community members from one another. Community members are so divided by "attack[s on] their characters" (*Robins*, at 28), by the ruin of "families and reputations and careers" (*Robins*, at 28), and by the "segment[ation] and fragment[ation of] litigation" (*Robins*, at 34). As in *Reserve-a* the purpose of division is to weaken the individual by forcing her to stand alone.

Other acts from which Robins executives separate themselves compound the harm caused by dividing community members from one another by also dividing the community from the courts. The executives prevent community members from obtaining the protection of the courts through their instructions to their attorneys to "clog court calendars" (*Robins*, at 34), to avoid "any proceeding which would give continuity or cohesiveness to this nationwide problem" (*Robins*, at 34), to ask that "cases be transferred to . . . judges unfamiliar with [them]" (*Robins*, at 35), and to "flee the jurisdiction" in which a judge "catches on" (*Robins*, at 36). However, as was not the case with Reserve, Lord finds it essential to note that the executives "go along stonewalling it" (*Robins*, at 40), denying that the corporation acts at their behest and in their names, and denying that they therefore are responsible for the corporation's acts. The executives rather than the corporation are the focus of the rhetoric of division.

In the context of courtroom rhetoric, Lord's identification of the source of division at first seems to present an insurmountable obstacle to unity. The cause of division is the separation of the Robins executives from their own individual responsibility as well as from other community members. But the construct of corporate personhood prevents Lord from reaching the Robins executives with a legal prescription for healing the division. The impediment to unity is not that the law treats the executives differently from other individuals but that the law does not treat the executives at all. In the eyes of the law the corporate person is accountable for its acts; as a result, the actual persons behind the corporation are not. However, Lord does not leave the problem of unity unaddressed. His rhetorical response to this obstacle is to place the requirement of justice before the law and to transform his judicial opinion into an appeal for which he takes personal responsibility. His rhetorical decisions fit the problem he faces. In this situation, unity can be achieved only by the decisions of individuals to recognize and take responsibility for the shared humanity that may bind them together in justice even if they are not so bound by law.

The *Reserve-a* and *Robins* opinions suggest that superficial similarities in legal conflicts do not limit the rhetorical choices to be made by judges in transforming seemingly divisive rhetoric into unifying discourse. Neither does dependence upon a single principle of justice to produce unity necessarily imply singularity in the rhetorical application of that principle. Lord's rhetoric illustrates that within such broad parameters lie a multitude of rhetorical possibilities and that those possibilities may be exploited to create a variety of avenues from division to unity.

COMMUNITY RELATIONSHIPS AND THE COURTS' LEGITIMACY

This analysis of Lord's rhetoric suggests that controversial judicial opinions seek new relationships among their various audiences. Each audience, including the public audience, is assigned a role in the pursuit of justice. However, each example of judicial speech examined here incorporates a unique audience emphasis and suggests somewhat different roles for the several audiences it addresses. For example, the *LaForge* opinion emphasizes the public's role in resolving societal conflicts that give rise to legal controversies. In that opinion the contrast between Lord's constrained judicial persona and his expansive treatment of political issues seems to subordinate the role of the courts and the legal community to that of the larger community. Although the courts and the government's lawyers are warned of inequities in the judicial system, they cannot solve the perceived underlying problem of militarism. In that opinion more than in the others the meaning of "the law" seems to be legislation that the public in its political role can influence more appropriately, more thoroughly, and more effectively than can Lord in his capacity as a judge.

The *Robins* opinion emphasizes equally the public audience and the judicial audience. It is notable for addressing all of its audiences as moral individuals; the judicial "sermon" it delivers suggests to all audiences that the law never can replace individual conscience. It calls upon each audience member, regardless of the group to which he or she belongs, to take moral responsibility for his or her individual actions regardless of what the law allows. The public is assigned the additional role of taking responsibility for monitoring their Congressional representatives. As in *LaForge*, the public can influence "the law" by instructing their legislators; in this case the instruction is that they will not tolerate laws that reward corporate wrongdoing. The opinion also constitutes a warning to the courts about what they have permitted to be done in the name of the law. It suggests for the courts a more active role in discovering facts and promoting justice. The injustices Lord's opinion describes continued because courts were susceptible to sophisticated legal tactics that placed the "game" of legal practice ahead of the goal of the law. Lord's appeal is not to justice instead of the law but to justice ahead of the law.

The *Reserve-a* opinion most clearly emphasizes the courts, inviting the public to "overhear" a judicial discussion. The dialogue between Lord and the Eighth Circuit Court of Appeals suggests an active role for lower courts in "instructing" the higher courts in matters of law as well as in matters of fact. The companion role for higher courts is, of course, to listen to lower courts, to accept the trial courts' hard-won expertise regarding litigants as well as facts.

The *Reserve-a* opinion also seems to insist that trial-court judges resist the models suggested by higher courts when they perceive those models to be contrary to justice. In his opinion Lord uses the "truth" of trial-court experience as his authority to challenge perceived factual and legal error in the higher courts. He uses the "truth" of life's experience as his authority to challenge the assumptions he perceives to be improperly influencing the higher court, making it readier to respond to economic appeals than to evidence of potential danger to the public health. In this case the public's "overhearing" role implies responsibility to expand their understanding of community beyond village or city limits so that they can make truly sound decisions regarding the community's long-term interest.

Lord's rhetoric also suggests the importance of a judge's rhetorical persona in supporting the courts' legitimacy while conceding that they do not always do justice. When judges speak for their courts they assume the status of representatives of the judicial system. When they criticize other judges or the judicial system, they implicitly offer themselves as exemplars of the fitting alternative to the conduct they criticize. Lord's rhetoric creates judicial personae tailored to the rhetorical problems of such situations. His persona becomes an actor in the tension-resolving "endings" to competing stories of litigants and in the continuing story of the pursuit of justice.

In the *Reserve* case, Lord presents himself as an advocate for the authority of federal judges to protect the community, and he demonstrates the strength of his conviction by risking removal to act on it. In *Robins* he presents himself in an expanded role. He is a member of the human community compelled by human decency to defend powerless victims. He also is a representative of the judicial system compelled to defend it from the insidious attacks of the powerful who use its rules to undermine its integrity. In *LaForge* Lord is a humble judge, with limits on his power that prevent him from correcting imbalances in either the justice system or the political system. This judge rhetorically joins the community, staying within his authority's limited scope but doing what "little" he can to mitigate injustice.

In each case Lord rhetorically shapes his persona to the needs he identifies and the actions he believes necessary. He becomes the model of a judge who would "do the right thing" in each situation. For audiences who accept his view of reality, he becomes the symbol of the judicial system's strength, even in instances of its error. As a representative of that system, he is proof of its capacity to endure in the face of challenges and to produce "good" judges.

J. B. White suggests that the "shared relations, attitudes and meanings" (1985, p. 42) that constitute a community can be maintained or modified by legal discourse in which "we make ourselves by making our language," addressing questions about communal values, motives, and aims in words and voices that enable community members to recognize themselves and their interests in the discourse (1984, pp. 272-273; 1985, pp. 40-44). The rhetoric of Miles Welton Lord provides examples of such discourse. He addressed multiple audiences regarding controversial issues, sacrificing neither legal clarity nor general comprehensibility. He appealed to fundamental principles, to notions of justice as well as to positive law, and to values that the community could recognize and accept as their own. Responses to his rhetoric suggest that he influenced public perceptions of the courts and the community and public discourse on issues related to legal controversies. Analyzing the rhetorical strategies Lord used to pursue his goals helps us to understand how judicial rhetoric can appeal to the community as well as to the courts and helps to shed light on the importance of trial courts in defining the role of courts in relation to the community.

NOTES

1. Parties to legal disputes are interested in specific judicial decisions and the reasons for them. Attorneys will account to their clients for the decisions and "translate" judicial reasoning supporting them; they and other lawyers will attempt to discern from judicial opinions what the law "is." Judges will use others' opinions as support or models for their own, and higher-court judges may be called on to review the opinions of lower-court colleagues. Legislatures and governmental agencies will study judicial opinions to learn what behavior is permitted and to plan the action needed to override judicially interpreted law. Finally, a public perceiving that judicial opinions affect its interests will attend to them as critics, students of argument, and as potential or actual political activists.

2. Within the oracular and scientific traditions the community's role is to bring its disputes to the courts after they have been distilled into legal concepts and translated into legal language by attorneys. The public will be told of and expected to comply with judicial decisions, but it will not be presumed to be capable of understanding judicial reasoning. In reasoned elaboration, "rational" legal discourse assumes a public audience but to a significant extent eschews controversiality. The community has played its role previous to the opinion; community consensus on issues falling within the special competence of the courts is a prerequisite to judicial consideration. The assumptions of sociological jurisprudence and legal realism are most closely associated with judicial conceptions of the community as audience for participants in judicial opinions.

3. The terms and phrases include action, advisement, agency, allege, allegation, appeal, bad or good faith, common law, complaint, conclusions of law, count, counterclaim, cross claim, cross examination, defendants, discovery, due process, duty of candor, enjoin, equity/equities/equitable powers, evidence adduced, exhibit,

finding of fact, hearing, injunction/injunctive, instrumentality, interposition of corporate entity, interrogatories, intervene/intervenor, joinder, jurisdiction (concurrent, equity, original, pendant), litigation, merits, motion, nuisance, order, *parens patriae*, plaintiff (party), police power, pray, prejudice, prima facie, privity, proceedings, produce documents, purge, pursuant, relief, remand, res judicata, reverse, review (appellate), rule, service, sovereign, statutory, stay, subpoena *duces tecum*, "substantial evidence" rule, temporary restraining order, testimony, and trier of fact.

4. An example of a quoted law is the following: "[T]he United States alleges that Reserve's discharge is in violation of 33 U.S.C. § 407 ("Refuse Act") which provides: It shall not be lawful to throw, discharge, or deposit, or cause, suffer or procure to be thrown, discharged, or deposited either from or out of any ship, barge, or other floating craft of any kind, or from the shore, wharf, manufacturing establishment, or mill of any kind or description whatever other than that flowing from streets and sewers and passing therefrom in a liquid state, into any navigable water of the United States . . . and provided further, that the Secretary of the Army whenever in the judgment of the Chief of Engineers anchorage and navigation will not be injured thereby, may permit the deposit of any material above-mentioned in navigable waters, within limits to be defined and under conditions to be prescribed by him provided application is made to him prior to depositing such material" (*Reserve-a*, at 24).

5. The paragraph reads: "It is the finding of this Court that the independent corporate identity of Reserve Mining Company must be and is disregarded since this Court cannot allow the interposition of corporate entity to frustrate the implementation of a judgment that is required by justice. *General Underwriters v. Kline*, 233 Minn. 345, 46 N.W.2d 794 (1951), citing *In Re Trust Under Will of Clarke*, 204 Minn. 574, 284 N.W. 876 (1939). The Court finds that this subsidiary is being used as a shield to protect the parents from the consequences of an illegal act. *United States v. Del Campo Baking Mfg. Co.*, 345 F. Supp. 1371 (D.Del. 1972). Finally the Court finds that complete relief cannot be accorded plaintiffs if Reserve is considered a separate entity. Fed.R.Civ.P. 19(a)(1)."

References

CASES

Adams v. Tanner, 244 U.S. 590 (1917).

Adkins v. Children's Hospital, 261 U.S. 525 (1923).

American Banana Company v. United Fruit Company, 213 U.S. 347 (1909).

Armco Steel Corporation v. United States of America, 490 F. 2d 688 (1974).

In re Arnold & McDowell, 566 F. Supp. 752 (1983).

Bennett v. Butz, 386 F. Supp. 1059 (1974)

Berends v. Butz, 357 F. Supp. 143 (1973).

Brenden v. Independent School District 742, 342 F. Supp. 1224 (1972).

Coordinated Pretrial Proceedings in Antibiotic Antitrust Actions, 410 F. Supp. 659 (1974). *Antibiotics-a.*

Coordinated Pretrial Proceedings in Antibiotic Antitrust Actions, 410 F. Supp. 669 (1974). *Antibiotics-b.*

Coordinated Pretrial Proceedings in Antibiotic Antitrust Actions, 410 F. Supp. 680 (1975). *Antibiotics-c.*

Coordinated Pretrial Proceedings in Antibiotic Antitrust Actions, 410 F. Supp. 722 (1975). *Antibiotics-d.*

Dean v. A. H. Robins Co., Inc., 101 F.R.D. 21 (1984).

DeFreitas v. Noot, 527 F. Supp. 147 (1981).

Gardiner v. Robins, 474 F. 2d 1180 (1984). *Gardiner.*

Gardiner v. Robins, Civ. 3-83-1025, 3-83-1060 (1984). *Robins.*

Hall v. University of Minnesota, 530 F. Supp. 104 (1982).

Hartmann v. Gaffney, 446 F. Supp. 809 (1977).

Kiphuth v. Heckler, 587 F. Supp. 1567 (1984).

LaBonne v. Heckler, 580 F. Supp. 558 (1984).

Le Tec Corp v. Johnson & Johnson, 1982-2 Trade Cas. (CCH) P64, 942, July 13, 1982).

Lochner v. New York, 198 U.S. 45 (1905).

Marathon Pipeline Company v. Northern Pipeline Construction Co., 7 Bankr. Ct. Dec. 1373 (1981).

Marbury v. Madison, 1 Cranch 137 (1803).

McDonald v. Johnson & Johnson, 537 F. Supp. 1282 (1982).

Minnesota Public Interest Research Group v. Butz, 401 F. Supp. 1276 (1975).

Muller v. Oregon, 208 U.S. 412 (1908).

National Association of Property Owners v. United States of America, 499 F. Supp. 1223 (1980).

Polaski v. Heckler, 585 F. Supp. 997, 1004 (1984).

Porter v. Schweiker, 527 F. Supp. 150 (1981).

Rajender v. University of Minnesota, 546 F. Supp. 158 (1982). *Rajender-a.*

Rajender v. University of Minnesota, 563 F. Supp. 401 (1983). *Rajender-b.*

Red School House, Inc. v. Office of Economic Opportunity, 386 F. Supp. 1177 (1973).

Reserve Mining Company v. Environmental Protection Agency, 514 F. 2d 492 (1975). *EPA,*

Reserve Mining Company v. Lord, 529 F. 2d 181 (1976). *Lord.*

Reserve Mining Company v. United States of America, 498 F. 2d 1073 (1974). *Reserve-b.*

Santa Clara County v. Southern Pacific Railway Co., 118 U.S. 394 (1886).

Scott v. Sanford, 19 How. 393 (1857).

United States of America v. Brown, 522 F. 2d 817 (1977).

United States of America v. LaForge, Cr. 4-84-66 (1984) [Transcript of Sentencing]. *LaForge.*

United States of America v. Reserve Mining Company, 408 F. Supp. 1212 (1976).

United States of America v. Reserve Mining Company, 380 F. Supp. 11 (1974). *Reserve-a.*

United States of America v. Reserve Mining Company, 56 F.R.D. 408 (1972).

Vickerman v. Hennepin County Probate Court, 543 F. Supp. 165 (1982).

BOOKS

Abraham, H. J. 1980. *The judiciary: The Supreme Court in the governmental process.* 5th ed. Boston: Allyn & Bacon.

Aristotle. 1954. *The rhetoric and the poetics of Aristotle.* Translated by W. Rhys Roberts. New York: Random House.

Ball, H. 1980. *Courts and politics: The federal judicial system.* Englewood Cliffs, NJ: Prentice-Hall.

Ball, M. S. (1985). *Lying down together: Law, metaphor, and theology.* Madison: University of Wisconsin Press.

Bartlett, R. V. 1980. *The Reserve Mining controversy: Science, technology, and environmental quality.* Bloomington: Indiana University Press.

Bartsh, T. C., F. M. Boddy, B. F. King, and P. N. Thompson. 1978. *A class-action suit that worked.* Lexington, MA: Lexington Books.

Bastow, T. F. 1986. *This vast pollution: United States of America v. Reserve Mining Company.* Washington, D. C.: Green Field Books.

Berkson, L. C. 1978. *The Supreme Court and its publics.* Lexington, MA: Lexington Books.

Bickel, A. M. 1962. *The least dangerous branch: The Supreme Court at the bar of politics.* New Haven: Yale University Press.

Blaustein, A. P. and R. M. Mersky. 1978. *The first one hundred justices: Statistical studies on the Supreme Court of the United States.* Hamden, CT: Archon Books.

Blegen, T. C. 1975. *Minnesota: A history of the state.* Minneapolis: University of Minnesota Press.

Bork, R. H. 1990. *The tempting of America: The political seduction of the law.* New York: Free Press.

Campbell, K. K. 1982. *The rhetorical act.* Belmont, CA: Wadsworth Publishing Co.

Carter, L. H. 1985. *Contemporary constitutional lawmaking: The Supreme Court and the art of politics.* New York: Pergamon Press.

Chase, H. W. 1972. *Federal judges: The appointing process.* Minneapolis: University of Minnesota Press.

Cicero, Marcus Tullius. 1970. *On oratory and orators.* Translated by J. S. Watson. Carbondale: Southern Illinois University Press.

Cortner, R. C. 1972. *The apportionment cases.* New York: W. W. Norton & Co.

Cowell, F. R. 1967. *Cicero and the Roman republic.* 4th ed. Baltimore: Penguin Books.

Davis, E. W. 1964. *Pioneering with taconite.* St. Paul: Minnesota Historical Society.

Douglas, W. O. 1980. *The court years 1939-1975: The autobiography of William O. Douglas.* New York: Random House.

Eisele, A. 1972. *Almost to the presidency: A biography of two American politicians.* Blue Earth, MN: Piper Co.

Eisenstein, J. 1973. *Politics and the legal process.* New York: Harper & Row, Publishers.

Engelmayer, S. and R. Wagman. 1985. *Lord's justice.* New York: Doubleday, Anchor Press.

Frank, J. [1949] 1969. *Courts on trial: Myth and reality in American justice.* New York: Atheneum.

Friedman, L. M. 1985. *A history of American law.* 2d ed. New York: Simon & Schuster.

Garraty, J. A. 1971. *The American nation: A history of the United States to 1877.* 2nd ed. New York: Harper & Row, Publishers.

Goldman, S. and T. P. Jahnige. 1976. *The federal courts as a political system.* 2nd ed. New York: Harper & Row, Publishers.

Grossman, J. B. 1965. *Lawyers and judges.* New York: John Wiley and Sons.

Hariman, R., ed. 1990. *Popular trials: Rhetoric, mass media, and the law.* Tuscaloosa: University of Alabama Press.

Holmes, O. W., Jr. [1881] 1963. *The common law.* Cambridge: Harvard University Press, Belknap Press.

Johnson, J. W. 1981. *American legal culture, 1908-1940.* Westport, CT: Greenwood Press.

Kelly, A. H., W. A. Harbison, and H. Belz. 1983. *The American Constitution: Its origins and development.* 6th ed. New York: W. W. Norton & Co.

Kitto, H. D. F. 1967. *The Greeks*. Baltimore: Penguin Books.

Lerner, M., ed. 1943. *The mind and faith of Justice Holmes: His speeches, essays, letters, and judicial opinions*. New York: Modern Library.

Lewis, F. 1980. *Mondale: Portrait of an American politician*. New York: Harper & Row, Publishers.

Matlon, R. J. and P. C. Facciola, P. C., eds. 1987. *Index to journals in communication studies through 1985*. Annandale, VA: Speech Communication Association.

McCloskey, R. G. 1960. *The American Supreme Court*. Chicago: University of Chicago Press.

McFeeley, N. D. 1987. *Appointment of judges: The Johnson presidency*. Austin: University of Texas Press.

McGuiness, E. A. 1988. *People waging peace*. San Pedro, CA: Alberti Press.

Mintz, M. 1985. *At any cost: Corporate greed, women, and the Dalkon Shield*. New York: Pantheon Books.

Murphy, W. F. 1961. *Elements of judicial strategy*. Chicago: University of Chicago Press.

Perelman, C. 1980. *Justice, law, and argument: Essays on moral and legal reasoning*. Boston: D. Reidel Publishing Co.

Perelman, C. and L. Olbrechts-Tyteca. [1958] 1971. *The new rhetoric: A treatise on argumentation*. Translated by J. Wilkinson and P. Weaver. Notre Dame, IN: University of Notre Dame Press.

Perry, S. and J. Dawson. 1985. *Nightmare: Women and the Dalkon Shield*. New York: MacMillan.

Presser, S. B. and J. S. Zainaldin, eds. 1980. *Law and American history: Cases and materials*. St. Paul: West Publishing Co.

Schaumberg, F. D. 1976. *Judgment reserved: A landmark environmental case*. Reston, VA: Reston Publishing.

Scheingold, S. A. 1974. *The politics of rights: Lawyers, public policy, and political change*. New Haven: Yale University Press.

Smith, C. A. 1990. *Political communication*. San Diego: Harcourt Brace Jovanovich.

Solberg, C. 1984. *Hubert Humphrey: A biography*. New York: W. W. Norton & Co.

Stites, F. N. 1981. *John Marshall: Defender of the Constitution*. Boston: Little, Brown & Co.

Stone, I. F. 1988. *The trial of Socrates*. Boston: Little, Brown & Co.

Strum, P. 1984. *Louis D. Brandeis: Justice for the people*. New York: Schocken Books.

Tocqueville, A. de. [1839] 1845. *Democracy in America*. Translated by H. Reeve. New York: Henry G. Langley.

Trefousse, H. L. 1968. *The Radical Republicans: Lincoln's vanguard for racial justice*. New York: Alfred A. Knopf.

Tulis, J. K. 1987. *The rhetorical presidency*. Princeton: Princeton University Press.

Westin, A. F. 1961. *The Supreme Court: Views from inside*. New York: W. W. Norton & Co.

White, G. E. 1976. *The American judicial tradition: Profiles of leading American judges*. New York: Oxford University Press.

White, J. B. 1984. *When words lose their meaning: Constitutions and reconstitutions of language, character, and community*. Chicago: University of Chicago Press.

———. 1985. *Heracles' Bow: Essays on the rhetoric and poetics of the law*. Madison: University of Wisconsin Press.

———. 1990. *Justice as translation: An essay in cultural and legal criticism*. Chicago: University of Chicago Press.

Wiebe, Robert H. 1967. *The search for order, 1877-1920*. New York: Hill & Wang.

Wiecek, W. M. 1985. *Constitutional development in a modernizing society: The United States, 1803 to 1917*. Washington, D.C.: American Historical Association.

CHAPTERS

Berman, H. J. 1971. Philosophical aspects of American law. In *Talks on American law*, edited by H. J. Berman, rev. ed. pp. 293-307. New York: Vintage Books.

Chase, H., S. Krislov, K. O. Boyum, and J. N Clark, compilers. 1976. Lord, Miles Welton. *Biographical dictionary of the federal judiciary*, p. 168. Detroit: Gale Research Co.

Dolbeare, K. 1968. The Supreme Court and the states: From abstract doctrine to local behavioral conformity. In *The impact of Supreme Court decisions*, edited by T. L. Becker, pp. 206-213. New York: Oxford University Press.

Holmes, O. W., Jr. [1897] 1943. The path of the law. In *The mind and faith of Justice Holmes: His speeches, essays, letters and judicial opinions*, edited by M. Lerner , pp. 71-89. New York: Modern Library.

[The] Judge ousted in the Reserve Mining case. 1976. In *New York Times biographical service*, p. 80. New York: New York Times.

Lord, Miles Welton. 1978. In *Judges of the United States*, p. 241. Washington, D.C.: The Bicentennial Committee of the Judicial Conference of the United States.

Rieke, R. D. 1982. Argumentation in the legal process. In *Advances in argumentation theory and research*, edited by J. R. Cox and C. A. Willard, pp. 363-376. Carbondale: Southern Illinois University.

Scheutz, J. and K. H. Snedaker. 1988. Courtroom drama: The trial of the Chicago Eight. In *Communication and litigation: Case studies of famous trials*, pp. 217-246. Carbondale: Southern Illinois University Press.

DISSERTATIONS

Corso, D. M. 1981. The rhetoric of the United States Supreme Court: A generic approach. University of Oregon.

Deutsch, E. F. 1971. Judicial rhetoric as persuasive communication: A study of the Supreme Court opinions in the *Escobedo* and *Miranda* cases and the responses in

the California press. University of California, Los Angeles. In *Dissertation Abstracts International* 32: 01-A.
Makau, J. M. 1979. The judicial opinion as rhetorical performance. University of California, Berkeley.
Vibbert, C. B. 1981. The Supreme Court and obscenity: The judicial opinion as rhetorical reconstitution. University of Iowa.

JOURNALS

Anapol, M. 1970. Rhetoric and law: An overview. *Today's Speech* 18:12-20.
Bartenan, K. M. 1987. The rhetoric of dissent in Justice O'Connor's Akron opinion. *Southern Speech Communication Journal* 52:240-262.
Beach, W. A. 1985. Temporal density in courtroom interaction: Constraints on the recovery of past events in legal discourse. *Communication Monographs* 52:1-18.
Bennett, W. L. 1978. Storytelling in criminal trials: A model of social judgment. *Quarterly Journal of Speech* 64:1-22.
———. 1979. Rhetorical transformation of evidence in criminal trials: Creating grounds for legal judgment. *Quarterly Journal of Speech* 65:311-323.
Brummett, B. 1979. Gary Gilmore, power, and the rhetoric of symbolic forms. *Western Journal of Speech Communication* 43:3-13.
———. 1984. Burkean comedy and tragedy, illustrated in reactions to the arrest of John DeLorean. *Central States Speech Journal* 35:217-227.
Condit, C. M. and J. A. Selzer. 1985. The rhetoric of objectivity in the newspaper coverage of a murder trial. *Critical Studies in Mass Communication* 2:197-216.
Corgan, V. C. 1986. Perelman's universal audience as critical tool. *Journal of the American Forensic Association* 23:147-157.
Crable, R. E. 1976. Models of argumentation and judicial judgment. *Journal of the American Forensic Association* 12:113-120.
Dicks, V. I. 1976. Courtroom controversy: A stasis/stock issues analog of the Angela Davis trial. *Journal of the American Forensic Association* 13:77-83.
———. 1981. Courtroom rhetorical strategies: Forensic and deliberative strategies. *Quarterly Journal of Speech* 67:178-192.
Galanter, M. 1988. The life and times of the Big Six; Or, the federal courts since the good old days. *Wisconsin Law Review* 6:921-954.
Gillmor, D. M. 1982. Justice William Brennan and the failed 'theory' of actual malice. *Journalism Quarterly* 59:249-255.
Hagan, M. R. 1976. *Roe v. Wade:* The rhetoric of fetal life. *Central States Speech Journal* 27:192-199.
Hample, D. 1979. Motives in law: An adaptation of legal realism. *Journal of the American Forensics Association* 15:156-158.
Harbinger, R. 1971. Trial by drama. *Judicature* 55:122-128.
Hosman, L. A. and J. W. Wright II. 1987. The effects of hedges and hesitations on impression formation in a simulated courtroom context. *Western Journal of Speech Communication* 51:173-188.

Hunsaker, D. M. 1978. The rhetoric of *Brown v. Board of Education*: Paradigm for contemporary social protest. *Southern Speech Communication Journal.* 43:91-109.

Jones, S. B. (1976). Justification in judicial opinions: A case study. *Journal of the American Forensic Association* 12:121-129.

Karpatkin, M. W. 1974. En route to "A gross conforming stupidity": Lamentations on the systematic suffocation of civil liberties in the declining days of the Nixon administration, as aided and abetted by the Supreme Court. *Today's Speech* 22:47-56.

Kaufer, D. 1980. Analyzing philosophy *in* rhetoric: Darrow's mechanism in the defense of Leopold and Loeb. *Southern Speech Communication Journal* 45:363-377.

LeDuc, D. R. 1976. "Free speech" decisions and the legal process: The judicial opinion in context. *Quarterly Journal of Speech* 62:277-287.

Levison, G. L. 1979. The rhetoric of oral argument in *The Regents of the University of California v. Bakke. Western Speech Communication Journal* 43:271-277.

Lucaites, J. L. 1990. Between rhetoric and "the law": Power, legitimacy, and social change (Review of *A guide to critical legal studies, The critical legal studies movement, and Interpreting law and literature: A hermeneutic reader*). *Quarterly Journal of Speech* 76:435-466.

Makau, J. 1984. The Supreme Court and reasonableness. *Quarterly Journal of Speech* 70:379-396.

McLean, D. 1979. Justice White and the First Amendment. *Journalism Quarterly* 56:305-310.

Rabin, D. A. 1978. Gottlieb's model of rule-guided reasoning: An analysis of *Griswold v. Connecticut. Journal of the American Forensic Association* 15:77-90.

Reinard, J. C. and R. A. Reynolds. 1978. The effects of inadmissible testimony objections and rulings on jury decisions. *Journal of the American Forensic Association* 15:91-109.

Rice, G. P. 1961. The meets and bounds of speech and law. *Central States Speech Journal* 13:7-10.

Rieke, R. D. 1970. The rhetoric of law: A bibliographic essay. *Today's Speech* 18:48-57.

Ritter, K. 1985. Drama and legal rhetoric: The perjury trials of Alger Hiss. *Western Journal of Speech Communication* 49:83-102.

Rodgers, R. S. 1982. Generic tendencies in majority and non-majority Supreme Court opinions: The case of Justice Douglas. *Communication Quarterly* 30:232-236.

Sanbonmatsu, A. 1971. Darrow and Rorke's use of Burkeian identification strategies in *New York v. Gitlow* (1920). *Speech Monographs* 38:64-72.

Scott, R. L. 1984. Chaim Perelman: Persona and accommodation in *The New Rhetoric. Pre/Text* 5:90-95.

Shaman, J. M. 1988. Judicial ethics. *Georgetown Journal of Legal Ethics* 2:1-20.

Shmukler, A. 1970. Some challenges to the student of rhetoric and law. *Today's Speech* 18:45-47.

Stempel, G. H., III. 1982. A Gutman Scale analysis of the Burger Court's press decisions. *Journalism Quarterly* 59:256-259.

Strother, D. B. 1963. Polemics and the reversal of the "separate but equal" doctrine. *Quarterly Journal of Speech* 44:50-56.
Stuart, C. L. 1974. The Constitution as "summational anecdote." *Central States Speech Journal* 25:111-118.
Tuttle, R. L. 1982. The Dalkon Shield disaster ten years later: A historical perspective. *Oklahoma Bar Journal* 54:2501-2505.
Ulrich, W. 1985. The creation of a legacy: Brandeis' concurring opinion in *Whitney v. California*. *Southern Speech Communication Journal* 50:143-155.
Washby, S. L., A. A. D'Amato, and, R. Metrailer. 1976. The functions of oral argument in the U.S. Supreme Court. *Quarterly Journal of Speech* 62:410-422.
Welch, C. 1976. Potential in legal communication: What's the verdict? *Journal of the American Forensic Association* 12:138-143.
Wright, W. E. 1964. Judicial rhetoric: A field for research. *Speech Monographs* 31:64-72.
Zarefsky, D. and V. J. Gallagher. 1990. From "conflict" to "constitutional question": Transformations in early American public discourse. *Quarterly Journal of Speech* 76:247-261.

PAPERS

Herbeck, D. A. 1984. Paradigms of legal thought: The rise and fall of the substantive due process doctrine. Paper presented at the meeting of the Speech Communication Association, November, Chicago.
Lindsey, J. J. 1985. Argumentation in *Miranda v. Arizona*. Paper presented at the meeting of the Speech Communication Association, November, Denver.

NEWSPAPERS AND MAGAZINES

ACLU backs Lord over Robins. 1984. *St. Paul Dispatch*, 7 August, p. 7C.
A. H. Robins chiefs agree not to block merger that could prevent bankruptcy. 1987. *Minneapolis Star and Tribune*, 3 October, p. 11B. Reprinted from *Washington Post*.
A. H. Robins hauls a judge into court. 1984. *Business Week*, 16 July, pp. 27-28.
Abortion hearing put off; Judge won't sit. 1974. *Minneapolis Star*, 28 March, p. 15B1.
Ackerberg, P. 1977. Judge Lord opinion: HUD "arrogant" on new town. *Minneapolis Star*, 13 July, p. 1B.
———. 1982. Just the facts. *Minneapolis Star*, 16 February, p. 11A.
Agreement backed in antitrust pact. 1973. *New York Times*, 27 September, p. 58.
Anderson, D. 1984. Judge Lord considers retiring, says Robins case not a factor. *Minneapolis Star and Tribune*, 25 July, pp. 1A, 10A.
Anderson, D. 1984a. Robins Co. lawyers fail in bid to halt IUD trial, oust Lord. *Minneapolis Star and Tribune*, 10 February, pp. 1B, 16B.
———. 1984b. Lord scolds Robins as 7 Dalkon suits settled. *Minneapolis Star and Tribune*, 1 March, pp. 1A, 8A.

Appelman, A. 1988. Robins reorganizing OK'd. *St. Paul Pioneer Press Dispatch*, 27 July, p. 9C.

Are judges too powerful? 1978. *Minneapolis Tribune*, 15 February, p. 13A. Reprinted from *U.S. News and World Report.*

Arguments on Judge Lord set. 1975. *Minneapolis Star*, 10 December, p. 2A.

Armed guards protect Judge Lord after call. 1979. *Minneapolis Star*, 10 April, p. 3A.

Armour, S. 1989. Miles Lord appeals to regents for reform. *Minnesota Daily*, 14 July, pp. 1, 3.

Associated Press. 1973a. Judge orders U.S. to reinstate Minnesota crop disaster loans. *New York Times*, 21 March, p. 23.

———. 1973b. Five drug concerns agree to pay $36-million to 6 states in suit. *New York Times*, 18 October, p. 50.

———. 1974a. Lord to interrupt Reserve trial. *Minneapolis Star*, 31 January, p. 7A.

———. 1974b. Disposal of waste on land foreseen. *New York Times*, 9 February, p. 32.

———. 1974c. Actor is released after 28 months in draft evasion. *New York Times*, 16 February, p. 34.

———. 1974d. Lake Superior town dismayed by ban on polluting ore plant. *New York Times*, 22 April, p. 70.

———. 1974e. Judge cites safety factor in Reserve Mining decision. *New York Times*, 13 May, p. 34.

———. 1974f. Reserve Mining permitted to continue lake dumping. *New York Times*, 15 June, p. 10.

———. 1974g. Reserve Mining granted delay in filing of proposal. *New York Times*, 17 June, p. 26.

———. 1974h. Ore waste hearing put off. *New York Times*, 18 June, p. 33.

———. 1974i. Court again backs dumping of iron ore. *New York Times*, 29 August, p. 29.

———. 1974j. Reserve Mining curb by higher court urged. *New York Times*, 8 October, p. 16.

———. 1974k. A U.S. judge scores tailings dump site. *New York Times*, 6 November, p. 90.

———. 1974m. Reserve Mining plea calls judge biased. *New York Times*, 17 November, p. 53.

———. 1974l. Reserve's parent firms call Judge Lord biased. *Minneapolis Tribune*, 17 November, p. 13B.

———. 1975a. Three states urge high court to close a taconite plant. *New York Times*, 6 March, p. 35.

———. 1975b. Judge withdraws from Reserve case. *New York Times*, 16 March, p. 64.

———. 1975c. E. P. A. panel to aid Minnesota clean-up. *New York Times*, 27 March, p. 34.

———. 1976a. No appeal expected in removal of Lord. *Minneapolis Star*, 10 January, p. 2A.

———. 1976b. Insurers accept antibiotic settlement. *New York Times*, 24 March, p. 55.

———. 1976c. Judge Lord kept on bank robbery trial. *Minneapolis Star*, 1 May, p. 7A.

———. 1976d. Reserve Mining fined $1 million in pollution case. *New York Times*, 5 May, p. 35.

———. 1976e. Appeals court will get text of Lord criticism. *Minneapolis Star*, 8 May, p. 7A.

———. 1976f. Prison gets week to improve conditions. *Minneapolis Star*, 28 May, p. 4B.

———. 1976g. Mistrial is declared in drug-maker suit. *New York Times*, 18 August, pp. 55, 64.

———. 1976h. Court-ordered halt in putting taconite into lake is upheld. *New York Times*, 29 October, p. 16.

———. 1977. Judge says HUD acted arrogantly. *Minneapolis Tribune*, 14 July, p. 8A.

———. 1979. Lord rejects land price unit for Voyageurs. *Minneapolis Tribune*, 22 June, pp. 2B, 4B.

———. 1980. U.S. Steel fined $3.5 million in suit. *New York Times*, 25 January, p. 4.

———. 1981. Lord: Corporations hid behind their anonymity in terms of pollution. *Minneapolis Tribune*, 9 April, p. 16B.

———. 1982a. Minnesota player retains eligibility. *New York Times*, 4 January, p. C11.

———. 1982b. Award upheld on Johnson. *New York Times*, 16 April, p. D11.

———. 1983. Court reverses Lord's hiring rule. *Minneapolis Star and Tribune*, 5 May, p. 19B.

———. 1984a. Lord says court can't act on his Robins remarks. *Minneapolis Star and Tribune*, 17 June, p. 9B.

———. 1984b. Trial lawyers will honor Lord for "long, distinguished career." *Minneapolis Star and Tribune*, 22 July, p. 10B.

———. 1984c. Ex-Robins attorney tells court he burned Dalkon Shield files. *St. Paul Dispatch*, 31 July, p. 9C.

———. 1984d. Robins board 'incredulous' at testimony. *St. Paul Dispatch*, 16 August, p. 8C.

———. 1984e. U.S. court demands 6 Dalkon Shield studies. *St. Paul Dispatch*, 20 September, p. 7C.

———. 1984f. Judge rebuked over remark. *New York Times*, 3 November, p. 46.

———. 1984g. Panel dismisses action against federal judge. *New York Times*, 27 December, p. A14.

———. 1985a. Judge Lord orders U.S. to reconsider benefit cuts. *Minneapolis Star and Tribune*, 16 April, p. 13B.

———. 1985b. Dalkon campaign to go overseas. *Minneapolis Star and Tribune*, 24 December, p. 7B.

———. 1986. Federal jury studying maker of contraceptive. *New York Times*, 21 November, p. 10Y.

———. 1987a. Judge gives A. H. Robins three weeks to hand over reorganization proposal. *Minneapolis Star and Tribune*, 14 January, p. 3M.

———. 1987b. Lawyers in Dalkon case want some secrets kept. *Minneapolis Star and Tribune*, 3 September, p. 11B.

———. 1987c. Dalkon settlement is $2.5 billion. *Star Tribune*, 12 December, pp. 5B, 9B.

———. 1988a. A. H. Robins selects Sanofi as merger partner. *Minneapolis Star Tribune*, 2 January, pp. 5B, 6B.

———. 1988b. Attorney to fight merger of A. H. Robins. *Minneapolis Star Tribune*, 3 January, p. 2A.

———. 1988c Shareholder group may block Robins merger. *Minneapolis Star Tribune*, 5 January, p. 2D.

———. 1988d. Two Robins suitors defer to American Home's Bid. *Minneapolis Star Tribune*, 21 January, p. 3D.

———. 1989. Bankruptcy reorganization approved for A. H. Robins. *Minneapolis Star Tribune*, 17 June, p. 13A.

Assuming the robes of power. 1987. *Minneapolis Star and Tribune*, 22 May, p. 3B.

At the Capitol. 1976. *Minneapolis Tribune*, 21 February, p. 5B.

Athletes and academic integrity at "U." 1982. *Minneapolis Tribune*, 11 January, p. 12A.

Berg, S. and D. Stone. 1976. The Lord of federal court and his life of "intrigue." *Minneapolis Tribune*, 9 December, pp. 1C, 8C, 9C.

Berkowitz, B. D. 1985. Justice with a spin on it. *National Review*, 9 August, pp. 35-36.

[The] Best and the worst federal judges. 1980. *The American lawyer*, July, pp. 16-30.

Bjerregaard, K. 1984. Ex-attorneys general debate Lord's courtroom behavior. *Minnesota Daily*, 11 July, p. 1.

Boschwitz backs off on product liability bill. 1984. *St. Paul Dispatch*, 16 August, pp. 1A, 4A.

Briefly. 1975. *Minneapolis Star*, 18 December, p. 2A.

Brody, J. E. 1974. Court bids company end dumping in Lake Superior. *New York Times*, 10 February, p. 39.

Brown, T. 1976. Lord calls Reserve aid plan "bribe." *Minneapolis Star*, 11 June, p. 17A.

Carideo, A. 1985. Firms must be more responsible, Judge Lord says. *Minneapolis Star and Tribune*, 29 April, p. 3B.

Carman, J. 1975. Reserve ruling criticized. *Minneapolis Star*, 15 March, pp. 1A, 6A.

Carr, D. 1984. Dalkon Shield: Robins faces burning issue. *Twin Cities Reader*, 8-14 August, pp. 4, 5.

———. 1990. Heaven can wait. *Minnesota Monthly*, January, pp. 23-29.

Cassano, D. 1973a. Judge Lord orders U.S. to produce prisoner. *Minneapolis Tribune*, 15 November, pp. 1A, 4A.

———. 1973b. Judge schedules hearing on authority over prisoner. *Minneapolis Tribune*, 16 November, p. 9C.

City bank wins Cuba-loan case. 1972. *New York Times*, 8 June, pp. 69, 72.

Classic conflict: Lake's pollution vs. "progress," editorial. 1974. *New York Times*, 28 April, p. 2.

Cohen, D. 1981. Lord's shot at corporations went astray, editorial. *Minneapolis Star*, 28 December, p. 8A.

Company is ordered to shift waste plan. 1974. *New York Times*, 6 February, p. 34.

Court bids Reserve Mining Co. end pollution of air and lake. 1975. *New York Times*, 15 March, p. 30.

Court to permit pollution by ore in Lake Superior. 1974. *New York Times*, 5 June, pp. 1, 26.

Dalkon claimants' group decries plan. 1988. *Minneapolis Star Tribune*, 3 May, p. 2D. Reprinted from *New York Times*.

Dalkon Shield maker to pay $15 million for fertility claims. 1987. *Minneapolis Star and Tribune*, 3 October, p. 3A. Reprinted from *Washington Post*.

Dalkon Shield victims told of options. 1990. *Minneapolis Star Tribune*, 18 March, p. 13A. Reprinted from *Los Angeles Times*.

[The] Danger of Judge Lord's misplaced anger, editorial. 1984. *Minneapolis Star and Tribune*, 11 November, p. 30A.

Dawson, G. 1984a. Ex-Dalkon lawyer alleges "fraud" acts. *St. Paul Dispatch*, 1 August, pp. 1A, 4A.

———. 1984b. Lawyer softens Dalkon testimony. *St. Paul Dispatch*, 3 August, p. 9B.

Decision to fight Dalkon case finally pays off. 1989. *Minneapolis Star Tribune*, 7 November, p. 8A.

Diaz, K. 1985. Lord moves into union's corner in Hormel fight. *Minneapolis Star and Tribune*, 23 December, pp. 1A, 4A.

Doliner, F. R. 1976. Furious at Lord's removal, letter to the editor. *Minneapolis Star*, 14 January, p. 14A.

Dornfeld, S. 1976. Judge: Politicians should not give aid to Reserve Mining. *Minneapolis Tribune*, 22 September, p. 2B.

Dornfeld, S. and D. Rebuffoni. 1975. Judge Lord says he won't "rule out" running for Senate. *Minneapolis Tribune*, 3 September, pp. 1B, 2B.

Dowie, M. and T. Johnston. 1976. A case of corporate malpractice. *Mother Jones*, November, pp. 36-39, 46-50.

Escaped patient charged. 1979. *Minneapolis Star*, 13 April, p. 3A.

Estimate on safe water. 1974. *New York Times*, 30 March, p. 28.

Farrell, W. E. 1974a. Trial on the discharge of ore wastes into Lake Superior is nearing completion. *New York Times*, 19 March, p. 18.

———. 1974b. Lake Superior ore plant ordered shut as polluter. *New York Times*, 21 April, pp. 1, 37.

———. 1974c. Ore company employees back on job, but uncertain. *New York Times*, 24 April, p. 26.

———. 1976. Long Reserve Mining dispute is far from resolved. *New York Times*, 3 February, p. 13.

[The] Federal judge who was ousted in the Reserve Mining Case. 1976. *New York Times*, 8 January, p. 24.

Foley, E. 1985. Judge hints he'll strike down Fridley law. *Minneapolis Star and Tribune*, 1 March, p. 6B.

Food stamp fund freed by judge. 1974. *New York Times*, 14 October, p. 19.

For Lord it's a highlight. 1981. *Minneapolis Star*, 29 July, p. 11A.

Fuller, J. 1973. NSP ordered to postpone mailing proxy statements. *Minneapolis Tribune*, 13 April, pp. 1A, 5A.

Furst, R. 1985. Well-wishers' verdict was unanimous: U.S. District Judge Lord will be missed. *Minneapolis Star and Tribune*, 27 August, p. 3B.

Furst, R., D. Peterson, and D. E. Gonzalez. 1984. Dalkon plaintiffs say money can't erase their pain. *Minneapolis Star and Tribune*, 16 November, p. 1A, 7A.

George, J. 1984. Dalkon firm says Lord abused office. *St. Paul Dispatch*, 15 May, pp. 1A, 4A.

Gladwell, M. 1989. Lawyer prolongs Dalkon Shield case in crusade against Robins officials. *Minneapolis Star Tribune*, 24 September, p. 12A.

Greene, W. 1974. Life vs. livelihood. *New York Times Magazine*, 24 November, pp. 17, 95, 96, 98, 99, 104, 106.

Grow, D. 1985. This time, Lord returns to ring for honors. *Minneapolis Star and Tribune*, 25 August, pp. 1C, 16C.

Hage, D. 1985. Personnel managers get an earful of Miles Lord. *Minneapolis Star and Tribune*, 17 September, pp. 7B, 11B.

Hamburger, T. 1992. Court limits citizen suits challenging policies on environment. *Minneapolis Star Tribune*, 13 June, pp. 1A, 9A.

High court denies plea on pollution. 1974. *New York Times*, 11 July, p. 9.

Hill, G. 1974a. E. P. A. acts to halt dumping in lake. *New York Times*, 30 March, p. 28.

———. 1974b. Three states ask court to halt dumping in Lake Superior. *New York Times*, 2 October, p. 50.

Hodowanic, J. 1982. Judge Lord's ruling encourages colleges to flout principles of higher education, editorial. *Minneapolis Star*, 7 January, p. 8A.

Hopfensperger, J. 1991. Patients say doctor's AIDS is like 'Russian roulette.' *Minneapolis Star and Tribune*, 18 June, pp. 1A, 6A.

Hurst, R. 1959a. Court calls Lord on DST action. *Minneapolis Morning Tribune*, 26 May, pp. 1, 7.

———. 1959b. High court plans action against Lord. *Minneapolis Morning Tribune*, 28 May, pp. 1, 11.

———. 1959c. High court issues strong censure of Lord in DST case. *Minneapolis Morning Tribune*, 29 May, pp. 1, 7.

[An] Institution called Miles Lord, editorial. 1985. *Minneapolis Star and Tribune*, 21 May, p. 14A.

IRs protest Judge Lord's Humphrey endorsement. 1982. *Minneapolis Star and Tribune*, 7 July, p. 4C.

IUD witness indicted for perjury. 1988. *Minneapolis Star Tribune*, 4 March, p. 1A. Reprinted from *New York Times*.

Johnson, C. 1985. Complaints against Judge Lord dismissed. *Minneapolis Star and Tribune*, 25 January, pp. 1B, 2B.

Johnson, M. 1976. Lord had guts, letter to the editor. *Minneapolis Star*, 14 January, p. 14A.

Judge called one of the worst. 1980. *Minneapolis Star*, 20 June, p. 15A.

Judge delays date of evictions from townhouse complex. 1976. *Minneapolis Star*, 11 June, p. 2A.

Judge holds Robins executive in contempt in bankruptcy case. 1987. *Minneapolis Star and Tribune*, 3 October, p. 11B. Reprinted from *Washington Post*.

Judge in Reserve Mining trial fighting disqualification move. 1975. *New York Times*, 20 December, p. 28.

Judge is removed over dumping ban. 1976. *New York Times*, 7 January, pp. 1, 9.

Judge Lord criticizes top appeals justice. 1984. *Minneapolis Star and Tribune*, 12 November, p. 1B.

Judge Lord orders change in AFDC eligibility rules. 1985. *Minneapolis Star and Tribune*, 31 March, p. 21A.

Judge Lord protests valuation on his home. 1975. *Minneapolis Tribune*, 21 September, pp. 1A, 12A.

Judge Lord rebuked. 1978. *Minneapolis Star*, 15 November, p. 3A.

Judge Lord to address attorneys general unit. 1976. *Minneapolis Tribune*, 27 February, p. 7C.

Judge Lord to speak. 1976. *Minneapolis Tribune*, 29 September, p. 5B.

Judge Lord to speak about "human power" at college symposium. 1976. *Minneapolis Star*, 20 September, p. 10A.

Judge Lord tours proposed disposal site. 1974. *Minneapolis Tribune*, 13 July, p. 11A.

Judge Lord was right, editorial. 1976. *New York Times*, 9 June, p. 38.

Judge Lord will address state Council of Churches. 1981. *Minneapolis Star*, 13 November, p. 10A.

Judge Lord's sense of propriety, editorial. 1974. *Minneapolis Star*, 20 March, p. 10A.

Judge overturns bankruptcy law. 1982. *Minneapolis Star and Tribune*, 16 April, p. 9C.

Judge pops for soft drinks, gets calm court. 1973. *Minneapolis Tribune*, 26 April, p. 6B.

Judge refuses to halt sale of book that is subject of reporter's suit. 1985. *Minneapolis Star and Tribune*, 29 August, p. 3B.

Judge takes stock of wife to stay on NSP case. 1973. *Minneapolis Tribune*, 13 April, p. 1A.

Judge to rule on logging. 1974. *Minneapolis Tribune*, 6 September, p. 14B.

Judge under guard following call. 1979. *Minneapolis Tribune*, 10 April, pp. 1B, 8B.

Judge's decision makes it certain: It's Lake Inferior, editorial. 1974. *New York Times*, 9 June, p. 2.

Justice Department joins plea on dumping in lake. 1974. *New York Times*, 5 October, p. 34.

Kaszaba, M. 1984. Lawyers criticize probe of Miles Lord. *Minneapolis Star and Tribune*, 4 July, p. 4B.

Kimball, J. 1978. Area judges confront the same dilemma. *Minneapolis Tribune*, 15 February, p. 13A.

Klobuchar, J. 1974a. The siege in Miles' courtroom. *Minneapolis Star*, 28 March, p. 1B.

———. 1974b. Miles Lord, judicial godfather to troubled environment. *Minneapolis Star*, 9 December, pp. 1B, 6B.

———. 1976a. Land of 67,000 tons—A new slogan. *Minneapolis Star*, 13 January, p. 1B.

———. 1976b. Reserve reactivates a villain. *Minneapolis Star*, 8 May, p. 9A.

———. 1978. Miles Lord returns to his ore dust. *Minneapolis Star*, 6 July, p. 1B.

———. 1979. Our Miles Lord discovers dignity. *Minneapolis Star*, 4 May, pp. 1C, 2C.

———. 1980a. A tree attacks the judge. *Minneapolis Star*, 29 January, pp. 1C, 2C.

———. 1980b. Gunsmoke in Miles' corral *Minneapolis Star*, 25 July, pp. 1C, 5C.

———. 1981. Justice overtakes Judge Lord. *Minneapolis Star*, 20 July, pp. 1B, 4B.

———. 1982. Friendly persuasion became federal case of bad judgment. *Minneapolis Star and Tribune*, 7 April, pp. 1C, 5C.

———. 1983a. Will Judge Lord someday spear dragons as a lawyer? *Minneapolis Star and Tribune*, 18 April, pp. 1B, 2B.

———. 1983b. Jim Klobuchar. *Minneapolis Star and Tribune*, 22 September, pp. 1B, 6B.

———. 1984. Jim Klobuchar. *Minneapolis Star and Tribune*, 10 November, pp. 1B, 3B.

———. 1985. He was hammy, gutsy, a pain and morally right—thanks, Miles Lord. *Minneapolis Star and Tribune*, 21 May, pp. 1B, 2B.

———. 1986. Lord's off the bench and into the fray. *Minneapolis Star and Tribune*, 14 January, p. 1B.

Lawrence, D. 1985. Look beyond the law to examine the motives of protesters. *Minneapolis Star and Tribune*, 11 January, p. 15A.

Lewin, T. 1988. New threat to A. H. Robins's plan. *New York Times*, 3 May, pp. 29Y, 34Y.

Lofstrand, W. S. 1976. Let's move at Lord's speed, letter to the editor. *Minneapolis Star*, 14 January, p. 14A.

Lord announces his retirement, says he'll enter private practice. 1985. *Minneapolis Star and Tribune*, 23 August, p. 3B.

Lord backs trademark for Jeno's. 1985. *Minneapolis Star and Tribune*, 24 July, p. 1M.

Lord delays decision on lake dredging. 1976. *Minneapolis Tribune*, 16 November, p. 8B.

Lord, M. 1986. Don't rob consumers of their best defense, editorial. *Minneapolis Star and Tribune*, 7 September, p. 23M.

Lord rejects honor dinner. 1976. *Minneapolis Star*, 23 January, p. 7B.

Lord removal hearing today. 1975. *Minneapolis Star*, 18 December, p. 2A.

Lord removed; Health issue remains, editorial. 1976. *Minneapolis Tribune*, 8 January, p. 8A.

Lord to stay on bench with senior status. 1985. *Minneapolis Star and Tribune*, 2 July, p. 6D.

Lord transfers FTC cases, citing overload. 1982. *Minneapolis Star and Tribune*, 6 October, p. 7B.

Lundegaard, B. 1972. Judge Lord is rebuked by appeals court panel. *Minneapolis Tribune*, 11 March, p. 5B.

Mack, M. 1984. Lord remarks in Dalkon trial stricken. *Minneapolis Star and Tribune*, 3 November, pp. 1A, 16A.

Many firms fail to turn over data, Lord says. 1984. *Minneapolis Star and Tribune*, 20 November, p. 14B.

Marcotty, J. 1984a. Lord lecture called "mild punishment." *Minneapolis Star and Tribune*, 7 July, p. 1B.

———. 1984b. Attention focuses on review of Lord. *Minneapolis Star and Tribune*, 9 July, pp. 1B, 5B.

———. 1984c. Legal experts testify reprimand of Lord would seriously harm judiciary. *Minneapolis Star and Tribune*, 10 July, pp. 1A, 12A.

———. 1984d. Judges challenge attorneys at Lord's hearing. *Minneapolis Star and Tribune*, 11 July, pp. 1B, 12B.

———. 1984e. Lord hearing halted until appeal heard. *Minneapolis Star and Tribune*, 12 July, pp. 1B, 7B.

———. 1984f. Suit says Dalkon Shield caused premature births, birth defects. *Minneapolis Star and Tribune*, 1 August, pp. 1B, 5B.

Margaret Morris. 1975. *Minneapolis Tribune*, 29 August, p. 3B.

Mark Hall, editorial. 1982. *Minnesota Daily*, 4 January, p. 4.

Maybe Judge Lord should quit. 1977. *Minneapolis Tribune*, 22 April, p. 6A. Editorial reprinted from Rochester, MN, *Post Bulletin*.

McAuliffe, B. 1986. Miles Lord recalls cases that made him people's hero, corporate scourge. *Minneapolis Star and Tribune*, 7 January, pp. 3B, 12B.

McCabe, M. 1975a. Governor backs Lord on Reserve tailings case. *Minneapolis Star*, 21 November, pp. 1A, 10A.

———. 1975b. Lord defends Reserve-case actions. *Minneapolis Star*, 19 December, pp. 1A, 4A.

———. 1976. Lord delays trial on removal motion. *Minneapolis Star*, 1 May, p. 16A.

McCarthy, C. 1984. Judge Lord's beautiful anger penetrates the corporate shield, editorial. *Minneapolis Star and Tribune*, 3 April, p. 10A.

———. 1985. Vindication for Judge Lord, editorial. *Minneapolis Star and Tribune*, 6 January, p. 14A.

McEnroe, P. 1983. File prompts Bouza, Lord to question Meshbesher conduct. *Minneapolis Star and Tribune*, 16 September, pp. 1A, 10A.

———. 1985. Miles Lord resigns as judge. *Minneapolis Star and Tribune*, 20 May, pp. 1A, 6A, 7A.

Merritt, G. J. 1990. Reserve Mining. *Minneapolis Star and Tribune*, 10 September, p. 12A.

[The] Miles Lord appointment, editorial. 1966. *Minneapolis Star*, 11 February, p. 14.

Miles Lord leaves federal bench. 1985. *Minneapolis Star and Tribune*, 12 September, p. 3B.

Miles Lord named to judicial advisory board. 1989. *Minneapolis Star Tribune*, 18 July, p. 3Bw.

Miles Lord's speech in the cause of justice, editorial. 1984. *Minneapolis Star and Tribune*, 18 May, p. 22A.

Minnesota communities asked to filter water. 1974. *New York Times*, 25 March, p. 46.

Nelson, D. and R. Furst. 1982. Judge halts dredging of river until dumping dispute settled. *Minneapolis Star and Tribune*, 28 July, pp. 1C, 4C.

Newlund, S. 1981a. Some to be put back on welfare. *Minneapolis Tribune*, 23 October, pp. 1A, 7A.

———. 1981b. Court stays Lord's welfare injunctions. *Minneapolis Tribune*, 11 November, pp. 1A, 8A.

———. 1982. Christmas with the Lords judged an utter delight. *Minneapolis Star and Tribune*, 24 November, p. 6T.

News Services. 1982. High court affirms Lord bankruptcy ruling. *Minneapolis Star and Tribune*, 29 June, pp. 5C, 10C.

———. 1989. Dalkon Shield settlement is upheld. *Minneapolis Star and Tribune*, 7 November, pp. 1A, 8A.

Now let's get moving, editorial. 1976. *Minneapolis Star*, 8 January, p. 6A.

Nygaard, C. H. 1966. Miles Lord thought good appointment, letter to the editor. *Minneapolis Tribune*, 15 February, p. 4.

Oakes, L. 1991. Union, Armco settle benefits case; ex-workers to split millions. *Minneapolis Star Tribune*, 10 September, p. 5B.

Oberdorfer, D. 1984a. Maker of Dalkon Shield lodges complaints against Judge Lord. *Minneapolis Star and Tribune*, 15 May, pp. 1A, 8A.

———. 1984b. Court panel hears testimony on firm's complaint against Lord. *Minneapolis Star and Tribune*, 15 September, p. 13A.

———. 1984c. Judge Lord assails "warmongers," gives suspended sentences to Sperry protesters. *Minneapolis Star and Tribune*, 9 November, pp. 1A, 10A.

———. 1984d. Robins complaints against Lord dismissed. *Minneapolis Star and Tribune*, 27 December, p. 1B.

———. 1985. The tangled saga of the Dalkon Shield/The final chapter. *Minneapolis Star and Tribune*, 15 September, pp. 1A, 10A.

———. 1987. Miles Lord happily switches from arbiter to advocate. *Minneapolis Star and Tribune*, 2 April, p. 1A, 10A, 11A, 12A.

Oslund, J. J. 1984. Is Lord antibusiness? *Minneapolis Star and Tribune*, 25 November, pp. 1A, 4A, 6A.

Panzer, U. 1985. Judges too often take revenge on those who question state, editorial. *Minneapolis Star and Tribune*, 11 January, p. 15A.

Parry, K. 1987. Circuit court takes parting shot at Lord. *Minneapolis Star and Tribune*, 3 April, pp. 1B, 2B.

Parsons, J. 1966a. Miles Lord nominated as U.S. judge. *Minneapolis Tribune*, 11 February, pp. 1, 6

———. 1966b. Miles Lord sworn in as federal judge. *Minneapolis Tribune*, 3 May, p. 1.

———. 1973. Judge Lord asks OEO, AIM to resolve dispute over funds for Indian schools. *Minneapolis Tribune*, 26 April, p. 6B.

———. 1984. Lord orders federal disability payments be reinstated. *Minneapolis Star and Tribune*, 28 April, pp. 1A, 8A.

———. 1987. Lawyers criticize proposal to handle Dalkon lawsuits. *Minneapolis Star and Tribune*, 29 April, p. 7B.

Perry, S. 1988. New contraceptive sparks memory of IUD's tragic history. *Minneapolis Star and Tribune*, 22 January, p. 15A.

Peterson, D. 1979. Miles Lord raps gavel on merit plan. *Minneapolis Star*, 27 February, pp. 1B, 4B.

——— 1980a. Sideline move keeps judge from "late hit." *Minneapolis Star*, 19 February, pp. 1A, 9A.

———. 1980b. Judge rules felon's tale of breaking leg untrue. *Minneapolis Star*, 21 March, pp. 1A, 8A.

———. 1980c. Lord scolds attorney for "unethical" conduct. *Minneapolis Star*, 20 June, p. 12A.

———. 1984. A. H. Robins to pay nearly $40 million in Dalkon Shield case. *Minneapolis Star and Tribune*, 15 November, pp. 1A, 7A.

Pfizer and others make a settlement in antibiotic suit. 1975. *New York Times*, 15 August, p. 49.

Phelps, D. 1987. Doty off to fast start at hearing. *Minneapolis Star and Tribune*, 2 April, p. 3A.

Phelps, D. and D. Oberdorfer. 1984. Court backs Judge Lord; NRA must list contributors. *Minneapolis Star and Tribune*, 14 November, pp. 3B, 15B.

Picone, L. 1975. Judge Lord orders permanent halt of logging in BWCA. *Minneapolis Tribune*, 14 August, pp. 1A, 4A.

[A] Plague of problems. 1974. *Forbes*, 15 August, p. 35.

Poll shows approval of Judge Miles Lord. 1976. *Minneapolis Tribune*, 11 April, p. 11A.

Pollution with Reserve, editorial. 1974. *New York Times*, 25 February, p. 26.

Rebuffoni, D. 1974a. Judge Lord to suggest fiber filtering. *Minneapolis Tribune*, 21 March, pp. 1B, 2B.

———. 1974b. Judge won't hear abortion-law suit. *Minneapolis Tribune*, 29 March, p. 4B.

———. 1974c. Lord studies Palisade Creek site. *Minneapolis Tribune*, 14 July, pp. 1B, 9B.

———. 1974d. Judge says high court may settle Reserve. *Minneapolis Tribune*, 16 July, pp. 1A, 14A.

———. 1974e. Lord asks if tailings can go into mines. *Minneapolis Tribune*, 17 July, pp. 1B, 10B.

———. 1974f. Lord doubts ruling's fate in U.S. high court. *Minneapolis Tribune*, 19 July, p. 2B.

———. 1974g. Lord indicates strong disfavor of creek site. *Minneapolis Tribune*, 24 July, pp. 1B, 2B.

———. 1974h. Lord to advise appeals court on site plan this week. *Minneapolis Tribune*, 30 July, p. 5B.

———. 1974i. Lord urges court reject Palisades discharge site. *Minneapolis Tribune*, 4 August, pp. 1A, 4A.

———. 1974j. MPIRG asks Judge Lord prevent logging in BWCA. *Minneapolis Tribune*, 20 August, p. 10B.

———. 1974k. Panel asks Lord find how tailings affect lake. *Minneapolis Tribune*, 20 August, pp. 1A, 10A.

———. 1974l. Lord will retain jurisdiction in key Reserve case issues. *Minneapolis Tribune*, 5 November, pp. 1B, 2B.

———. 1975a. Lord ordered out of Reserve talks. *Minneapolis Tribune*, 9 April, pp. 1A, 6A.

———. 1975b. Lord says officials ignore rulings, please Reserve. *Minneapolis Tribune*, 1 August, pp. 1B, 2B.

———. 1975c. Lord, Anderson at odds on Reserve. *Minneapolis Tribune*, 19 November, pp. 1A, 4A

———. 1975d. Appeals court tells Lord to halt further Reserve hearings. *Minneapolis Tribune*, 21 November, pp. 1A, 15A.

———. 1975e. Anderson denies being "cozy" with Reserve, rift with Lord. *Minneapolis Tribune*, 22 November, p. 1A.

———. 1975f. Judges to hear bid to take case from Lord. *Minneapolis Tribune*, 11 December, p. 11B.

———. 1975g. State asks court keep Lord over fiber case. *Minneapolis Tribune*, 18 December, pp. 1A, 16A.

———. 1975h. Judge Lord faces appeals court. *Minneapolis Tribune*, 19 December, pp. 1A, 10A.

———. 1976a. Appeals court will consider another Lord decision. *Minneapolis Tribune*, 8 February, pp. 1B, 5B.

———. 1976b. Reserve seeks more time. *Minneapolis Tribune*, 14 October, pp. 1B, 2B.

———. 1980a. Judge Lord takes over 3 BWCA lawsuits. *Minneapolis Tribune*, 18 April, pp. 1B, 4B.

———. 1980b. Judge lets cameras roll for "history." *Minneapolis Tribune*, 25 July, p. 4A.

———. 1980c. Lord dismisses 3 BWCA lawsuits. *Minneapolis Tribune*, 25 July, pp. 1A, 4A.

———. 1984. Judge Lord bans trapping of wolves. *Minneapolis Star and Tribune*, 6 January, pp. 1A, 4A.

———. 1985. Judge Lord's decision blocking wolf trapping upheld by appeals court. *Minneapolis Star and Tribune*, 20 February, pp. 1A, 6A.

Rebuffoni, D. and L. Picone. 1975. Judge Lord considers leaving U. S. bench. *Minneapolis Tribune*, 6 August, pp. 1B, 2B.

[The] Reserve scandal, editorial. 1976. *New York Times*, 10 January, p. 24.

Robins plans merger; Dalkon victims disapprove. 1987. *Minneapolis Star and Tribune*, 4 July, p. 9B. Reprinted from *New York Times*.

Robins top 2 executives to give to fund for victims. 1988. *Minneapolis Star and Tribune*, 3 February, p. 2D. Reprinted from *New York Times*.

Sandler, L. 1987. Some Robins holders are seen awaiting rival suitors to better American Home's bid. *Wall Street Journal*, 6 February, p. 20.

Savage, D. G. 1989. U.S. law, society reflect Brennan's vision. *Minneapolis Star Tribune*, 2 October, p. 2A.

———. 1992. Experts detect Supreme Court tilting toward executive branch. *Minneapolis Star Tribune*, 15 June, p. 7A.

Schwadel, F. 1985. Robins files for protection of Chapter 11. *Wall Street Journal*, 22 August, p. 3.

Seifert, J. J. 1986. Miles Lord's skewed view of the world and the law, editorial. *Minneapolis Star and Tribune*, 20 April, p. 19A.

Serrill, M. S. 1984. A panel tries to judge a judge. *Time*, 23 July, p. 88.

Shenon, P. 1988. Professor is charged with lying for maker of birth control device. *New York Times*, 4 March, p. 1.

Shoop, J. 1975. Governor says he'll inspect tailings site. *Minneapolis Star*, 18 March, pp. 1A, 4A.

Showdown at Superior, editorial. 1974. *New York Times*, 28 April, p. 20.

Silar, J. F. 1988. Tenacity, precision make Ciresi tops in torts. *St. Paul Pioneer Press Dispatch*, 10 October, p. 8.

Smith, M. L. 1989. "U" women still are fighting bias. *Minneapolis Star Tribune*, 31 July, pp. 1A, 8A.

Social conscience in Reserve case, editorial. 1974. *Minneapolis Tribune*, 12 July, p. 10A.

Stone, D. 1976a. Lord declines dinner in his honor. *Minneapolis Tribune*, 23 January, p. 4B.

———. 1976b. Appeals court tells Lord to complete action in drug case. *Minneapolis Tribune*, 3 August, p. 2B.

———. 1976c. Mistrial declared in antitrust suit. *Minneapolis Tribune*, 17 August, pp. 1A, 8A.
———. 1979a. Lord removes himself from Upper Great Lakes trial. *Minneapolis Tribune*, 22 June, p. 2B.
———. 1979b. Lord removes self from Piper retrial. *Minneapolis Tribune*, 6 July, pp. 1B, 5B.
———. 1980. Survey calls Lord one of 11 "worst" federal judges. *Minneapolis Tribune*, 26 June, pp. 1B, 5B.
———. 1981. U.S. lawyers select Lord as top trial judge. *Minneapolis Tribune*, 18 July, pp. 1A, 5A.
Strick, S. 1974a. Lord thinks cancer, tailings tied. *Minneapolis Star*, 22 March, p. 5A.
———. 1974b. Reserve chief lauds judge's idea to part water, tailings. *Minneapolis Star*, 30 March, pp. 1A, 2A.
Sturdevant, L. 1976. Judge to teach ethics from lectern, bench. *Minneapolis Tribune*, 12 July, p. 1B.
———. 1984. Boschwitz pulls his name off product-liability bill. *Minneapolis Star and Tribune*, 16 August, pp. 1A, 9A.
Superior, private dump? editorial. 1974. *New York Times*, 7 July, p. 14.
Swearing in is a family affair. 1981. *Minneapolis Star*, 25 November, p. 11A.
Tai, W. S. 1984. IUD firm spending $4 million on ad effort. *Minneapolis Star and Tribune*, 15 November, p. 7A.
Thorkelson, W. 1976. ALC district backs equality amendment. *Minneapolis Star*, 3 April, p. 10A.
———. 1981. Judge Lord urges corporations to mend sinful ways. *Minneapolis Star*, 20 November, p. 10A.
Trial lawyers to honor Lord. 1976. *Minneapolis Star*, 22 January, p. 9A.
Try it—It may be safe, editorial. 1974. *New York Times*, 4 October, p. 38.
Tubert, J. 1985. Civil suit challenging Fridley's prostitution ordinance dismissed. *Minneapolis Star and Tribune*, 25 July, p. 5B.
———. 1986. Keller, Reagan and industry not without warts, sayeth Lord. *Minneapolis Star and Tribune*, 9 April, pp. 3B, 8B.
$2.3 billion in Dalkon fund unclaimed. 1990. *Minneapolis Star Tribune*, 23 August, p. 1D.
United Press International. 1974a. Panel overturns taconite closing. *New York Times*, 23 April, p. 55.
———. 1974b. High court rejects antipollution plea. *New York Times*, 13 October, p. 92.
———. 1975. Judge is criticized by Appeals Court on lakes hearing. *New York Times*, 9 April, p. 22.
———. 1976a. Reserve Mining Co. held liable for cost of water filtration. *New York Times*, 22 February, p. 23.
———. 1976b. Court bars moving of U.S. drug suit. *New York Times*, 2 August, p. 45.
———. 1976c. Judge kills major part of U.S. drug trust suit. *New York Times*, 3 November, p. 83.
———. 1984a. Judge rebuked over remark. *New York Times*, 3 November, p. 46.

———. 1984b. Panel dismisses action against federal judge. *New York Times*, 27 December, p. A14.
———. 1987. A. H. Robins reports receiving buyout offer. *Minneapolis Star and Tribune*, 5 February, p. 3M.
Upon talking too much, editorial. 1977. *Minneapolis Star*, 5 May, p. 16A.
Walsh, M. W. 1984. Jurist's tactics hasten the pace of litigation in Dalkon Shield cases. *Wall Street Journal*, 14 September, pp. 1, 20.
Walsh, M. W. and F. Schwadel. 1984. Bizarre twist in lawsuits on contraceptive is provided by ex-A. H. Robins attorney. *Wall Street Journal*, 3 August, p. 13.
Wargin, B. 1976. Decision is appalling, letter to the editor. *Minneapolis Star*, 4 January, p. 14A.
Wascoe, D., Jr. 1987. Law firm uses its celebrities for TV ads. *Minneapolis Star and Tribune*, 9 February, p. 3M.
Weaver, W., Jr. 1975. Supreme Court rejects a ban on dumping by Reserve Mining. *New York Times*, 1 April, p. 24.
Wehrwein, A. C. 1976. The extraordinary case of Judge Miles Lord, editorial. *Minneapolis Star*, 14 January, p. 14A.
———. 1979. Judge Lord was out of bounds, editorial. *Minneapolis Star*, 18 April, p. 8A.
———. 1981a. Lord shows real creativity in mentally ill case, editorial. *Minneapolis Star*, 8 January, p. 7A.
———. 1981b. Judge Lord throws the book at corporate irresponsibility, editorial. *Minneapolis Star*, 10 December, p. 12A.
———. 1982. Here's a way to drive hypocrisy out of university sports, editorial. *Minneapolis Star*, 7 January, p. 8A.
Weinstein, H. 1975. $20-million refunds due for drug overcharges. *New York Times*, 9 July, pp. 51, 57.
Whose risk? editorial. 1975. *New York Times*, 20 April, p. 16.
Wilson, B. 1977. Lord wants Wendy opposed. *Minneapolis Star*, 13 April, pp. 1A, 4A.
———. 1985. Mattson proposes Lord be named member of divestment task force. *Minneapolis Star and Tribune*, 17 September, p. 3B.
Wolkerstorfer, T. 1975a. Lord's Reserve moves rebuked. *Minneapolis Star*, 9 April, p. 1A.
———. 1975b. Judge unsure of Reserve role. *Minneapolis Star*, 2 May, p. 30B.
———. 1975c. Reserve to test whether Lord exceeded authority. *Minneapolis Star*, 17 November, pp. 1A, 5A.
———. 1975d. State backs Judge Lord on Reserve. *Minneapolis Star*, 18 November, pp. 1A, 4A.
———. 1975e. Governor fears Lord acts on Reserve. *Minneapolis Star*, 19 November, pp. 1A, 3A.
———. 1975f. Motion to close Reserve tabled. *Minneapolis Star*, 25 November, pp. 1A, 4A.
———. 1976a. Order removing Lord clouds appeal by state. *Minneapolis Star*, 7 January, pp. 1A, 16A.
———. 1976b. Judge Devitt to take over Reserve case. *Minneapolis Star*, 9 January, pp. 1A, 4A.
Worth Noting. 1974. *Minneapolis Star*, 26 December, p. 4C.

———. 1975. *Minneapolis Star*, 6 February, p. 2C.

———. 1976a. *Minneapolis Star*, 19 March, p. 3B.

———. 1976b. *Minneapolis Star*, 24 April, p. 7A.

Zack, M. 1983a. Meshbesher lashes out in court at misconduct allegations. *Minneapolis Star and Tribune*, 17 September, pp. 1A, 8A.

———. 1983b. Meshbesher asks Judge Murphy to disqualify herself from case. *Minneapolis Star and Tribune*, 21 September, pp. 1A, 10A.

———. 1984a. Ex-Robins attorney says he destroyed IUD files. *Minneapolis Star and Tribune*, 31 July, pp. 1A, 5A.

———. 1984b. Company withheld information, former Robins attorney testifies. *Minneapolis Star and Tribune*, 1 August, p. 5B.

———. 1984c. Ex-Robins attorney suggests firm lied. *Minneapolis Star and Tribune*, 3 August, pp. 1B, 4B.

———. 1984d. Lord's remarks in Dalkon trial stricken. *Minneapolis Star and Tribune*, 3 November, pp. 1A, 16A.

———. 1985a. Alsop provides a sharp judicial contrast to Lord. *Minneapolis Star and Tribune*, 21 May, pp. 1B, 2B.

———. 1985b. Lord might continue on bench. *Minneapolis Star and Tribune*, 23 May, p. 3B.

———. 1985c. Judicial panel declines to take up misconduct complaint against Lord. *Minneapolis Star and Tribune*, 6 June, p. 22A.

———. 1985d. Lord's successor on bench shuns public eye. *Minneapolis Star and Tribune*, 10 June, pp. 1B, 10B.

Zack, M. and D. Phelps. 1983. Prosecutors got, kept Mesbesher defense file. *Minneapolis Star and Tribune*, 15 September, pp. 1A, 8A.

OTHER

Lord, M. W. 1984. Interview by Mike Wallace. "60 minutes." CBS. 11 November.

———. 1988a. Interview by Dean Stephen Young. "Portraits of justice." Regional Channel 6, Minneapolis, 9 September.

———. 1988b. Interview by author, Minneapolis. 30 November.

———. 1990. Conversation on ethics with Miles Lord. Public discussion. University of Minnesota, Minneapolis, 21 May.

———. 1992. Interview by Beth Friend. "Portrait: Miles Lord." KTCA Twin Cities Public Television, Minneapolis-St. Paul. 17 May.

Index

About the Author

VERNA C. CORGAN, Associate Professor in the Department of Theatre and Communication Arts at Hamline University, has a Ph.D. in speech communication from the University of Minnesota. She has been concentrating on studies of judicial rhetoric at the trial court level.

www.ingramcontent.com/pod-product-compliance
Ingram Content Group UK Ltd.
Pitfield, Milton Keynes, MK11 3LW, UK
UKHW020814290926
15470UKWH00003B/1156

9 780313 292477